In Your Loving Is Your Knowing

Front cover picture: *Since long I expected you*
Dag Magne Staurheim, etching, 1979
Courtesy of the Student Christian Movement of Norway

The poem (which is inverted in the etching) translates:

Since long
I expected you
like a wind
you came
threw all
stones and fences away

But I
I could not
in spite of my longing
meet you
in your whirling stream
Trembling with loneliness
I will be standing

In Your Loving
Is Your Knowing

Elizabeth Templeton – Prophet of our Times

Edited by Peter Matheson and Alastair Hulbert

BIRLINN

First published in 2019 by
Birlinn Limited
West Newington House
10 Newington Road
Edinburgh
EH9 1QS

www.birlinn.co.uk

The Editors and Publisher gratefully acknowledge financial assistance
from the Drummond Trust towards the publication of this book.

ISBN: 978 1 78027 563 5

British Library Cataloguing-in-Publication Data
A catalogue record for this book is available from the British Library.

Typeset by Hewer Text UK Ltd, Edinburgh
Printed and bound by Gutenberg Press, Malta

For Douglas, Kirsten, Alan and Calum Templeton
and with grateful thanks to Vivian Baker

Contents

List of Illustrations

Elizabeth and her brother Peter on holiday.

As a pupil at Hutchesons' Girls' Grammar School in Glasgow.

Meeting the Duke of Edinburgh at the opening of the English Speaking Union Debating Society in Edinburgh.

Elizabeth Anne McLaren, as she was then, at her graduation at Glasgow University, 1967.

Meeting the Pope as part of a British Council of Churches delegation to the Vatican in April 1983.

With members of the British Council of Churches delegation and Pope John Paul II.

Douglas and Elizabeth with Kirsten and Alan on the beach at Southend, Mull of Kintyre.

Elizabeth with Kirsten, Alan and Calum and their friend Catherine Hepburn in 1984.

Elizabeth and her friend Catriona Matheson from Dunedin, New Zealand.

Elizabeth and Douglas with Alan at his graduation from Aberystwyth University, July 2003.

Elizabeth and Douglas with their friend Ute Fleming and her two children, and their dog Donald.

Elizabeth was active in the charity Missing People after the disappearance of Alan in 2006.

The *Promise* conference, at which Elizabeth delivered the address, *Angels in the Trees? A Theology for Today*.

With participants of one of the two very successful International Theological Summer Schools at Scottish Churches House.

The Interim Management Group of Scottish Churches House in 2005.

Elizabeth and Donald Smith, Director of the Scottish Storytelling Centre in Edinburgh.

On holiday on the Isle of Gigha.

With friends Heinke and Peter Matheson during a visit to New Zealand in 1991.

Elizabeth and Douglas outside their house at Milton of Pitgur, near Pitlochry.

Elizabeth Templeton.

'My *whole vision of theology is a convivial, energising conversation, engaging every aspect of the self, and open to every partner from any quarter. That it is so often experienced, inside and outside the Church, as a dry, remote, eccentric and restrictive discipline is tragic and needs remedy!'*

– Elizabeth Templeton

Preface

Not long after Elizabeth Templeton died in April 2015, a round-table conversation was organised by the Centre for Theology and Public Issues at New College, Edinburgh, to remember her, review her life and work, and suggest what might be a fitting way to keep her vision and insight alive for succeeding generations of students. Her involvement in the fields of theology, Church, education, broadcasting, ecumenism and inter-faith dialogue, as well as elements of her life story, were the themes discussed. Rather than seeking someone to write a biography of her, it was agreed that an anthology of her talks, addresses and sermons would be more appropriate and useful. An editorial group was appointed to carry forward this intention, composed of Alison Elliot, Richard Holloway, Alastair Hulbert, Lesley Orr and Donald Smith.

However, without the extraordinary perseverance and imagination of Elizabeth's friend Vivian Baker, who gathered together over a hundred scattered papers – lectures, talks, sermons, addresses, meditations – this book would never have appeared. Many of them had to be transcribed from Elizabeth's handwriting, and this was graciously done by Alison Elliot, Sheilagh Kesting and Johnston McKay. The editorial group agreed to invite Peter Matheson, an old friend of Elizabeth's and a former lecturer at New College, now Professor Emeritus of Church History in Dunedin, New Zealand, to select and edit the texts and write an introduction. In this he was helped by his wife Heinke, for many years a close friend and confidante of Elizabeth's. Peter's edit allows for some overlap in the texts, given the wide variety of audiences and occasions represented by the addressees. Gendered language is left as in the original context. The language also reflects the times in which the pieces were written. Incidental comments which are no longer relevant have been edited out.

Alastair Hulbert ensured e-mail communication between Peter and

Heinke and the editorial group in Edinburgh. Elizabeth's brother, Peter McLaren, contributed much-appreciated support for the book project, including biographical information and photographs of Elizabeth, while Richard Nicodème of Creative Context lent his artistic and graphic skills to develop the imagery of the book.

Warm thanks are due to the Drummond Trust, 3 Pitt Terrace, Stirling, for its generous financial assistance in publishing the book. Thanks too to Ann Crawford and her colleagues at Birlinn Limited who were keen to publish it.

The book's contents are divided into six thematic parts, with each part being introduced by a member of the editorial group to provide context and commentary. The group was joined by three other contributors: Tim Duffy, Charlotte Methuen and Rowan Williams.

Thanks go to all these good people and organisations who have contributed to making *In Your Loving Is Your Knowing* a challenging memorial to Elizabeth Templeton. The New College Library will maintain an archive of her work. Kirsten and Calum Templeton, Elizabeth and Douglas's two surviving children, have asked that royalties from the sale of the book be given to the charity Missing People, in memory of their brother Alan.

Peter Matheson and Alastair Hulbert

Introduction

Elizabeth Templeton – An Appreciation

Peter Matheson

Elizabeth Templeton was a freelance theologian, engaged like Don Quixote in the knight-errantry of the heart. Her being and thought was consistently lived on the edge, symbolised by the remote cottage near Pitlochry which was her home in later years. She was never captured by the establishment; rather, she captivated it. Her life was rich in contradictions. Although in demand as a speaker on the world scene, she was probably most at home in informal local gatherings. Often impatient with her own Church, she was chosen to convene a key working party of the Church of Scotland as it struggled for doctrinal coherence on issues of human sexuality. She was Scottish and indisputably Glaswegian, but found attentive listeners in England, Ireland, the continent of Europe, Australia, the USA and elsewhere.

Elizabeth was excited about theology, and committed to the Academy, but her real passion ignited when theology illumined and was fed by the lives of young people and their parents, by poets and professionals, lay people and those alienated from the Church. Again and again in her books, lectures and broadcasts, one is reminded that here a busy mother is speaking, a genial host at hastily improvised meals, a wife, a special friend, the compassionate carer for an apparently endless succession of the lost and the lame.

Post-war Scotland with its rationing was not the easiest of places in which to grow up, especially as her father, Peter McLaren, had been in Barlinnie Prison for the whole of 1942 and more briefly later because of his unflinching pacifism. Yet her brother Peter, three years younger than Elizabeth, comments: 'As children we had a very secure existence. We weren't rich, materially, but we never had a sense of being deprived of anything. We lived in Govan on the edge of one of Glasgow's poorest districts, but in a big, old, end terrace house, with a front and back garden. There was no TV, no car, and the phone arrived relatively late on. Books mattered, doing well at school brought praise . . .'

Elizabeth's mother, also Elizabeth, a primary-school teacher, ran house and family while holding down a full-time job. Her father, a clerk in the Water Department, went to university as a mature student, and after a teacher-training year became a secondary-school teacher.

The family would go on trips by tramcar or bus to places round Glasgow – the Red Smiddy at Inchinnan, the Fossil Grove in Victoria Park, Hogganfield Loch ('You can see Barlinnie from here,' her dad would say), the art galleries, criss-crossing the Clyde from Govan to Finnieston on one of the little passenger ferries that took shipyard workers or football fans north or south of the river. Walking under the Clyde by the Finnieston Tunnel was a special thrill!

They played in the street, 'heidie' football or chases, swapped scraps and football cards, played ball against the Co-op wall, wore Clarks sandals in the summer. Saturday meant a walk through Bellahouston Park, a visit to Ibrox for the last twenty minutes of a Rangers match when the gates opened, a trip to Mosspark Library: there were no distractions to dilute the thirst for reading. Summer holidays were spent in boarding house or rented flat, *doon the watter* – in Rothesay, Arran, St Monans, Nairn, Grange over Sands, St Anne's on Sea.

Anne (Elizabeth's name at home) sat the entrance exam for Hutchesons' Girls' Grammar School and started her secondary education at this selective, fee-paying institution. It may seem surprising that a lifelong socialist like her father should send his children there. Yet it was what you did at that time. She embraced the competitive and academic culture of Hutchesons', earning the accolade of school Dux, joined the English-Speaking Union Debating Society and won competitions with Katie Thomson, her lifelong friend. She was invited to the ESU headquarters when it was opened by the Duke of Edinburgh. *The Scotsman* featured a photograph of her in school uniform, complete with hat, under the headline: 'Talkative Schoolgirl Meets Duke'. She won the Britain-wide competition organised by *Time and Tide: John o' London's* magazine with the essay 'The Strength to Dream'.

Their father never talked about his experiences in Barlinnie Prison, but every week he sent out a dozen copies of *Peace News*. This involved careful folding of the paper into its printed paper wrapper, and a trip to the nearest post office, where a long tail of 1d and ½d stamps was obtained from the stamp machine. Her parents visited several churches until they found one where the minister – the Rev. Gilbert George – chimed in with their own political pacifist beliefs. Her father was the Sunday School Superintendent there – it was a conventional orthodox religious upbringing. Elizabeth even succumbed for a short time to zealous pietistic pressures.

At Glasgow University, poetry entered her bloodstream. She relished the renaissance of Scottish literature, and wrote poems herself, though none, alas, have survived. Later in life, her talks were invariably enlivened by poetry and by the fables she composed. Favourite poets were Iain Crichton Smith, Edwin Muir, Norman MacCaig, e e cummings, T.S. Eliot, Zbigniew Herbert, W.H. Auden, R.S. Thomas, Philip Larkin, John O'Donoghue. She was to become an avid reader of Iris Murdoch and Graham Greene, but also of Australasian writers such as Janet Frame and Patrick White.

Literature walked hand in hand, however, with philosophy. She put herself through the mangle of the logical positivism which then dominated the academic scene. Little if anything of the gentle piety of her childhood and adolescence survived. Her lecturers' critique of religious language and thought hit home. There emerged, however, a lasting delight in cleanness of thought, an intellectual gutsiness, whatever it cost. Professor Keith Ward, then lecturer in logic at Glasgow, recalled that she was the brightest student he had ever taught.

The clash of head and heart led her to New College, Edinburgh University, not so much with any thoughts of becoming a minister, though she took the pastoral courses, but to see if faith, as represented by a strong and diverse theological faculty, could answer the questions which had become her own. While enjoying her time there, major questions remained unresolved: what was meant by discourse about God, what to make of the reality of evil, of prayer, worship, the Church? Despite her doubts, she was appointed to be a lecturer in the philosophy of religion at New College, her sharp and adventurous intellect obvious to all. She shone as a teacher. As Lesley Orr, who was one of her students, has commented, 'Her inspirational dialogical teaching, fearless encouragement to explore, and gift for friendship had a deep and enduring impact on a generation of students.'

A turning point in her personal religious quest was the deepening engagement with Greek Orthodox thought, mediated to her by a new colleague, John Zizioulas, as is obvious from the frequent references to him in the papers in this book. She also gathered around her a group of radical friends, who explored different patterns of Church life. Contacts with Eastern Europe, and the exploration of Christian–Marxist dialogue, became important for her.

One story from the early 1970s illustrates her confidence that risk-taking could puncture the doublespeak which followed the collapse of the Prague Spring. Her friend, Vlastá Nosova, worked as a secretary in the offices of the Church of Czech Brethren. 'With typical Czech passive resistance, the office staff worked out a plan to show their hostility to the regime. Each year, one member would be deputed to take the inspectors round. The rest would sit at their desks or typewriters, stonily working. Not a smile, not an eye contact, not a word of greeting. The year it was Vlastá's turn, after half an hour, she could bear it no longer. "How can you do this job, where everybody hates you?" she asked. At that, one of the men burst into tears, and the two of them began to describe what it was like to work as quislings for the central bureaucracy. And in the end, the whole office was talking with them, exploring how to live with the pain of occupation.'

In 1977, Elizabeth married a colleague, the New Testament lecturer Douglas Templeton, after a whirlwind romance which took her out to his beloved Greece to rescue him from a hospital where he had been incarcerated. Douglas was highly cultured and erudite, with a deep love for the classics. He was generous to a fault, and, like Elizabeth, deeply devoted to his students. Having done his national service in the Black Watch, his everyday dress was a kilt of the Black Watch tartan. An eccentric traditionalist, he was in many ways a rebel against the mores of his affluent Glasgow background. But he was not a feminist – and Elizabeth, who wasn't either, carried the main load of family responsibilities which came with marriage. They shared a love of the wilderness, of art, music, literature, of friendship and hospitality and good food. Yet evident too were their differing social and political backgrounds, disparate approaches to child-rearing and education, to lifestyle and work routines. Elizabeth left New College in 1980 to care for the growing family; and, though later on she applied for several jobs, including at least one professorship in a Scottish university, she remained freelance all her life.

They had three bright and beloved children, Kirsten, Alan and Calum, who, like many others of such gifted and driven parents, bore the weight of their parents' professional commitments. For years, Elizabeth managed to juggle an often chaotic domestic life with a growing international reputation as a teacher, author and speaker. Frequently she would be up at the crack of dawn to meet a deadline for a book or lecture.

Somewhere, honest with herself, she describes Christian faith as being about the unmanageable.

In the 1970s, she was the secretary of the General Assembly's so-called Committee of Forty, set up to make recommendations for the reshaping of the Church of Scotland. Along with the committee's convener, Professor Robin Barbour, the two made a formidable combination. They had the satisfaction of seeing their radical proposals for the reform of the Church approved in 1978, but little came of them in the end.

Her first book, *The Nature of Belief* (1976), one of a series to introduce students, senior pupils and the general public to major issues in religious studies, was partly in dialogue form, and peppered with quotations from poets and novelists. All manner of questions about the evidence for, or indeed the possibility of, belief were opened up by her earthy, engaging manner. A flurry of books followed in the 1990s. They included *God's February* (1991), a biography of Archie Craig, pacifist and ecumenist, and a rather saintly Moderator of the Church of Scotland, though no friend of affectation, as seen in his comment on 'Barthian cockerels crowing in front of every theological barn door'. Elizabeth admired his rare quality of humanity.

Travelling with Resilience (2002), her edition of essays for Alastair Haggart, Primus of the Scottish Episcopal Church, offered an empathetic, differentiated picture of this determined man who, perhaps more than any other, transformed his Church. God, Haggart would insist, created us with a brain as well as a nose. He was utterly committed to the alliance of faith and scholarship.

Elizabeth was greatly influenced by these male 'fathers in God': Gilbert George, her old parish minister; the future Moderators, Robin Barbour and Archie Craig; Bishop Alastair Haggart; and John Zizioulas. In 1993, however, she edited *A Woman's Place: Women and Work*, which opened up the issues of sexism in the workforce, and brought together an intriguing group of women involved in industry and in the churches. Also in 1993 came her most allusive work, *The Strangeness of God*, a passionate call to dig deeper, to go behind our often trite language about God to the actual allegiances and longings which make us what we are.

She was making a name for herself by 1980 as a lively and provocative speaker, a public intellectual. She toured the world like a concert pianist, addressing the Lambeth Conference of Bishops, the Faith and Order Conference of the World Council of Churches (WCC), and clergy refresher courses in Ireland, the USA and Australia. She prepared these addresses and courses meticulously, often sending off material well in advance. It was a costly business in time and effort. Her energy was prodigious. She was also, however, a skilled networker. Without the willing support of key figures within the Church of Scotland and the Scottish Episcopal Church, none of this would have been possible.

At the heart of her concerns, however, was the promotion of lay access to, and appreciation of, theology. This extended from editing *Trust*, the newsletter of the SCM Press, to founding Threshold, a drop-in centre for theological discussion in Tollcross, Edinburgh. On the face of it, this was a totally unrealistic undertaking, but it was carefully planned, and it really took off. Ron Beasley, a friend and leading layman, contributed his organisational skills, and many others were involved as well.

Another grassroots educational venture close to her heart was the Adult Learning Project (ALP), the initiative of community workers like Stan Reeves and Gerri Kirkwood in the Gorgie/Dalry area of Edinburgh. Their work with groups of people at local, national and international levels was influenced by the pedagogy of the Brazilian educationalist Paulo Freire. From systematic studies of social issues, the ALP groups would determine a programme of learning and action in the community. In this very secular setting, Elizabeth's input on the history – and development of the theology – of Protestantism in its particular Scottish context proved very insightful for those trying to make sense of Scotland's culture. Her ability to clarify, in simple language, these powerful cultural forces was always valued in the project.

She tutored the postgraduate work of an inmate in one of Her Majesty's prisons. She was in demand as a religious broadcaster. Aware of the challenges facing religious educators in schools in the new pluralist Britain, she was also drawn increasingly into the area of inter-faith dialogue. She threw herself into the promotion of Scottish Churches House in Dunblane, and the brave ecumenical experiment, Action of Churches Together in Scotland. The Churches' attitudes to sexuality was another area on which she began to gather expertise. The controversies around gender issues in the Churches led her from convening a working group of the Church of Scotland's Panel on Doctrine on sexuality into unexpected directions, including a growing solidarity with LGBT groups. She had a gift for helping quite traditional people to open up. In her view, everything was ultimately determined by how personhood and indeed the nature of God was perceived, and she sought to bring theological perspectives to bear on the controversies.

In 2006, Elizabeth and Douglas's son Alan disappeared. He was twenty-five. It was not until 2012 that his remains were found. Throughout that dreadful time of searching and waiting, there had always been the hope that he might be alive, and Elizabeth played a leading role in the charity Missing People. She continued to preach in her local church, and was active in the work of Scottish Churches House, but much of the old vibrancy had gone. The stigmata of Alan's disappearance and death were deep in her and Douglas's souls. Living, simply living, had become an often overwhelming task; something was lost that could never be found. Both theologians, biblical scholars, in the grief and terror of Alan's loss, she and Douglas would sit by a lighted candle in the window of their house at Milton of Pitgur, and read together from the Psalms. A supportive circle of friends and family became increasingly important to them, and nothing gave her greater joy than the arrival of Judith, a wonderful granddaughter.

It would be a mistake, however, to explain her gradual withdrawal from the larger scene by this personal tragedy. Other factors were in play. She was now in her late sixties. Politically and ecclesiastically, it was a very difficult time. Her father would have despaired of what had become of the Labour Party. The high hopes of the ecumenical movement were increasingly a thing of the past, and it was a particularly savage blow for her when Scottish Churches House was closed in 2011. She had fought for it tooth and nail. It had been a beacon for the universal appeal of the Gospel and for a renewal of the life of the Churches. So, her last years, and then the long months in hospital after the diagnosis of liver cancer, were very difficult.

At her funeral in Dunkeld Cathedral in April 2015, it was as if all Scotland mourned. As Professor Stewart Brown expressed it: 'She was one of Scotland's leading theologians – and a woman of great compassion and humanity, who worked tirelessly to make Scotland, Britain and indeed the world more open, inclusive and caring.' He recalled, too, at the dedication of the Elizabeth Templeton Lecture Theatre at New College in October 2016, that with her political concern for the disadvantaged and marginalised went a personal practice of generosity and hospitality. 'From the 1970s until the late 1990s, she and her husband Douglas hosted a weekly informal "at home" in their Edinburgh flat, inviting all New College students, spouses and friends to drop by for conversation over a cup of coffee or a dram. For many students, especially students from overseas, these gatherings helped to make Edinburgh a home.'

Freedom, community and inclusiveness as the pointers to the boundless generosity of God were her bywords. Over four decades, her intellectual courage and perceptiveness had opened up theology in a new way, and not only for lay people. She had asked many of the right questions about the future shape of the Church and offered suggestions about the way ahead. If the projects she was involved in, such as Threshold, or indeed Scottish Churches House, did not outlast her, the signals they sent out remain as relevant as ever. It seems altogether fitting that a lecture room in New College has been named after her, and will perpetuate her memory.

PART 1

CHRIST AND CULTURE

Introduction

Richard Holloway

For readers unfamiliar with the technical language of Christian theology, the title of this section requires some explanation. Behind the shorthand phrase *Christ and Culture* lie centuries of conflict and disagreement, so I'd better begin by trying to define the terms.

Christ is the Greek version of the Hebrew word *messiah*, meaning 'anointed one'. In the last days, according to the Jewish Bible, God would send his Christ to establish a reign of justice and peace on earth. And, according to the Christian Bible, a first-century Jew from Nazareth called Jesus was the Messiah so promised, hence the name by which he is known in history, Jesus Christ or Jesus the Messiah. But theological development did not stop with the identification of Jesus as the Messiah. It went on to define him as the incarnate presence of God in history, now represented on earth by the Christian Church. So, the term 'Christ' in the phrase *Christ and Culture* carries a hefty punch. It is shorthand for the mind and will of God as revealed or made known to the world through the agency of the Christian Church.

The opposing pole in our phrase, the term *culture*, is a more slippery word. The most useful definition I know is that it is any widespread behaviour transmitted by learning rather than acquired by inheritance. But even that definition needs further explanation. Speaking very broadly, culture is what distinguishes humans from the other animals on the planet. Like them, we acquire much by inheritance, including the natural instincts that drive our behaviour. The difference between us and them is that we are not entirely programmed by these drives. We have more self-conscious agency than they do, so we are not completely dominated by instinct. This enables us to transcend nature and make our own mark on the world. The shorthand term for this agency and the way it changes the world is *culture*. It includes everything that is transmitted by human learning, such as how to build bridges and fly aeroplanes and compose symphonies and write theological essays. It would be no exaggeration to say that *culture* includes everything that is distinctively or uniquely human, everything we have invented, including religion – though, as we'll see, there are versions of religion that believe they are exempt from this description and think of themselves not as standing within human history but as outside or against or in judgement over it.

Another way of translating the phrase *Christ and Culture* would be as *God and Human History*, the tension being that while God is thought of as constant, human history is marked by unceasing change. So, what is the nature of the relationship between them? How does the Eternal God – or the body on earth that claims to represent God – relate to the social and moral flux of human history? The classic book on the subject, published in 1951, was written by the American theologian Richard Niebuhr. Niebuhr claimed that historically there had been five responses to the duality or tension between Christ and culture. Two of them were polar opposites, while the other three were attempts to mediate between these two extremes. Any neat classification system should provoke wariness in the observer, but Niebuhr's opposing polarities offer us a helpful way to enter this ancient debate.

Niebuhr's first pole, which he labels *Christ against Culture*, is stark and dramatic. It rejects human culture as intrinsically and enduringly sinful: 'fallen' is the theological shorthand for this state. Therefore God's servants should withdraw themselves from contact with this fallen world and live in communities that are separated from it. As the saying goes, they may be in but they should never be of the world. The cleanest versions of this position are seen in sects who allow themselves only minimal contact with the surrounding culture, such as the Amish in Pennsylvania or the Exclusive Brethren in North-East Scotland. Interestingly, in mainstream Christianity today, there are voices calling again for this kind of separation. The world is so far gone in sinfulness and disorder that the only safe bet for Christians is to withdraw from it and serve God in faithfulness, letting the world go to hell in its own way. A sophisticated version of this neo-sectarian position, as we shall see shortly, was the target of a powerful polemic by Elizabeth Templeton.

At the other pole of his typology, Niebuhr placed a response called *Christ of Culture*. Those who occupy this position see the movement of history not as the enemy but as the mode of God's continuing revelation. God did not stop engaging with human society some 2,000 years ago, so the Church, far from turning its back on history, should study it to see where God is active today. This means that Christians should always be alert to shifts in humanity's moral and social evolution. An illustration will help make the point.

For most of its history, the Christian Church taught that the only permissible locus for sexual intercourse was within the bond of marriage. Sex outside marriage was sinful. Since 'marriage', by definition, was between a man and a woman, it followed that there was no way in which homosexuals could ever be sexually active. God had endowed them with needs and longings, but had forbidden them any legitimate physical expression of those needs. So, homosexuals were sentenced to an asexual, celibate existence, whether or not they wanted it or were capable of it.

In my lifetime, every aspect of that traditional attitude to sex has been abandoned by secular society. The sexual revolution has plunged the Christian community into a state of internal warfare, with the battle lines drawn between Niebuhr's two competing polarities. And the rhetoric of their disagreement captures the tone of his main protagonists. Christian opponents of these liberalising trends say those who adopt them are following not the divine spirit, but the spirit of the age. They are conforming themselves to the world because they have been seduced by its wiles and lack the courage to withstand them.

On the other side, those who have adapted to these changes in the moral economy of society, and who support gay liberation, claim that conservative Christians have confused the incidental cultural norms of late Bronze Age society with the eternal will of God. They say that Christians have to distinguish between the unchanging essence of the revelation of God that entered history 2,000 years ago and the conventions of the community into which it came at the time. And, just as we have abandoned the science of 2,000 years ago, so we should discard its social norms. To refuse to do this is not faithfulness; it is stupidity. It ties Christians into unnecessary knots and lands them in unnecessary conflicts.

This was a debate in which Elizabeth Templeton was passionately engaged. She rejected the *Christ against Culture* position and proclaimed her opposition to it in a letter to one of its modern exponents, Professor Thomas Torrance, at the time Scotland's leading theologian and Moderator of the General Assembly of the Church of Scotland. In the Kirk's magazine *Life and Work*, Professor Torrance had called upon Christians to withdraw into the pure citadel of faith and pull up the drawbridge against the rampant secularism of a corrupt and corrupting world. Elizabeth fired off a reply included in this section of the book under the title *Don't Shut out the World!*

Come off it, Tom, the history of Christendom has as much to be ashamed of as post-war secular Europe. And, indeed, it was in the past our 'Christian' oppression, our bigotry, our vicious dogmatisms which alienated European culture from faith, and nudged it towards the humanism of the Renaissance and the secularising tendencies of the Enlightenment.

She tells Professor Torrance that his

account of the 'crisis' stands as one interpretation of how Christ and culture relate. It is one in which some of us would suffocate. There are many other theological voices . . . who document more creative inter-actions between God and this present, secular world.

But she is also wary of the pure *Christ of Culture* position. In her lecture on *Worldly Ministry*, she says:

I am well aware, in principle at least, of the risks of confusing revela-tion with human self-understanding, Christ with culture and so on. But I am no longer persuaded that these exist in mutually exclusive spaces . . . at any point, the presence of God is liable to destabilise the complacencies of our shared and broken existence.

Though she never quite said it, in almost everything she wrote she implied a fundamental distinction between God and *religion*. Religion is best understood as a human construct, a cultural creation, even if it is prompted by humanity's response to the mystery of God. She was always keen to point out that all human knowledge was precarious and uncer-tain, even if it was knowledge of God.

That meant that all our religious and moral claims should be held *provisionally* – a favourite word of hers – because we can never be sure what in them comes from God and what comes from our own fear and hatred of change. And it is why we should reject any claim of the Church to exclusive rights in the detection of God's presence in the world. As she writes in *Don't Shut out the World!*:

[God] is present in the consulting rooms of agnostic psychotherapists who enact for many – more actually than the Church – what listening and acceptance and healing and transformation of the past means. He is present in the scripts and poems and films of secular men and women who articulate truthfully aspects of human freedom and un-freedom, life and longing and brokenness.

In *Worldly Ministry*, she tells us how the Orthodox theologian John Zizioulas had influenced her thinking on these matters, because he rejected any fundamental separation between God and the world:

> I have learned, as it were on a deeper register, what it means, in the light of the cosmic Christ, to hold all matter as capable of Transfiguration, indeed as transparent of God . . . because it is all touched by the relational event of what in the trade is called 'incarnation', the strange, unimaginable earthing of God in flesh, blood, place, time, in such a way as to invite all of it to newness.

It was that same cosmic generosity that enabled her to embrace even those, such as Tom Torrance, with whom she had profound theological disagreements – because they too were held in the mystery of God's teasing and surprising relationship with the world. Implicit in all her work is what I can only describe as a dynamic intellectual and spiritual ecology or struggle for balance.

Whatever else it may be, Christian theology is a human art. And all art operates within the dialectic of preservation and development; holding to the best of the past while being open to a future that may at any time overturn and redirect it. This is why theology is inescapably contentious and uncertain – and exhilarating, when played well. It is why Elizabeth Templeton dared to challenge Tom Torrance, a man she revered, a man who had bequeathed insights to her that nourished her until the end of her life. Because that was how the dialectical art of theology worked. It called its practitioners to a radical openness to the presence of God in the world and to the surprises it might spring on them at any time.

And that's why it helped to have a sense of humour, something Elizabeth had in glorious abundance. As I write these words, I can see her smile and hear her laugh. I miss them. But it comforts me to think that, even if religion just turns out to be a trick we all played on ourselves, Elizabeth Templeton was probably in on the joke from the beginning.

I

Theology and Experience*

We must retrieve theology for the non-theologians, those to whom the tradition is non-existent, dead or actually pernicious: the atheist, the secular empiricists of our day, the rich and the poor. For them it may be, at least initially, vital to forge a language which excludes the tradition, which speaks in terms of the bitter-sweetness of mundane existence, and lets men and women explore their rage and shame and boredom and ecstasy to the full.

When I was teaching at New College, I set a second-year class an exercise. 'Imagine', I said, 'that you sailed far away across the sea and chanced to arrive on an unknown island. You stayed there for a year and were able to live with the people of the island. You learned their language a bit, enough to have a fairly complex conversation, say at the level of a five- or six-year-old child. One fact was clear. They had no word for "God". Suppose you could witness every aspect of their life together – how would you decide whether or not these people knew the same God as you?'

Then I gave them bits of paper. Their faces registered bewilderment, dismay, paralysis. 'You can think for as much of the hour as you want,' I said. Hollow laughter. Nevertheless, they thought, and the exercise as well as its conclusions proved a rich theological agenda, which you might like to try out if you have a spare moment.

What provoked me to try it out was a growing conviction which I came to as a theological teacher – that theology was being constantly reduced to verbal assertion; and that the verbal assertions people made to themselves and others were very haphazardly related to any specific experience, let alone to a common experience. It was like a whispers

---

* Address to the European Student Chaplains Conference, London, 6 May 1985.

game, I used to think. If I said any sentence using the word 'God', that would be heard in about thirteen different ways. And the next sentence would double the number of variant hearings, and by the end of the lecture, people would have heard multiple meanings which I had never dreamed of, because of the networks of interpretation behind their hearing of any word I used.

My exercise was designed to try to undercut this, to push people to *explore* what is existence, rather than making assertions they took to be knowledge of God, and to lay bare conflict or convergence at that level rather than at the level of doctrinal affirmation, where it would have emerged fast and furious, but with no existential connections.

I will try to illustrate what I mean by this by selecting some episodes in my theological history, not because they are specially interesting, but because they serve as a case study. My family context was securely religious. But church was for me a word associated early with patterns of light through bright glass, friendly people, and occasional surprising words. (I remember, of all my Sundays, one sermon on the Revelation text, 'And there shall be no more sea.') Retrospectively, I appreciate, the minister was a generous, literate, ecumenically open, socially passionate man. There was no sense of being cramped in this environment. Sundays of course had their ups and downs. I can remember minor crescendos of irritation and short temper as collar studs wouldn't go in on communion Sundays and we were supposed to be there early to cut up the bread. But I never really had the sense that the brushed-hair, clean-shoes, washed-face scene was phoney. That was partly because the deepest core of my father's faith was a Christian pacifism which had taken him to prison for fifteen months during the Second World War, and in a pre-articulate way I knew that something more vital than collar studs took him into this ritual of Sundays. At any rate, it was an unobtrusive enough part of my childhood which was in general unselfconscious, a bit overprotected and a trifle priggish. But, by comparison with other people, as I later discovered, I was happy and confident. That may be my deepest debt to my parents in terms of the roots of theology.

In spite of that, when I was about fourteen, I fell hook, line and sinker for the evangelical ravings of those organising a school children's camp I went to. Such is the power of theology! For nothing in my experience corresponded to these new categories of guilt, judgement, being bought with blood; and yet something in my pre-adolescent psyche, along with the peer-group pressure of close friends all around me being saved at twelve-hour intervals, toppled before this attack! With some tiny twinges of uneasiness, promptly interpreted by the new faith as demonic temptations to backslide, I decided to ask to be saved – and then it all happened! Euphoria, congratulations from all my friends, public thanksgiving, initiation into new rituals at Bible study, prayer, self-examination, and a complete re-mapping of the world, including my parental and church worlds. They could not be real Christians since they didn't say the right words, didn't read the right books, didn't move in circles of twice-born men and women. My job was to go back armed with my new faith to convert them.

This little episode must be so commonplace among teenage girls in certain circles of Anglo-Saxon education that it needs no comment. It might have been punk or horse-riding or computer games in a different context. Nevertheless, it exposes one feature of our 'experience' of which we must be aware if we want to make that a control on theology.

'Experience' is never neat, uninterpreted data: it comes to us already shot through and laden with theories, convictions, idioms of thought and speech which give it its colour. My 'encounter with Jesus' in those evangelical months, which certainly was not faked from my subjective point of view, was nevertheless a fabric of language, of images, of psychic expectations, of subtle group sanctions. And it was watertight: scripture, Church traditions, common sense, world affairs were all reinterpreted in the light of the new faith.

The invulnerability of the martyr was ours. Parental anxiety about incipient religious fanaticism, school pressure to persist in criminal activities like doing French homework on Sundays – all confirmed the new experience of being embattled soldiers fighting for a Christ rejected by 'the world'. Our fervour was self-confirming.

Such teenage fantasy, for such I judge it to have been, came to an end not from any explicit external threat – my parents' worries were muted, lest I become more entrenched – but in one internal episode at the next camp I went back to, when we were assessing our first year as Christians, how we had fared, what challenges we had met. The camp commandant heard our stories and made assessments. Out came all my proud crusades to make my parents say the magic formula about accepting Christ as Lord and Saviour, my witness among Laodicean church people who had the trappings of religion and no first-hand knowledge of the Lord.

Instead of rapping me on the spiritual knuckles for intolerable arrogance and naivety, this well-meaning and bigoted woman commended me for my endeavours. 'Do not be afraid of conflict,' she said, 'for did not Christ say, "I have come not to bring peace, but a sword"?' I do not know quite how to describe my response to that, but it was pre-conscious, unreflecting. The whole constructed world in which I had been living collapsed. Reflecting later, I suppose it was years of living with my father's costly, conflict-making stand for peace, weighed against this facile justification of religious bickering. But somehow, at every level of my being, this assessment rang false. Perhaps it had only been skin-deep, though it had been intense. At any rate, the whole world of evangelical theology dismantled quickly, and I returned with relief to the more tentative exploratory style of faith I was used to, in the context of family and church.

By the time I actually became a committed member of our parish, I still had questions a-plenty – and only a generous and mature minister would have welcomed as a confirmed member one who asked so many questions about received doctrine – I was a very late developer on praxis. Going to university and doing philosophy cultivated the questions, especially since my main tutor was an intelligent, sensitive, humane agnostic. I had already had the experience of a mini-religious world disintegrating from nerve-tingling, self-authenticating fervour to a heap of untenanted words. Might this be the fate of my deeper-rooted belief as well? Who was this God? I thought I glimpsed him in conscience and the sense of mystery, in compassion, in hope. But could these feelings or intuitions not be better explained in human terms?

How would God's existence ever be verified or falsified? How could the diversity, the contradictoriness of belief about him, be reconciled with his caring about whether people knew him? Either he was careless or incompetent in his self-disclosure: in neither case was he God. Again, better to believe that explanation lay on the human level, with psychology, sociology and anthropology all showing how people and communities project their needs, fears, hopes and self-analysis on to eternity.

While logic could make us question our confidence in the existence of the eternal world, what hope was there for God's survival? What I had taken to be prayer discontinued. All that may be emerging from this is that I am peculiarly vulnerable to ideological suggestion. For certainly behind much of this philosophy lay a particular hard British dogma which made cats on mats the standard of reality and dissolved in its empiricist acid such abstractions as 'mind', 'freedom', 'truth' and 'meaning', to name but a few.

While I feel that I have, after many years, outgrown that particular philosophical worldview, I still owe it much in terms of the integrity of questioning which, from its admittedly limited perspective, it demonstrated. I still believe that experience is not ever self-evident. I still believe that people must face intellectually what threatens to undo them. My evangelical conversion and subsequent deconversion had the same quality of conviction, psychologically speaking. Yet, if one was true, the other could not be. The recognition of incompatibility in experience is not just, I think, a matter of logical rigour. It is a fact of human meeting. Either we account for it by postulating an endless number of self-contained private worlds, systematically isolated from one another, each 'authentic' in experiential terms – or else we are committed to 'exploring the web', the tissue of thought and language and vision which goes into our experience, constructs it, cradles it and articulates it. So far, my own experience of encounter at the level where it counts, with other human beings, persuades me that the second way is worth it – 'exploring the web', and that it is a slow, painstaking business, but exhilarating as you begin to discover what it is to inhabit a common world, where previously you thought you were separate.

Also, this was all happening in the late 1960s. At last I became aware of the range and depth of political questioning which was involved in radical theology, and of the questions which had to be put to academics as a class and liberal British academics in particular. I have found this happen particularly in the Christian–Marxist dialogue as a teacher.

As you may very well be recognising, such a way of perceiving or experiencing the human questions comes from a very individualising culture, the outcome, I think, of certain strands in classical Greek thought, taken over in Western Christendom and secularised by the Enlightenment and the Romantic movement. If you live in Crossroads, a shanty town in South Africa, or in Tigre in Buenos Aires, you start off, in one sense, with a head start on solidarity as your experience of the world. Even the strenuous moralising which urges us to care for sisters and brothers in the Third World itself confirms the anthropology of individualism. You are you alone. You are capable of relating to x and y. Relate to them. Take up that option. My experiences, apparently shifting, apparently 'self-authenticating', had clearly the emotional and intellectual horizons of a twentieth-century Western person.

If you can stand one more autobiographical episode, I will then draw some conclusions and some questions to focus our further thinking. Having finished a philosophy degree, my intellectual relation to Christianity was that of someone hanging onto a cliff by the toenails. I still have no major emotional disgust at the scandals of Christendom – the obscenities of missionary imperialism and the complacencies of established social order (I told you I was a late developer on praxis). Or rather, I was confident in my 'practical' distinction between real Christianity, like Jesus and the Sermon on the Mount, and the phoney sort – establishment, conformist and self-protective. Whatever force empiricism had in questioning the actuality of God, the actuality of Christian history troubled me little enough.

I went then, being a glutton for punishment, to do theology, mainly wanting to ask the theologians how they defended themselves against the onslaught of the philosophers. To my amazement, they were largely untroubled by them. Either they engaged in skirmishes which they took to be drawn, if not actually won, on the intellectual level: the ontological argument, the cosmological argument, the argument from design, the argument from religious experience, and so on, or else they conceded that there was no way to 'win' intellectually against the philosophers on grounds of logic, and that faith was a very different ball game, a self-validating encounter, a gift of divine self-disclosure, warranted by scripture and tradition. A very Protestant response.

None of these seemed to me to help my agnostic alter ego. The 'arguments' were manifestly unsatisfactory or question-begging. I flailed around trying to keep the questions biting, but in fact finding more freshness in the new ground of biblical exegesis – the creativity of these early Christian communities and the panoramic nightmare of Church history. I was invited on graduating to lecture – you have before you a genuine hothouse academic, redeemed only by intensive nappy-washing in the last five years – and I remember saying to my prospective professor in a panic, 'But I can't take my money for telling people what the truth is!' 'Don't worry,' came the reply, 'there are plenty of other folk around who can do that.'

So, I began to teach, terrified that I was going to grow old and stale reproducing debates which I found increasingly sterile, but could see no way round.

It was at this point that I met someone who exploded my ideological captivity and set in motion a not-yet-completed process. He was a colleague, Greek Orthodox, called John Zizioulas, but with an extraordinary range of human and intellectual energies, who could move from the non-availability of non-fluoride toothpaste in Boots to theology. He knew, of course, the Patristic traditions which I had learned as obedient geometry as a student. But he read them as existentially vital: not as external, constraining authorities, but as writings which clarified and made articulate the dilemmas and passion and direction of being human.

I can hardly begin to describe the difference it made to do theology with him as mentor.

For instance, the central problem for Western philosophers of religion is to identify the personal co-ordinates of God: how do you isolate God distinctively from anything else or anyone else? John undercut the issue by refusing to equate personal presence with empirical presence. If it's God, you don't bump into him like Joe Bloggs. He noted the episode in Sartre's *Being and Nothingness* where a man waits in a café for the friend with whom he has an appointment. No friend appears. The café is full of people. They are, however, absent to the man waiting. His friend, empirically absent, fills the café. Like my earlier 'de-conversion', it was a kind of gear change, opening up new possibilities of movement. To think of God as significant absence rather than detectable presence offered new leverage on many contexts. The yearnings for righteousness unattained by our corporate structures and particular selfishnesses; the trivialisation of God in the individualistic piety of 'having a supernatural running mate'; the crisis for all forms of sectarianism presented by a catholic God significantly absent from squabbling Churches; the sheer existential pain of an uncherished world. Here the change in thinking allowed all sorts of experience to voice itself unashamed.

Gradually, from that point, I began to explore what was for me a new theology, and in that process what I had taken to be my non-experience of God, and perhaps even my experience of no God, became again reinforced as a kind of wrestling with the significantly absent God. The fantasy conversations of my adolescence could go, and their silencing was not necessarily proof of the atheist case, but a faithful enough hearing of the active silence of God. The 'religious experience' which separated human beings into massive classes, religious and non-religious, could go, and the common ground for knowing God, significantly absent, was existence itself: existence with its shared though variable pressures and possibilities; being born, not having asked to be being born in a family, a place, of one sex, in one class, having to grow old; being in competition for the world's resources, winning or losing that competition, loving someone who doesn't love you, having to choose between the people you love, not having enough time to be free for yourself, having to choose between two vocations/two causes, having to die, having to choose to die sooner or later, having to choose between enforcing justice and restricting freedom, having no choices (the existential importance of suicide).

Of course, these things can be analysed simply on the level of human phenomenology – they need not be read theologically. Yet even this alarming reticence of God about his own existence could be re-experienced as the crisis of freedom offered to a world made out of nothing: not God 'expressing himself' but making something so free, so 'other' that it could not be coerced into dependence or belief. Not a God who was jealous of the world's freedom, resentful of our eating the fruit of the tree, but a God whose invitation was that we would participate in his freedom, his knowledge, would transcend all the limits and frustrations of causality which destroy us, a God whose pain was seeing us reject that invitation in favour of a more intact and manageable identity, nameable and detached from and in favour of death.

I had no new data – yet all the theological map changed. So far, I am more than stretched, intellectually, emotionally and politically by the implications of this shift, and I can only hint at some of these. It is not that any of my specific experiences have changed. There are no special glows or tingles, no privileged communications, no semi-private sixth sense of anything which some people have and others lack. Rather, I find myself challenged to interpret my total experience in relation to a God whose meaning is a catholic community of freedom: a community without constraint, to which all are invited.

I have come to believe that this is the historical intention behind some of the classical expressions of trinitarian doctrine and the doctrine of the personhood of Christ, though I am far from mastering the detailed intricacies of some of that. But it means that I no longer think there is a terrible either/or between 'academic theology' and the quest for fullness of life for the poor and the oppressed. Whichever end you start from, I think, if you do the job with fullness of dedication, you have to engage with the other end – though of course it is a typical pain of existence that you are liable to finish up submerged towards one end or the other with the weight of your agenda. But I do not believe that the only 'sharp end' is the actual putting of food into hungry mouths, or conscientisation.

A domesticated theology/piety fuelled the empires which exploited the Third World. Guilt and contrition alone will not, I believe, be enough to undo the evils of that past. We need to do better theology to experience the world better, not just the other way round. Now I speak to you as chaplains, that is to say, as people who have tamed the tradition, more or less: who carry it on your backs in your unworn dog-collars and your theological training and perhaps your ordination. To you, and others who still have contact with Christian tradition, I believe there are ways of transforming theology from a furtive, defensive, parenthetical enterprise to a lively and critically innovative one.

But more importantly, I think we must retrieve theology for the non-theologians, those to whom the tradition is non-existent, dead or actually pernicious: the atheist, the secular empiricists of our day, the rich and the poor. For them it may be, at least initially, vital to forge a language which excludes the tradition, which speaks in terms of the bitter-sweetness of mundane existence, and lets men and women explore their rage and shame and boredom and ecstasy to the full.

Such a theology will not simply reflect experience: it will alter experience put in crisis, generate it. The British normative experience (for which nation is it not?) of the love of God cosily nurtured by hubby, wife and two-point-something children will be challenged, not just by sociological shifts, but by evangelical questions about a Kingdom of God in which marriage is impossible. The security of pietistic introspective prayer will be dislodged by the challenge to pray meeting the eyes of the significant other, the one whose existence threatens yours, whom yours threatens. The utopianism of some political agendas will be forced to confront the intransigence of evil and the cost of drawing its sting: in terms of both, commonsense utilitarianism will reel. The marginal – children, lunatics, criminals, sexual deviants – will be there to question our experience of 'normality', and all this will follow from exploring the God who is 'the significantly absent other'. To incarnate that seems to me our agenda.

To return then to my visited island, what things would I explore, existentially, and what questions would I ask about their community?

- I would ask to examine whether they were entirely content with their community, either domestic or corporate.
- I would ask what things dissatisfied them. Are they only dismayed by rational and manageable problems, e.g. the distribution of resources? Or do they express concern at unmanageable things in song/poetry/ritual, e.g. at the irreversibility of time, at not being able to be in two places at once, at being subject to causal necessity?
- How do they meet 'significant others'? Who are their enemies? Who could be? How are they met? Does this generate pain? Or are they happy that their enemies are contained?
- What do they make of children/criminals/mental defectives/the mentally ill?
- Do their systems of education, criminal justice and medicine social-ise such people towards adult normality, or enable their lives to pose

questions to the adult norms, to be effectively subversive? Can they make room for the anarchy of admitting unsocialised persons to the world?
- Can they operate between complacency and neurosis in relation to social problems? What role does humour, especially self-deflating humour, play in their existence as a community?
- How do they express their dreams, and what do they express in them? Does their art represent reality as transformable or merely reproduce it as it is?
- What, if anything, would they be willing to die for?
- At what point in their social structure is constraint most manifest? Does this worry them? How do they 'map' such constraint?

From such questions as these, or the observations and experiences they articulate, I believe one could clarify what, for a given community, were its significant absences. The distances between its experience and what it longed for, its direction: its eschatology. If the direction was towards a community without constraint/freedom without isolating individualism, then I would take that as recognition of the God whose significant absence I explore.

In my own Scottish community, I find few formal theologians who move along these lines, but many in the artistic world who seem to have intuitions of what I mean, and some in fields like education and psychiatry. The interface for you in your community may be quite different, but I am interested to see whether you can recognise anything of your experience in this theology, or any of your theology in this experience?

Finally, to give you a whiff of the idiom I would choose for my theological encounters, here is a poem by Iain Crichton Smith – an overtly atheist son of the Western Hebridean Free Church tradition. It has no theological words, yet I believe it touches the core of many issues which I would regard as theological – the irreplaceability of any human, the pain of their apparent irretrievability – the need, however, to celebrate, cherish it and the need to meet to encounter the significant other who, in the end, some call God.

'None is the same as another'

None is the same as another,
O none is the same.

That none is the same as another
is matter for crying
since never again will you see
that one, once gone

In their brown hoods
the pilgrims are crossing the land
and many will look the same
but all are different

and their ideas fly to them
on accidental winds
perching awhile in their minds
from different valleys.

None is the same as another,
O none is the same.

And that none is the same is not
a matter for crying.

Stranger, I take your hand,
O changing stranger.

2

*Don't Shut Out the World!**

The Gospel cannot be preached to a world encouraged to hate itself.

Dear Tom,

As one of my teachers in the 1960s, you urged that theology at its best was a passionate and intelligent activity. And you spoke unforgettably about the generosity of the Incarnation as God's catching up our humanness into his own life, embracing, judging and transforming us.

My dismay at your somewhat sclerotic articles (October, November and December) about our present 'crisis' is that the passion is thinned by petulance, the intelligence infiltrated by unworthy prejudices, and the generosity overlaid by the kind of superior scolding of the secular world which seems so often the best the Church can do in lieu of prophecy.

Your contention is that some spreading rot set in somewhere after the renewal of belief in the great truths of the Gospel. What renewal was that? From then, you urge, we have seen 'a steady retreat from the high ground of doctrinal certainties to the low ground of socio-political utilitarianism without much evangelical substance'. (That's the welfare state, is it?) Rampant secularism, with rejection of belief in the supernatural, is the primary enemy, seducing ministers into serving up to congregations 'the sentimental religious froth of a popular socialism' instead of the Gospel.

Return to the intellectual straight-and-narrow involves rejection of the 'backward social sciences' and the 'obsolete preconceptions' of

---

* This is a remarkable open letter to the towering figure of Professor Tom Torrance, then Moderator of the General Assembly of the Church of Scotland, from Elizabeth Templeton, an unordained female theologian. It follows Professor Torrance's three articles in *Life and Work*, the Church's official magazine, in October, November and December 1976.

historical-critical method, and acceptance of the triumphant witness of named modern scientists that physical virgin birth and resurrection present no problems to the scientifically enlightened mind.

From our seduction by bad science, you argue, ethical and social corruption follow. The detachment of ethics from its grounding in scientifically acceptable evangelical truth sends the young plunging down Gadarene slopes of sexual decline, goaded by the erotic music of the '60s and later. Moral bankruptcy, social chaos, family breakdown, vandalism, cynicism are rife.

And through it all runs the central polarisation between Church and world. Church generates community, society involves individuals. Social 'mechanisms' compete with 'the unifying and transforming operation of divine love'. In earlier times 'Christianity provided healing for [society's] pathological states, and the Church gave society the inner cohesion it needed'. Now a sort of 'cultural hybrid between Christianity and secular society' means that 'the Church is infected with the same wasting sickness as the world around it'.

And so, with the billing of a prophet, you rest your diagnosis.

Dear Tom, my children enjoyed a story where a quick-witted girl sets out to rescue her wimpish prince from a local dragon. She invites the dragon to prove his fire-blowing powers; and when he has huffed and puffed himself to fireless exhaustion, she steps round him to rescue her prince. I'm afraid that I kept finding this dragon image popping into my mind as I read your account.

But I am also distressed that many theologically innocent members of the Church of Scotland may succumb not to your arguments but to your reputation as scholar prophet, theological maestro, and may swallow your account whole in modesty and awe, even though they cannot theologically or humanly digest it.

I share with you the conviction that God was/is in Christ, not just symbolically but actually; that God, disclosing himself as Father, Son, Spirit, is present in space and time, not just 'symbolically' but actually.

I believe that the Church is called to proclaim and anticipate and serve a kingdom which constantly puts 'the world' in crisis, challenging our axioms of individualism, normality, sanity, prudence, property, success, to name a few.

I am sure that we all need to beware of complacency about any particular socio-political norm thrown up by particular cultures.

But it is precisely insofar as I believe these things that I disbelieve almost every specific allegation you make in these articles. And I venture to open up some critical questions.

First, you, who call for intellectual rigour, should be more sparing in the vocabulary of rhetorical manipulation. 'Rampant', 'obsession', 'cheap', 'bandwagon', 'outmoded', 'cynical', 'schizophrenic', and above all 'obsolete'. Over and over again, surreptitious personal opinions are presented as descriptive terms.

Of course you believe them to be descriptive. But they are all contestable, as much in terms of the dismissive scorn of your typewriter's tone as of their justice and accuracy. You are entitled to throw down any intellectual gauntlet to social scientists, politicians, biblical critics or whoever. But if you want serious duelling, you should not pre-assassinate people by innuendo.

Second, you, who have always insisted that we should question our statements and presuppositions, let yourself off with undocumented assertions and generalisations, which deserve scrutiny. When, exactly, was the Church giving society the inner cohesion it needed? Was it when the Crusades whooped their way through the holy places of Islam? When the prelates and clergy of the late Middle Ages pauperised the unlettered masses? When Calvin's elders pulled girls and boys out of bed with one another and executed the odd heretic? When witch-burning was the social equivalent of Sunday-school picnics? When Victorian England got its poorer children up on Sunday an hour earlier for factory work so that they could go mid-morning to church? When the sexual needs of Christian heads of impeccably authoritarian families were met, without benefit of the Beatles, by maidservants and prostitutes?

Come off it, Tom, the history of Christendom has as much to be ashamed of as post-war secular Europe. And, indeed, it was in the past our 'Christian' oppression, our bigotry, our vicious dogmatisms which alienated European culture from faith, and nudged it towards the humanism of the Renaissance and the secularising tendencies of the Enlightenment.

It was no trendy radical but the devotedly evangelical Archie Craig who was wont to remark on how revolting an institution the Church could be. Your indiscriminate machine-gun assaults may hit the odd deserving target, but in the process you annihilate generations of good, truth-loving and open-minded scholars and practitioners, some Christian, some not, who have no chance to defend themselves. Of course, there are grave questions to put to our fragile and vulnerably human culture. But no one will listen to us – and rightly not – if we demonise and caricature others who are also passionately concerned for truth. How absurd, for instance, to suggest that secular society is a matter of our 'enforced submission to collective ends'. Not even a Hobbesian account of total depravity could ignore the natural desire in people for structures of belonging – the deep, basic human need to share language and laughter and value and the weight of existence.

We make politics, as we make love and art and law, because that is the sort of beings we are. And the ends are, in intention if not always in effect, as often for our 'mutual care and comfort' as for some alien collective tyranny. Of course psychologists and historians may have limited perspectives, even distorting ones. But cosmic vantage points belong only to God, not to even the most confident theologians, and it is no demeaning of a contribution to the search for truth to say it is from a point of view!

But third, and most dismaying to me, is that the God of these articles is so much less generous and flexible and world-loving than the God you helped me to find credible. Your hero Barth saw God in a much more affirming and freedom-conferring relation to the diversity of human culture than you suggest with your unqualified 'No!' to the secular world.

All your images are confrontational, whereas evangelical imagination explores metaphors of leaven and salt, and quiet interpretation where no lines can be drawn between the salutary and the damnable. I am sure that God is alive and well in Scotland, but mercifully not dependent on the Church of Scotland for his effective self-disclosure. He is present in the consulting rooms of agnostic psychotherapists who enact for many – more actually than the Church – what listening and acceptance and healing and transformation of the past mean. He is present in the scripts and poems and films of secular men and women who articulate truthfully aspects of human freedom and un-freedom, life and longing and brokenness. He is present in political questions asked by responsible journalists; in the urgency of the young for a less exploitative world; in the painstaking un-utopian attempts of secular politicians, diplomats, negotiators to handle the complexities of a manifestly finite world; in the untutored subversiveness of small children; in the love-making of those who learn through it to grapple with the costliness of loving or to recognise joy when they meet it.

The Gospel cannot be preached in a world encouraged to hate itself. For the sifting and transformation we need to be fit for the Kingdom is in the context of learning to love our specificity and diversity of being.

Deeper than our self-doubt at our tarnished past and ambiguous present, we are invited into the delight of being cherished as we are recreated in the community of the Resurrection.

You, dear Tom, taught us that. I think you did. But in these nagging, denunciatory, polarising articles I can hardly hear that. I wish I could. It worries me that such an analysis is presented as the main theological banquet available to the Church of Scotland's faithful members, let alone to a hungry world that hardly knows what it hungers for.

I think Church and world could do much more mutual nourishing if we sat down together and listened to one another – really listened – not with converting and de-converting designs on one another but with the fascination of discovery which would really stop Church and world being effective strangers.

We in the Churches need to hear more, not less, from the dramatists, the sociologists, the psychiatrists, the philosophers who think we kid ourselves and other people. And perhaps they might then relax in Christian company enough to explore the limits and possible dead-ends of their own disciplines and experience, once we had acknowledged their gifts to our marginal and often ghetto-minded Church.

Your account of the 'crisis' stands as one interpretation of how Christ and culture relate. It is one in which some of us would suffocate. There are many other theological voices, historical and contemporary, who document more creative interaction between God and this present, secular world. The readers of *Life and Work* deserve access to them also.

3

*Worldly Ministry**

Our ministry is about letting the world discover itself.

I would like to dedicate this lecture to Dennis Potter, the playwright, best known perhaps for his play *The Singing Detective*. As some of you may know, Dennis Potter was diagnosed last February as having inoperable cancer of the pancreas, and given a probable three months to live. He died on 7 June. In a final TV interview with Melvyn Bragg, he spoke about his life and work, and his vocation to let the wistfulness of passing music-hall song be seen as the Psalms of David. That interview confirmed the sense I have long had that he is, in a completely secular idiom, a holy man, and that his writing is a kind of priesthood of creation, a worldly ministry, from which professional clergy might learn much.

Some of you may never have encountered his television dramas, or have met them only as causes of critical scandal: too much explicit sex, bad language, vulgarity. And there is no way to paraphrase in print the psychic force of his dramatic imagery and the surrealism of his imagination. But in his truthfulness about the pain and vulnerability and the preciousness of life, he seems to me to touch much deeper levels than any moralising can reach.

What I want to try to do in this lecture is offer a theological commentary on 'worldly ministry' and its implications for our ways of operating.

* This paper was given by Elizabeth Templeton at the first Summer School of the Theological Institute of the Scottish Episcopal Church in 1994. She is described by the organisers of the conference as 'a notable freelance theologian, currently the Secretary of Action of Churches Together in Scotland (ACTS). Frequently on the frontiers of Christian mission she writes, broadcasts and lectures from a perception of theology as an exploratory discipline, not delivering dogma, but making connections between human experience and the depth reality which some people name as "God".' In her paper, she suggests ways in which the world recognises and gives voice to theological thought.

Not because it needs the commentary to be worthwhile. Indeed not, but because, for a group whose profession involves explicit religious speech, it is, I think, a rare gift to be able to recognise vision and ministry in secular idioms.

It's a matter of concern, undergirding the thrust of this paper, that most of the people with whom we deal in the big wide world actually find our religious language a kind of code, albeit one they sometimes learn devoutly, until it becomes a vehicle for their thought and prayer and practice. But still it remains often an internalised code. We spend a great deal of time, as preachers, catechisers and apologists, trying to decode this language for people (and sometimes for ourselves). But we are, I suspect, less skilled at recognising the freshness and immediacy of theological truth in the world's own language, and are sometimes even resentful at its disregard of our code.

I've come to think that some of our agonies about communicating faith, our proper embarrassment about a Decade of Evangelism (which strikes not too many people as good news), are self-imposed. And that if we could really learn to look and listen around, with courage and freedom, at the explorations of the so-called secular world, we would be hugely enriched.

For a brief period in the 1960s, under the influence of Bonhoeffer and some of his followers – Gregor Smith, Van Buren and other near-forgotten names – the secular enjoyed a theological boom. Those tantalising hints at the end of *Letters and Papers from Prison* about religionless Christianity were explored with some excitement: the secular city was celebrated as the shared symbolic home of humankind, even if it lived in Auchtermuchty or sub-Saharan Africa; and the distinction between faith and religion, the former positive and the latter negative in the parlance of the day, was a commonplace of the theological *Guardian*-reading public! (Harvey Cox's influential book, *The Secular City*, appeared in 1965.)

We are a long way from there, thirty years on. Today, it is religion which is enjoying a comeback. At worst, it is hard-line fundamentalism, or a kind of supermarket, consumerist religion, a pick-'n'-mix range of esoteric insider knowledge, best glimpsed on the shelves of secular bookshops, where New Age thinking jostles with Zen meditation techniques, apocryphal gospels and a variety of yogic manuals. At best, it is a recognition that there is a perennial openness to something more than the give-and-take of business life and lowest-common-denominator values. Even at the sociological level, the rootedness and cultural vitality of traditions deep in religious symbolism is recognised as part of people's authentic identity if they have it, and of their proper wistfulness if they don't.

And theologically, partly because of the impact of dialogues with other faiths which have not gone through the European Enlightenment experience, and partly because of the ecological theology which seeks to re-sanctify the earth as a bulwark against its abuse, we are much more willing to recognise sacred space, sacred time, and the whole area which the cabbage-growers of Findhorn would call 'geometaphysics'. In such contexts, 'secular' has been dragged towards negativity by its cousin secularism, and has associations for many with the anti-religious, the anti-faith, with brash vaunting humanism and careless consumerist worldliness.

My own first nurturing theologically as an adult was in the 1960s, but it would hurt my pride to think that I was merely indulging here in middle-aged nostalgia. And indeed, the form in which I would now wish to argue for a worldly ministry would, paradoxically, be more theological than it would have been, or could have been in the 1960s. For I have since then been deeply influenced by the theological vision of the Eastern Orthodox Churches, and from that I have learned, as it were on a deeper register, what it means, in the light of the cosmic Christ, to hold all matter as capable of transfiguration, indeed as transparent of God, not by virtue of some pantheistic principle, but because it is all touched by the relational event of what in the trade is called 'incarnation', the strange, unimaginable earthing of God in flesh, blood, place, time, in such a way as to invite all of it to newness.

It is, perhaps surprisingly, my sense that the Eastern Churches actually are less caught on the hop by the processes sociologists call 'secularisation' than we are in the West. One reading of this, the cynical one, is that it just hasn't happened to them yet, but I suspect it may be because there is already a deep secularity in their celebration of the earth, a delight that it should be itself, and a lack of desire to alter it in any sense except to give it freedom from death. That may be significantly connected with the relative absence of an identity crisis among their professional clergy!

At any rate, it seems to me to be a component of secularity, in the good sense in which I want to use the term, that the Judaeo–Christian creation myth does not suggest that the world is God, nor part of God, nor made out of God's substance. It is not divine. That is often read these days as a flawed myth, in the sense that it is tied in, in some quarters, with the abuse of the earth both in technological and commercial rape. Unlike Aboriginal Australians, or Native Americans with their sensitivity to the divine spirits of tree or water, Christians are sometimes accused, sometimes rightly, of a cavalier dismissal of the earth as a tool of human gratification, producing food and fuel and wealth. The ethical judgement may stand, but the theological point about the de-sacralising force of the Christian myth is that it guarantees the earth's freedom to be itself. As correlative with that, the Adamic task of naming the earth suggests a radical responsibility for the structuring of the reality we inhabit. We are not placed in an environment in which we are passive recipients of what happens to be. We are charged with making. Our ministry is about letting creation discover itself.

In this context, theology has to challenge the infantile religiosity which wants to have truth on a plate, pre-packed and vacuum-sealed – and I believe ordained clergy need to challenge it! (It is also, I am sure, an insult to infants to call such an attitude infantile, since children are among the most robustly Adamic people in terms of their refusal to accept second-hand truth. Whatever lay behind the Gospel commendation of them as those to whom the Kingdom belongs, I am sure it was not the virtue of unquestioning dependence!)

Truth emerges in tasting the world, not as a dilettante, but as one who has been invited to live, therefore to co-exist, with all the hope, joy, pain and passion that that engenders. It demands radical openness to whatever 'other' is there. For without that, truth is ghettoised. The world shrinks to an enclave. The complex depths of its integrity are missed. Things are tidied up, made manageable. This holding of the world in its awful marvellousness is indeed characteristic of the child, much deeper than sentimental enjoyment. Norman MacCaig catches it well in his poem, 'Grandchild':

> She stumbles upon every day
> as though it were a four-leaf clover
> ringed in a horseshoe.

> The light is her luck – and its thickening
> into chair, postman, poodle
> with a ribbon round its neck.

> She plays among godsends
> and becomes one. Watch her being
> a seal or a sleepy book.

Yet sometimes she wakes in the night
terrified, staring
at somewhere else.

She's learning that ancestors
refuse to be dead. Their resurrection
is her terror.

We soothe the little godsend
back to us
and pray, despairingly –

May the clover be
a true prophet. May her light be
without history.

For a so-called atheist poet, that seems to me remarkable, so accurate in
its sense of the giftedness of things. Over and over again he does it in his
poems, as if his noticing, his attentiveness were almost a metaphysical
apprehension.

And sometimes he even explicitly challenges the kind of fawning over
the world which tries to make it mean something other than its own being:

'A Man I Agreed With'

He knew better than to admire a chair
and say *What does it mean?*

He loved everything that accepted
the unfailing hospitality of his five senses
He would say *Hello, caterpillar* or
So long, Loch Fewin.

He wanted to know
how they came to be what they are:
But he never insulted them by saying
Caterpillar, Loch Fewin, what do you mean?

In this respect he was like God,
though he was godless. – He knew the difference

between *What does it mean to me?*
and *What does it mean?*

That's why he said, half smiling
Of course, God, like me,
is an atheist.

I suspect that MacCaig might hoot and put it into Pseud's Corner were one to suggest that this was anything to do with priesthood, but I'd like to risk it. For I cannot easily imagine a better account of how to present the *anaphora* aspect of how we minister to the creation than the lines: 'He loved everything that accepted / the unfailing hospitality of his five senses'.

But MacCaig is not alone. Time and time again, novels, films, plays which are in no way didactic, and certainly not specifically Christian, enlarge our sense of reality and give us all kinds of new sharpness of insight and recognition.

William McIlvanney's *Walking Wounded* strikes me as a piece of secular intercession, like the Australian author Patrick White's *The Burnt Ones*.

This openness to the moment is echoed in some of Dennis Potter's comments to Melvyn Bragg, where, when he was asked how it felt to be facing his dying, he spoke of how he was learning to enter the nowness of things, the blossom on the plum tree in his garden, the ten pages of work he could do that day.

The interesting thing is that it does not seem to matter whether or not these creators are Christian. They seem able to communicate in an idiom which undercuts the distinction between Christian and non-Christian without excluding either: naming the human, naming the earth, with a delicacy and precision which fulfils the Adamic task of active response to the world in love and knowledge.

For me, it is vital that priesthood begins with Adam/Eve and not with Aaron. For some theologians and some Christians, this is not enough to rescue the situation from being one of mere humanism, since there is no explicit naming of Christ. But this judgement seems to me to underestimate rather than overvalue the presence of Christ in the freedom of the spirit moving over the face of creation. The New Zealand author Janet Frame's autobiography, for example, filmed as *An Angel at My Table*, or any of her amazing works of fiction, *Owls Do Cry*, *Scented Gardens for the Blind* and so on, tear the throat with pity for the fragility of things, the locked-in-ness of people in scenarios of distress, disease or isolation. If this is not what we would call, theologically, 'a diagnosis of sin', I don't know what is. And its potency is that it moves, with the giftedness of fresh, exhilarating, stretching words from the abstraction of the label 'sin' to the concreteness of our co-existence. In something like the technical Methodist sense, it convicts us, but with such clear-eyed tenderness that it goes beyond description towards a horizon which I can only describe as intercession. When I try to imagine how, so to speak, God sees creation, how he enters it, unscoldingly, with love blazing, and yet with the restraint of his desire for our freedom and integrity, I find reading a Janet Frame novel a significant hint of it.

Having cut my theological teeth in a Dogmatics department headed by a teacher who thought the truth ran directly from God to Athanasius to Calvin to Barth, I am well aware, in principle at least, of the risks of confusing revelation with human self-understanding, Christ with culture and so on. But I am no longer persuaded that these exist in mutually exclusive spaces – though, at any point, the presence of God is liable to destabilise the complacencies of our shared and broken existence.

But the secular world also knows its own limits. Here is Janet Frame again:

'The Pure Truth Act requires a label to be added to each truth, stating the known percentage of adulteration.'

The microcosm of her novel, *Scented Gardens for the Blind*, searches the untruthful heart more penetratingly than many a homily on original sin, and more graphically, yet without hostile dissociation, somehow taking the reader into a deeper awareness of how partial and partisan our seeings and convictions are liable to be.

Whether or not this is named Christianity (and it is not), the significant question seems to me to be whether it helps people to recognise, in their own human condition, what the Gospel names as 'sin', to wince at it, to be quickened to pity and shame at its pervasiveness. That seems to me to be priesting, even if no Christian formulary is used.

Perhaps it is so hard for the Church to make public acknowledgement of this kind of worldly ministry because we still operate, subliminally if not consciously, with the old, medieval dualism of sacred and profane. But that assumes that there is privileged space, privileged company; that some things are intrinsically more holy than others. My sense is that, at its best, Christian faith invites people to unlearn that distinction, even if the sociologists suggest that it is endemic in human religious consciousness. The problem is not with the category of the holy, but with its use to delimit and segregate. And the same is true, I suspect, of the way we inherit the phrase 'holy orders'.

Again, Eastern theology may serve us better here, perhaps only paralleled in the west by Celtic spirituality, with a much stronger sense than Augustine or Calvin could allow of relational glory in creation. This is different from pantheism, which makes sacredness a property of nature. The distinctively Christian account of the matter is rather a relational one, in which sacredness is conferred in the love and freedom of God, and acknowledged, owned, in the love and freedom of our stewarding of creation.

Without that dynamic of communion, there is nothing holy. With it, everything is. I rejoice that this insight is enjoying something of a renaissance at present in ecumenical theology, where the idea of communion or *koinonia* is moving to centre stage in the work of Faith and Order. But it may be one which our Church cultures have barely been faithful to in thought, word or deed. And in some cases it has virtually disappeared.

I still remember the shock, in the course of some Baptist/Presbyterian conversations in Scotland a few years ago, when something had been said, I think about the child's natural instincts for relationship, and one of the participants burst out: 'But it's a damned world!' I was so stunned that I was uncharacteristically silenced for longer than it took to reply. But that may be fortunate, for the sentence retrospectively seemed to me so blasphemous, such a denial of God's restoring love, that I could only have wounded the man by saying how un-evangelical it seemed to me. For, surely it is not a damned world, post-incarnation and post-resurrection, however we decode these affirmatives.

If our Churches could relearn this in their bones, perhaps the tone of Church–world encounter might change for the better. And perhaps the world could find good breathing space in the orbit of the Church in which it actually learned to love and cherish itself at deeper levels instead of expecting to be scolded and nagged all the time for not being good enough, not being faithful, not being responsible and so on. The trivialisation of God to a moral nanny, with multiple binoculars trained mainly on the bedrooms of the world, rightly alienates people. And it alienates them, not because, as the Moral Majority would have it, they cannot bear the scrutiny of the judging God, but because they know in their bones that such a God is not God but Blake's Nobodaddy, a God constructed out of human fear and guilt.

If we could undo the expectation that we, who are Church, are somehow in competition with the world for the souls of men and women, not only would we get off the world's back, but also we might be more open to receiving the gifts of sanity, wit and freshness which are there as worldly gifts in so many contexts. At present, of course, even church people, in their private lives, recreate themselves by climbing mountains, or folk-singing, or reading a good book, or bird-watching, and many conscientiously thank God for such possibilities, although more perhaps simply enjoy an unspoken and slightly furtive relief at the various modes of being human which are less restrictive and claustrophobic than church sometimes is.

We have got out of the habit, in our ecclesiastical mode, of recognising that we receive gifts from the worldliness of the world, and are not simply relating to it as would-be converters, improvers and spiritual blood donors. A worldly ministry would have its pores open in receptivity to all that potential. It would not romanticise or idealise the world. No one with eyes open in the hurly-burly of politics or global economics, or in the rooms of counselling agencies, would pretend that we are unblemished. But the world can be trusted to discover that in its own life whenever it tends to utopian self-idealising.

It was one of the fascinating insights of Christian–Marxist dialogue in East Germany in the 1970s, in the days when Marxists were less rare than Martians, that the Marxists came to the Christians making unsolicited enquiries about this word 'sin' that they had overheard, because they could not understand the failure of a system into which love and careful strategy had been invested. Perhaps if we could recover the fullness of celebration that we are world, we might recover also a more authentic and inviting vocation as Church, which might include unforced confession and the yearning for shared and inclusive newness, rather than the pursuit of ghettoised righteousness.

Worldliness, then, needs to be recovered, if we have lost it, as a manifestation of the incarnational mandate, and as a corollary of faith in the pervasiveness of the living Spirit. If world is set against Church, demonised, distrusted, despised, we betray the love which generated both old and new creations. If the world is called to become, in the end, Church, it will not be by ceasing to be world, but by being caught into the newness which can resist and transform time, attrition, death, without loss of specificity and form.

The basic ministry of the Church is to hold the whole cosmos sacramentally, offering it to its future in the love of God by our uncoerced solidarity with it. Given that solidarity, humanism and even paganism (if by that you mean the fierce and tender identification with the earth) become important, not as the whole story, but as apprehensions of worth and goodness which Christian hope wants to cherish and enlarge, not to remove and deny. Worldly ministry then becomes something very holistic, more a way of being than a role or a range of specialised functions. It is above all about how to be a whole community which manifests and enables this transformation to be accessible. Clerical ministries are justified only by their structural importance for this new way of being. What all this means for the nitty-gritty detail about patterns of ministry remains to be explored in its specifics. Let me just suggest some starting points.

Whatever priesthood or ministry mean, in such a theologically positive account of the world, they do not mean being superhuman, far less sub-human, but as human as possible. This means realism about the joys and pains of actual existence, not an evasion of any of them. The minister's professional participation in being human, as well as his/her personal one, cannot simply be vicarious, if by that one means that one simply overhears news of sin, hope, death, love. It involves earthed solidarity deep enough to be recognisable as being like rather than unlike. For some, this may be primarily by imaginative empathy. We can't all be whisky priests, or sexually chaotic individuals, but we might stop demonising those who are, for they surely bear in their own lives the sin of the world.

It involves a deep attentiveness to those who live exposed to pressures we hardly know, protected as we are by education, wealth or status – the jargon is 'marginal people'.

It involves a constant alertness to those who have humane imagination – we neglect artists and poets and children and film-makers at our peril.

It involves modelling our co-existence in ways which are non-hierarchical. This is not simply a Presbyterian twitchy warning against the evils of medieval prelacy. There are many more subtle and pervasive clerical sins, including the patronising of lay people by excluding them from the exploration of an adult faith, and the fear of one's own vulnerability being manifest. We need to work in every sphere of ministry for modes of being which are genuinely enabling, participatory and convivial. Illich's *Tools for Conviviality* is still seminal here.

All of this, I hope, might dispel the slight queasiness that some robustly worldly people feel in clerical company, the sense that they are being invited into ethereal realms, where somehow their humanness is thinned, their intelligence underrated, or their adulthood in the area of moral integrity demeaned.

It seems to me that Christianity in its named manifestations has forfeited, perhaps for the foreseeable future, the possibility of attracting in our culture many thousands of wholehearted, caring and thoughtful people. I am not sure that it is a primary task of the Church in the short term to try to reverse that, either by decades of evangelism or by subtler attempts at apologetics. I think that there are shoots of exciting and tough recovery around, but not to be forced.

The Ecumenical Spirituality Project of the Council of Churches for Britain and Ireland, based in Milton Keynes, has unearthed scores of attempts to recover some kind of integrated and unsanctimonious discipleship. Inter-faith life in Britain is likely to put more and more pressure on us to recover a ministry which we share, albeit not uncritically, with other faith communities. It would, I suspect, be good and scary for us to go beyond the ethos of polite toleration, to search whether and how the truth of the one God is manifest in other faiths. And so long as that does not become a ganging-up of the religious against the non-religious.

That should give us access to models of recovering the truth of God in secular idioms as well. And, of course, the momentum of Liberation Theology, with its insistence that we attend to the outsider, the weak, the poor, the marginal, will, if risked, continue to challenge our ecclesiastical complacencies and teach us the cost of solidarity.

But it is not, for me, any longer of primary importance that people should be able to recognise their situation, their predicaments, their hope in the language of Christian faith. It is that they should encounter Christ-shaped love, and love it more than they fear it. I suspect that for decades yet in this culture, that might mean great reticence on the part of the Churches: partly the reticence of atonement for the clumsy, moralising, intellectually flabby, humourless, politically compromised life we so often lead, palpably at odds with our claims to enjoy abundance of life. And partly the reticence of a faith which may be surprised by God if it does not identify the growth of our ecclesiastical institutions with the growth of the Kingdom, but waits, like a spring gardener, to see where the shoots are coming up. It is that imaginative openness, the relaxation to explore the unfamiliar idioms where there is no protected language, the confidence that our shared humanness is deeper than even our deepest divisions of dogma and form, which I long for in the Church, and see as the nerve of our common ministry.

On the strength of my confidence that God is more spacious than our largest hope, I am encouraged to keep exploring worlds of shared discourse and experience with whatever other, not needing to grab them into my idiom of faith. So, I can read a secular essay in the local paper which catches the poignancy of the closing of paths our human choices force on us, and recognise it as theologically truthful even though it has no religious reference whatsoever.

I can be glad that it will ring bells with many people who might never be in a position to hear a sermon on the pathos of finitude. For it is in our openness to truth in whatever shape it comes that we are preparing for the ultimate openness some name, mythologically, as the day of judgement. It is in our resistance to falsehood, in whatever shape it comes, that we fight off what some name, mythologically, as Satan.

And the deepest falsehood is not to do with telling lies about this or that; not even with misnaming God. It is to do with the denial of belonging together which God invites us to, and which we as Church need to realise and to taste and to service, if creation is to be cradled into any permanent healing.

4

Becoming and Belonging[*]

Where is home for the postmodern generation?

Let me begin by introducing to you a sociologist called Zygmunt Bauman, Polish by birth; his book is called *Postmodernity and its Discontents*.

The second chapter, hauntingly called 'The Making and Unmaking of Strangers', sets the scene for us. He writes: 'The image of the world daily generated by present-day life-concerns is devoid of genuine or assumed solidity and continuity. By cautious, and if anything, conservative calculations, rich Europe counts among its citizens about three million homeless, twenty million evicted from the labour market, thirty million living below the poverty-line.'

The switch from the project of community as the guardian of the universal right to decent and dignified life, to the promotion of the market as the sufficient guarantee of the universal choice of self-enrichment, deepens further the suffering of the new poor, adding insult to their injury, glossing poverty with humiliation and with denial of consumer freedom, now identical with humanity. 'Tesco ergo sum: I buy therefore I am.'

Only the few powerful enough to blackmail the other powerful into the obligation of a golden handshake can be sure that their home, however prosperous and imposing it may seem today, is not haunted by the spectre of tomorrow's downfall. No jobs are guaranteed, no positions are foolproof, no skills are of lasting utility. Experience and know-how turn into liabilities as soon as they become assets; seductive careers all too often prove to be suicide tracks.

The other safety nets (neighbourhood or family) have been considerably weakened. The changing pragmatics of interpersonal relations, now

* Extracts from a talk given in Kirkwall, Orkney, 18–19 January 2000.

permeated by the ruling spirit of consumerism, and thus casting the other as the potential source of pleasurable experience, is partly to blame: whatever else the new pragmatics is good at, it cannot generate lasting bonds, and most certainly not the bonds which are *presumed* as lasting and treated as such. The bonds which it does generate in profusion have inbuilt until-further-notice and unilateral withdrawal-at-will clauses, and promise neither the granting nor the acquisition of rights and obligations.

The image, the mask, the role, the replayable video – all these, Bauman suggests, replace the sense of stable identity which medieval man had: a fixed place in an eternal scheme of things. It might be at the bottom of the heap, but it was still a given place. You knew where you were.

Today, our children inherit a world in which 'belonging' is problematic. Last year, I heard an Irish Jesuit sketch the feel of young people in Dublin. He began by showing a slide of a terraced house in an inner-city street. Coming down the road, pulling a shopping trolley, was a wee Dublin wife, drab coat, boots and a headscarf, an image of modest, undemanding, colourless life. In the garden of one of the houses, four young people were emerging – all more or less punk-style. One had a Mohican haircut. All were studded with earrings, lip rings and metalled leather. They wore mostly black with odd flashes of shocking pink or orange. One girl wore dangling suspenders over skin-tight leggings with ten inches of bare thigh. Their faces were masks of make-up: huge eyes, pale faces, dark lips. Across the low garden hedge, the woman stared at them and they stared back at her as if they came from different planets. Yet only six yards separated them, and they were living simultaneously as far as the clock went. Michael-Paul went on to describe the terrifying statistics of young people, especially young men in Dublin who attempted suicide, in a city where poverty wasn't a significant element, and said that he had come to understand the inescapable sense of rootlessness which pervaded their generation. His summary was: no sense of place; no sense of history; no sense of belonging.

Many years ago, the sociologist Peter Berger published a little paperback called *The Homeless Mind*, which was a vivid account of this sense of the fragmentation of identity that was beginning to so characterise our culture. I remember discussing this book in a group which included a former missionary from Kenya. His first comment was illuminating. 'This title', he said, 'could not be translated in the language of the people I was working with. First, they had no word for "mind": they didn't think of people as a combination of two or three bits, "body", "mind", "soul". Nor did they have a word for "homeless": the nearest approximation to that in their language would have been a worse meaning, "He who is far away from where he belongs".'

That was, for me, a startling reflection on my culture, that I inherit a language which makes room for homelessness as a state of being, and that there are (or were) cultures where that was impossible. One could only be lost, or far away, not without a home.

As so often, I find it is the poets and novelists who often catch the situation with a precision which eludes the theologian. One of my treasured resources is the writing of R.S. Thomas, poet-priest of Wales. He has one poignant little poem:

'The Word'

A pen appeared, and the god said:
'Write what it is to be
man.' And my hand hovered
long over the bare page,

until there, like footprints
of the lost traveller, letters
took shape on the page's
blankness, and I spelled out

the word 'lonely'. And my hand moved
to erase it: but the voices
of all those waiting at life's
window cried out loud: 'It is true.'

That poem comes from a collection called *Laboratories of the Spirit* in which the poet accepts that he cannot return to the old stories, the old forms of prayer, the old expectations of healing, the old self-blame. In the last four lines of the first poem in the collection, 'Emerging', he writes:

Circular as our way
is, it leads not back to that snake-haunted
garden, but onward to the tall city
of glass that is the laboratory of the spirit.

But where *is* home for the postmodern generation? An e-mail address? Light, portable, placeless, timeless, insubstantial? You may also begin to wonder if there really is a common world anywhere, or whether we only inhabit various shifting tectonic plates which slide past each other with occasional volcanic or earthquake causing collisions. Where does one belong in such a world? What does one hope for? What are the ways, if any, of creative becoming amid such complexity, such rapidity of change, such a plurality of vantage points?

5

Angels in the Trees? A Theology for Today[*]

The hunger for theology is as deep as the hunger for spirituality.

I met Milan Opočenský once or twice in the context of the Christian Peace Conference in the 1970s as my ecumenical horizon and sense of history were expanding. As a young man, Milan was assistant to Professor Josef Hromádka, founder of the Christian Peace Conference; and, after a spell as European Secretary of the World Student Christian Federation and later as professor in the Comenius Faculty of the Church of Czech Brethren in Prague, he became General Secretary of the World Alliance of Reformed Churches. I met him when I applied for his position as General Secretary of WARC! There are probably many reasons why I didn't get it; but the most obvious point where Milan blinked in the interview was when he asked me if I believed in the Protestant principle of *sola scriptura*, and I confessed that I didn't and tried to say why.

Of course, for anyone theologically schooled in Protestant Scotland, 'the Word' was probably *the* central category. It was, admittedly, occasionally hinted that the Word was Christ, rather than scripture, but in effect it was the Bible that was the safe gatekeeper to that Word, the criterion of truth. So, hermeneutics was the battleground. And the whole complex of issues about whether 'scripture interprets itself' or is only interpretable when we recognise a whole range of dimensions – language, culture, politics and so on – which bear on our understanding, is dense and almost frightening.

But it's also exciting, and it seems to me one of the biggest ecumenical challenges. So really, I'm trying to articulate that challenge and to test

* A talk given by Elizabeth Templeton in Scottish Churches House on 25 March 2008 at *Promise*, an international conference on the ecumenical movement in honour of the Czech theologian Milan Opočenský (1931–2007).

whether you find it convincingly named – and, if Milan is overhearing, it's a rather longer reply than I could give at my interview!

When the poet William Blake was eight, or ten perhaps, he had his first vision as he wandered the outskirts of eighteenth-century London which he found so fascinating. In 1797, parental anxiety about a child going off for the day was less acute than now! Sauntering along on Peckham Rye, by Dulwich Hill – Margaret and Denis Thatcher might not have bought their retirement home had they known – he looked up and saw a mulberry tree, filled with angels, 'bright angelic wings bespangling every bough like stars'. Coming home, he related this incident, and only escaped a thrashing from his father for telling a lie by his mother's intercession, though she too, on occasions, beat him for his precocious claims, e.g. that he saw the prophet Ezekiel in a tree under the fields.

We seem to be experiencing, at least in the West, a revival of 'spirituality', unthinkable in the 1960s, when many of us here were theologically being formed; when 'secular' was a positive and resourceful concept, rather than a negative and demonised word, as in current Vatican discourse. So, Blakean visions might get a more sympathetic response from many of the population than a few decades ago. But there is a corresponding *loss* of sympathy for doctrine or dogma, associated as they are with the negative adjectives in English, 'doctrinaire' and 'dogmatic'. So, the 'W'ord is suspect, under siege.

Probably not one in a thousand will have heard of, far less read, the big names of postmodernism like Foucault and Derrida, but the hermeneutic of distrust and deconstruction is in the air now. Every apprentice reporter and news interviewer learns how to interrogate for the subtext – and the general suspicion of spin in every political utterance is deep in public life, with corrosive effect.

One of my most significant theological teachers was Tom Torrance, who recently died. He distrusted the social sciences, but believed that theology was 'up there' with the natural sciences as disclosing 'objective truth'. (It will be interesting to hear the eventual heavenly dialogue between him and Richard Dawkins!) Tom had a kind of theological apostolic succession which jumped the centuries from Christ to Athanasius, Athanasius to Calvin, Calvin to Barth, and Barth to Torrance, with a few minor links in between. 'His' theocratic Barth was deeply conservative, disapproved of long hair, beards, modern music and Picasso. So, for me it was a revelation and a wonder to arrive in Prague in 1969 – and revisit it for the next five years in a row – and discover the other European Barth: of Milan Opočenský and Hromádka and Helmut Gollwitzer – the

radical Barth, undergirding conversations with Communism which terrified most Western liberal theologians.

Interestingly enough, several of Tom's students, Alastair Hulbert
among them, took off into front-line situations like the French Protestant
Industrial Mission, resisting both Tom's politics and his somewhat
authoritarian churchmanship. Another New College teacher/colleague,
Roland Walls, had a typically imaginative account of Tom's bewilderment and dismay as these able students of his went zooming off into
radical ministries. It was, said Roland, as if Tom had constructed a
powerful theological motorbike, and sat there in the garden, revving it
up! Vroom, Vroom! Then various students, appreciating the bike's power,
took off in all directions, and went! Leaving Tom, perplexed, still revving
up in his garden!

Who sees what angels in what strange trees? And how, if at all, is it
connected to theological discourse? That's my lead question. First, I
want to say something about language, in the face of much Christian
malaise – again from the Vatican down – but also in Presbyterian 'W'ord-
land that we are losing it; and that we need to battle to retrieve the
ground invaded by postmodernity, with its apparent dissolving of
'T'ruth, of grand narrative, of objectivity and certainty.

I am convinced that we should be seeing this dissolution of certainty
not as threat but as gift, and that it needs to be used creatively to make
tentative 'raids on the inarticulate' for a while yet. Without panic, and
with a sense of serious exploratory play, as children play. But I also
believe we need to be more *confident* about language, about the wondrous
power and grace of good words; and part of the 'decoding theology'
business is finding intermediaries who use words with freshness, and
force the clichés of piety to be dismantled, and the rumours of angels to
be overheard.

I'd like to start with a vision of the diversity of language as gift –
'angels in the trees' – from the Jewish philosopher, George Steiner. In
1975, he wrote a short, sharp essay called *After Babel*. (This year [2008],
he revisited and elaborated on the theme in *My Unwritten Books*.) 'I
have argued in *After Babel* that the thousandfold multiplicity of incom-
prehensible languages once spoken on this earth – so many are now
extinct or disappearing – is not, as mythologies and allegories of disaster
would have it, a curse. It is, on the contrary, a blessing and a jubilation.'

He goes on: 'Each and every human tongue is a window on being, on
creation. A window like no other. There are no "small" languages,
however reduced their demographic or environmental setting. Certain

languages spoken in the Kalahari desert feature more and subtler ramifications of the subjunctive than were available to Aristotle. Hopi grammars possess nuances of temporality and motion more consonant with the physics of relativity and undecidability than our own Indo-European and Anglo-Saxon resources.'

Now that's a scholar's mouthful, especially after a Scottish Churches House breakfast! But his conclusion is magical, I think: 'The consequence is a boundless wealth of possibility. Every human tongue challenges reality in its own unique manner. There are as many constellations of futurity, of hope, of religious, metaphysical and political projection – "dreaming forward" – as there are optative and counterfactual verb forms. Hope is empowered by syntax.'

That maybe doesn't sound too much like *sola scriptura*, but it seems to me to have a finesse and subtlety, that words are among the huge gifts of humankind to resist authoritarian absolutes – to name the garden, the Adamic gift: 'It is the seemingly wasteful plethora of languages which allows us to articulate alternatives to reality, to speak freedom within servitude, to programme plenty within destitution . . . Without the great octave of possible grammars, such negation and "alterity", this wager on tomorrow, would not be feasible.'

Now, why would one want to articulate 'alternatives to reality'? The idea, of course, is not about fantasy but about *resistance*, which is why I find the subtitle of Dorothee Sölle's *The Silent Cry: Mysticism and Resistance* (2001) so haunting. The 'and' is fascinating. It is her testimony to the link between the angels in the trees and the energy to challenge every status quo of contemporary life which is so impressive.

She writes: 'In feminist discussion there is often a critique of religion's fixation on transcendence, including ecstasy, which is said to be just another attempt by patriarchal culture to abandon the body. Here, religion is suspect, as one of the most effective instruments for keeping the body, sensuousness, and women under the suppression of the mind and the male. Does religion not instil denial of and hostility toward the body? And does this not then serve the interest of strategies of social control of women?

'Such a totalising suspicion overlooks both the reality of oppression and liberation. The mystical ecstasy of losing oneself does not dismiss the body as an ill-functioning machine: rather it sets the body free for a different and new self-expression.

'In order to comprehend the mystical element in religion, we have to go beyond the hermeneutic of suspicion. Suspicion is appropriate wherever religion exercises unrestricted total power over the life of women. In our situation, one in which organised religion appears to be negligible, to say the least, and irrelevant for the majority of people, our enquiry needs a different point of departure. Rather than asking what political dominion religious power uses to consolidate its own power, we need to ask what it is that women and men are looking for in their cry for a different spirituality. I try to depict a hermeneutic of hunger.

'It has been described often enough, this search for meaning, or the bottomless emptiness into which consumerism plunges people. Depression and isolation transport women and men into a kind of spiritual anorexia where any kind of nourishment is nauseating. Suspicion can no longer release such people from the constraints of tradition: what drives them on is a yearning to lead a different kind of life.'

Here at Scottish Churches House over the past few years, we have had several series of conversations about spirituality which bear out the reality of that hunger. It's also conspicuous how often one hears people, for instance in radio interviews, saying the likes of 'I'm spiritual but I'm not religious'. But if 'religious' has a negative undertone in much common perception, 'theological' is even worse – a word to send people shifting away from you on the bus. (Though, interestingly, when we recently visited Sydney, the immigration officer, as well as inspecting my boots, spent a good two minutes commenting on the 'theologian' I had put down on my visa card. 'We don't get many of these in a year.' 'Do you work in a university?' 'No, I used to but now I work freelance.' 'Who wants a freelance theologian?' and so on.)

Now, I believe that the hunger for theology is as deep as the hunger for spirituality: indeed that they are two faces of the same coin, and that either without the other is weakened and liable to corruption. But culturally, here at least, the *word* 'theology' suffers on the pavement from associations of aridity, sterility, stuff about angels dancing on pinheads, not in mulberry trees, and theoretical debate that has nothing to do with life or death.

Around 1971, the aforementioned Tom Torrance appointed a forty-odd-year-old Greek Orthodox lay theologian called John Zizioulas. John would begin a class by asking: 'If we look at John's phrase "The Word became flesh", what would you say "became" meant?' And he would wait, minutes if need be, until the paralysis subsided and someone risked saying something. Then he would pick it up and run with it. 'Well, if that's what it means, what would the implication be for . . .?' And the class would be rolling.

I, who had the good fortune to have my staffroom adjacent to the classroom where this was going on, remember two students passing my open door after one such lecture; students who were proudly fundamentalist, and one saying to the other in some bewilderment, 'Do you know, I think I was thinking in that class!' John has argued in his two major books, *Being as Communion* and *Communion and Otherness*, that the bipolar integration of freedom and reciprocity (a kind of shorthand naming of his vision of the Trinity) was the test and the benchmark of truth.

For me, who had been languishing for seven years in a kind of post-analytic-philosophy agnosticism, the theological encounter with John was liberating beyond belief. He decoded theology for me. Not only the shadowy remnants of my Calvinist culture with its determinist God, but also the limitations of my rationalist, individualistic, measuring, classifying, secular culture were undercut by this account of God as utterly free: utterly open, even to becoming not-God, utterly unlike the Superbloke of popular religious imagination.

The importance of the *apophatic* tradition, that deep sense in Orthodoxy that when you say something of God you have to unsay it – though I had glimpsed it in some of the Western mystical tradition – struck me with a new force and credibility. That sounds esoteric; and on one level it is. You won't get snappy soundbites in *Communion and Otherness*. But you will get the sense that there is *nothing* in creation made to be separate, though much made to be distinct and particular. For John, Christology is a tool not for exclusivity but for inclusivity: from the dust of the stars to the marine life of the Black Sea, from the cosmic to the *humanum* and back again.

It would take me much more time than I have to expand on all that. But, in closing, I would just like to testify that I find the most remarkable resonance between many of the insights of secular culture and encounter and this deeply Orthodox theologian, who has done so much to make *koinonia* fundamental to the theology/ecclesiology and anthropology of contemporary ecumenism.

The ideological battle between theism and atheism is, I suspect, now an anachronism, sterile and pointless. Nicholas Lash in *The Beginning and End of Religion* (1999) makes that one clear. What it means to 'believe in God' is not tested by the concepts you can affirm, any more than atheism is tested by the concepts you can't swallow. The issue is on another level: about what you long for, to the extent that you would die for it. Being 'godless' is having nothing you would die for.

In Scotland, traditional theology falls more and more on deaf ears, both in church and in society. Almost all of Scotland's major poets for decades have been formally atheist, shaking off the brutalisations of their childhood's merciless, punitive deities who still stalk the corridors of schools and church halls, though with diminishing purchase!

That is not just because we have failed to *live* convincingly, though it is partly that, of course. It is also that we have not engaged intellectually with the tides of culture of which someone like George Steiner is a creative and suggestive interpreter. We have let theological and even biblical language fossilise, become arterially sclerotic.

For freshness, I find, at present, the most helpful place to be looking is to the custodians of the imagination: the artists, poets, novelists, filmmakers who pay attention to the world in ways which create new awareness of what Steiner himself calls 'real presences', and Peter Berger five decades back called 'rumours of angels'. These are not 'full-blown' theology. But they are experiences, awarenesses, sensitivities which open up, for example, to the sheer irreducible otherness of another, to the fragility of the cosmos, to the sense of communion with the stuff of the world, and so on.

We have forfeited, for various reasons, mulberry trees full of angels. But I believe that we should/can hold the waiting time for a new theological discourse quietly and with an intent to be ready. I don't quite believe we can *make* it. That would be too Pelagian! But I dare to hope that it will come upon us if we listen with attention: both to the world and to the Bible, and to tradition and to the creativities of human experiences. *Sola scriptura* won't quite do!

6

*Are the Christians Still Among the Prophets?** *

If you speak of God-informed existence, you cannot distinguish your knowing of someone from your loving of them. You do not have two things, knowing and loving. In your loving is your knowing, your capacity to speak the truth. And out of love you know nothing.

'Among all forms of mistake,' according to George Eliot, 'prophecy is the most gratuitous', and, according to St Paul, 'it will pass away'. A risky and provisional job, then, prophesying! Certainly from a philosopher of religion trained to answer in terms of 'on the one hand . . . on the other . . . depending on what you mean by . . .' you must not expect anything so bold.

But as soon as the sentence is out, ghosts of Amos stalk the campus and rebuke: 'He who forms the mountains and creates the wind and declares to man what is his thought gives not a fig for your critical reflection. For while you reflect, injustice is done to my poor, saith the Lord of Hosts, and they die.' What is to be said to these ghosts? Or is any answer 'alibi-ism'?

I was asked to speak about the question in relation to academic life and particularly about chaplaincy work. There may, of course, be important differences between teaching staff and chaplains, particularly if the chaplain is not on the university payroll, but a 'resident alien'. However, I am going to speak for most of the time as if Christian, chaplain and theologian were synonyms – a rash assumption which many on the earth might doubt. I am also going to restrict myself to the rather parochial Scottish scene, which I hope may serve as a case study.

---

* Address to the European Student Chaplains Conference, Brezje (former Yugoslavia, now Slovenia), May 1978.

The absurd theological question I want to ask is: 'What has God to do with the University of Edinburgh?' For, unless that is provisionally answered, the question of who the prophets are or how the Christians relate to them can scarcely be tackled. The question sounds bizarre, like asking how the laws of thermodynamics have to do with my aunt's budgerigar. But I take it that any university is a paradigmatic institution, and that any institution is a microcosm of our structural existence in the world.

There is, of course, a kind of formal piety which would say that, like everywhere else, the University of Edinburgh depends on God for its continuing existence. This supposition is feebly implied by the fact that the Senatus Academicus opens with prayer, even if half of its members stand with their eyes embarrassedly open. Every intent theologian knows that God is omnipresent. He must therefore be present also in the University of Edinburgh. *Quod erat demonstrandum.*

If, however, we resist the blandness of abstract theism, and return to the brutalities of the prophet Amos, the presence of God is not a uniformly supportive relation. There are places, it seems, whose dust he will shake from off his omnipotent feet: things he cannot digest and spits out. Is the University of Edinburgh one of them?

If one moves even timidly on the fringe of radical circles, the answer 'yes' seems the likeliest one to emerge from prophets and the trainers of prophets. There we are, a palpably elitist structure, daily reversing all the Beatitudes, cultivating the intellectual excellence of the naturally clever and already well-educated. There we are, diligently pursuing, so the story goes, truth for truth's sake, aloof from the sordid ideologies of lesser minds. There we go providing bits of paper to increase and reinforce the division between professional and non-professional in a world where esteem and power lie with the former.

For seven years now, I have discussed the problem of evil in leisured classrooms, half a mile away from alcoholic-filled hostels and night shelters for the homeless. None of that is remotely like those images of community we call the Kingdom of God, and one could go on cataloguing the greater and lesser inanities and barbarisms of the place for much of the evening. But, for me at least, that would be the rhetoric of indignation and sedentary guilt. It would not be prophecy. Nor do I think it would be prophecy for you, because you expect it, and could take it for granted, and would clap. That would be my first clue for the detection of prophets. Their hearers are surprised, and do not like what is said. That is no guarantee of prophecy, but a minimal indication.

So, I will not say much about the obvious educational reforms which anyone of humane thoughtfulness would be fighting for: that students should not be spoon-fed, and subjected to ridiculous examinations which prevent thought rather than encourage it; that subjects should not be artificially so isolated that a question cannot be followed where it organically leads; or that departments should not all belong to one provincial school of thought (as, for instance, British philosophy currently does) so that students should have no choice of courses.

Nor will I say much about the more controversial political prophets, because I doubt if for you they are controversial. How does the university relate to the local community? (Edinburgh, for instance, has a building policy which seriously affects housing in the city centre.) The quadrangle of the divinity faculty is now the way into the Sheriff Court, which has the use of Church premises on the other side. Where does university finance come from? Where does it go to? What will become of work done by science staff on biological warfare techniques?

Why should everyone not go to university? Are present policies not just dictated by a stupid government trying to disguise unemployment levels? Should students not appoint and assess staff rather than being assessed by them? Whatever the implications of these questions, I am sure that they need to be squarely faced, and battle done about them if need be.

I am going to explore a worry with you. I am terrified that there is in a certain kind of political theology a new puritanism with two attendant dangers. The first is self-righteousness, and the second is shame at enjoyment. The first is heard in the constant prayer: O God, I thank you that I am not as this Liberal is. And the second may, I suspect, be present in the demand, shared by radicals and the British Department of Education and Science, that the university should further some specific social end, or stand unjustifiable.

I will not sound like the Vice-Chancellor on speech day, but suppose for a moment that you thought of intellectual delight as something like making music or making love: a kind of play between people which is not a means to something else. I have a friend who, because of his commitment to the working-class area he lives in, feels he must not play his cello any more.

Now, I find it a little hard to offer you proof-texts, but I think he is wrong. God likes cello-playing. And I suspect that it is being more niggardly than God to ask an artist or a lover or a delighted thinker to justify his activity. Of course I am terrified that I am simply saying something obscene. But I throw it at you. And I report, as a matter of autobiography, that my main professional pain is that we so rarely teach in a way which lets people be exhilarated in learning.

But what then about God, or any proof-texts! What I will not sketch is a conviction which I regard as distinctively New Testament. I am a New Testament scholar only by matrimony, but I am rather convinced that the New Testament is significantly different from the Old in some matters, and I would just plead for one thing. If Christians really find the Old Testament the base of their commitment, they should be frank about that. But it is neither frank nor free to say 'I believe *x* to be true, as the OT says, therefore I must show that the NT says it.' Actually, I believe that both Old and New Testaments often say internally diverse and even contradictory things (and here we would need a big debate about hermeneutics), but I am willing to give you my canon within the canon.

God, then, if I read it straight, is inviting the world to a new identity where freedom and love will converge, i.e. where no one's relation to anyone else will be burdensome or coerced, and yet where no one's existence will be dispensable or un-delightful to anyone else. Even more boldly, he is inviting it towards a future which death does not decisively frustrate, so that there is no need for the panic-stricken self-protectiveness which is our natural way of living.

Such a possibility, however, does not, according to much of the New Testament, belong to our moral endeavour, nor is it wholly continuous with our present world. That is not to say it is another world altogether. But it is this world more radically transformed than human doing can transform it. It is this world with no institutions which classify and segregate people (and which institution, by creating a boundary between those who belong and those who do not, does not?); the end of assessment in terms of success and failure, and the end of that limitation of the nerve-ends which, for us, makes privacy necessary.

If that vision is not a piece of Gnostic escapism, then the distinctive vocation of a Christian or Christian community would be in fact to manifest certain strangenesses. The first strangeness would be that everything is appraised against the Kingdom of God. More basic dissatisfactions than those of the most zealous revolutionary, though including his, are warranted, because the hope for the *eschaton* is restless not only about the ethically manageable, but also about the morally unmanageable. (Man) is addressed as not-yet-his-proper-self in the context of necessity and limitation and death which apparently define his possibilities. (This, incidentally, seems to me one of the most important areas in

Christian–Marxist dialogue: whether our obvious subjection to causality, economic, biological, psychological, is to be welcomed as part of our true humanness or deplored as part of the distortion of creation which theologians call 'Fall'.)

The second, compounding strangeness is that this recognition of distance between the world and the Kingdom is not translatable into blame or judgement. If there are any Christian prophets, then I suspect they are prophetic by not judging others. This is not merely a question of accidental ignorance, that one doesn't have access to the complexity of need and motivation in oneself or others. It is, I think, a more novel and far-reaching suggestion of Christian epistemology that if you speak of God-informed existence you cannot distinguish your knowing of someone from your loving of them. You do not have two things, knowing and loving. In your loving is your knowing, your capacity to speak the truth. And out of love you know nothing. Or, put differently, you cannot want to exclude the other from your existence and know him.

From this strangeness, I think Christianity might make a distinctive input to the discussions of 'objectivity' which are part of any university's self-consciousness, for it comes back to suggesting an inseparable bond between knowledge and delight. But then, if judgement disappears, are the Christians still among the prophets?

Perhaps: there is a distinction between judging as wanting to exclude, to punish, to make culpable, and being so inclusively 'for everyone' that those who are really against co-existence have to take themselves off.

The third strangeness is that Christians should not go mad under the strain of living 'between two worlds', manic when they anticipate the hilarity of their *eschaton*, and depressive when they see no sign of its arrival. Perhaps it is the main distinction between the Christian and either Stoic or Manichean that he is sometimes allowed to relax. His incapacities and his neighbours are neither the end of the world, nor the resigning of the world to hopelessness. It strikes me sometimes when I see the faces of those who feel so urgent to renew the world that they are entirely taut, they cannot let up for a moment without guilt.

The fourth strangeness is that the first three together do not make Christians inert. While none of our doing, on my reading, constitutes the Kingdom, since none of our doing undoes death, there is a gift of being which signals the hope of its coming. It is, however, no longer obligation. It is more like being unable to avoid laughter, a kind of making love to the world which sees it in the light of its unprogrammable future, and is not defeated by how it now is. Quite rarely one meets people who leave that impression in the amount of space they make around them for others.

If we call these strangenesses 'eschatological existence', or life with a toe in an alternative future, what shape would it, or does it, or can it take in the University of Edinburgh?

Above all, as anywhere in Scotland, it would be against the moralising self-righteousness of the culture, which may be due to too little sunlight, or to the shadow of Calvinism. People brought up in Scotland learn early to know themselves as decent or not. If they have a job, they are decent; if they are out of work, they are not. If they say 'I did' and 'I have gone', they are decent. If they say 'I done' and 'I've went', they are not. Decent people who drink gin and tonic at home in decent districts hold veto polls to stop pubs being built there, so that they do not meet the indecent mobile drinking population which might invade the area. The Residents Association in one Edinburgh street petitioned against the Scottish Minorities Group (which campaigns for Gay Liberation) being allowed to put up a nameplate, because they did not want the area contaminated by the publicly announced traffic of homosexuals. Decent children are taught to respect teachers and policemen and property. Decent people go to church. And, as an example of a repressed, violent, puritan culture, it would be hard to beat. It is hard to know how you undo or even unmask a culture. Prophetic debauchery might be one way, though more liable than most to misinterpretation. Cultural comparison might be another, more easily undertaken in a university context, where social psychology, sociology of ideas, history and theology departments might fruitfully collaborate. Even more constructive would be to provide ways where people come up against the humanness of those they have never had to take seriously. But that probably means sustained meeting, since slogans can survive occasional contact and immense amounts of information.

Prophets need above all imagination, to find the Nathan story, or enact the telling parable, and for that, probably, their only allies are the artists. Of course, the strategic difficulty is how to welcome the people dehumanised by these absurd norms without hating existentially those who defend them (who presumably need salvation even more). Can you eat with the Pharisees and with the Publicans? Is that perhaps the distinctive agitation which a Christian prophet creates, by refusing to let either lot think themselves valuable at the expense of the other? Or is that out-Christing Christ, and getting fat with weak liberalism? What anyway is the analogue to eating with the Pharisees? Letting the National Front, or the Lord's Day Observance Society, use the chaplaincy centre as well as

Students for Socialism and Third World First, and going to the meeting to protest? Or letting anyone use it who applies, and not going to the meeting to protest? Can such permissiveness with one's enemies reflect the love of God, or only disguise it? The question is not rhetorical. I cannot answer it, and would like to share some concentration on it.

I am influenced enough by Marxist teaching to think that people are often incapable of thinking certain thoughts because they live where they do and as they do. And influenced enough by Freudian teaching to believe that rationalisation is not confined to the upper classes. But I do not believe that the influence between ideas and praxis is unidirectional. An idea is potent in shaping existence, not just vice versa.

To undermine moralism and class-consciousness therefore, one also needs to unpick ideas, and this seems to me the particular job of the Christian in an intellectual context. For certainly in Scotland, the way things are is caused in part by the conviction that God is behind the order of things. The immediate protest against this is made most often by the poets and novelists, who have no option but to abolish God.

Thus, in one novel, Iain Crichton Smith, not in his own judgement a Christian, describes an episode where a boy goes round his girlfriend's classroom in the primary school where she teaches: 'They walked round and they looked at drawings and paintings; they saw magazines and newspapers lying about on desks, they saw piles of bright books, crayons, tape recorders, record players. The painting on the walls, she told him, were by the children themselves. Everywhere were bright colours, a higgledy-piggledy storm of creativity as if ideas were being picked out of the air . . . There was no sense of a forced order, no sense of anyone looking for a theology that would unite the data, that would arrange the world. Everything incomplete, disorderly, sprawling.'

To endorse this theologically, one has, I think, to go a long, long way back behind medieval Europe and the Protestant Reformation to some of the quite early Greek writings, which centuries later produced Dostoevsky and his resistance to tidy boundaries. And access to such vastly different readings of Christian tradition is, sadly, only slowly acquired.

But is it worth it? Why not just leave the prophesying to the atheists or the Marxists, and let the slow erosion of God-talk go on irrelevantly? Why not leave the religious language with the bogey-man behind the Protestant work-ethic and lace curtains? Why not let the theologians cover their theistic nakedness with Marxist fig leaves? Why even try to expose people to explicit Christians, a policy which is so frequently fatal to their health as human beings?

My conviction at the moment is that I do not trust any other context quite so much to keep me uncomplacent about my identity, to insist that I am homeless so long as I am not at home with anyone I meet, not welcoming his entrance. Of course, I cannot do it psychologically, politically, ethically. There I stand for and against, and my existence is partisan. But I will be discontented with the state of affairs, even if I can do nothing about it; and I will encourage others to be discontented. And my only alternative image is of the Kingdom of God: an absence, but an absence which exerts leverage on all my political possibilities.

You must be now convinced that living in one ivory tower has made me project it onto the cosmos, and of course I have real fear that you may be right. (Incidentally, the only literary reference I know to towers of ivory is to the Queen of Sheba's neck, and I would be interested to know how and when it became a term of abuse for scholastic isolation.)

If however I am not altogether wrong, how does my eschatological ivory tower affect my existence in the northern hemisphere, if that is the direction of influence? It gives me a perspective from which to criticise, to challenge and to generate restlessness. It convinces me that I have not understood someone who disagrees with me until I can be so inside his skin that I can see myself as him. It persuades me that, as a teacher, I must move in the direction of giving my students infinite space and infinite time.

It makes the notion of homelessness, of not having things taped, mandatory. It invites me to imaginative excess, to lunacy, to eliminating all boundaries, to leaving all my willed and necessary isolations. It makes me recognise that children are crucial to the Kingdom, and promiscuous lovers, and mental defectives, and the impotent. For all these are unselfconscious. They have no idea that their failures are fatal. They sleep without guilt. And in that, they are Christian prophets. But by now, Jews, Greeks and Marxists must be tearing their un-utopian collective hair, so I will stop, before you are all quite bald.

PART 2

MAKING SENSE
OF THEOLOGY

Introduction

Charlotte Methuen

Elizabeth Templeton never taught me in a classroom, but she became for me a theological teacher, mentor and guide through the weekly 'At Homes' to which she and Douglas were still, in the late 1980s, inviting any New College students who wished to attend. These offered space to explore the kind of questions which too often seemed beyond the university's curriculum, and to make connections between different fields within and outside theology, while drinking wine and sharing a large sofa with the Templeton children and dog. Pondering God as both *A* and not *A* (heady stuff for a recent mathematician), considering the boundaries of knowing and knowability, wondering how the language of systematic theology meshed (or not) with the lived experience of faith: these were important evenings during which the conversation might lead anywhere (indeed it took me, in 1989, to Germany), and the process of getting there – the questions asked, the stones turned, the experience reflected and the books pored over – was as important as (probably more important than) any end result. This focus on the way of getting there is evident from the papers collected in this section, which show Elizabeth's passion for considering the ways in which theological, or religious, thought is in reality constructed, and the context in which that thought emerges, in people's actual, lived lives.

For Elizabeth, theology was never a series of syllogisms, but a matter of questions which arose from the realities of living life and all the challenges that this entails. Her vision of theology, as the epigraph to this book reminds us, was as a 'convivial, energising conversation, engaging every aspect of the self, and open to every partner'. In 1977, she published an essay entitled 'The Defence of Disorder' (*Theology* vol. 80, pp. 413–22), in which she laid out the approach which underlay her theology. Concluding that article, she summarised:

This negative placing of order which I recommend for theological attention would affect the whole range of attitudes and political stances we take to the artist, the criminal, the madman, the State, the Church, the university, the limits of our nature, and perhaps (though this will be my last ditch) the law of non-contradiction. At any rate, it strikes me currently as one of the few theological suggestions I have encountered which combines realism about how-the-world-is with the refusal to identify that with how-God-wants-it-to-be. (p. 422)

'Realism about how-the-world-is' combined with 'the refusal to identify that with how-God-wants-it-to-be': the lectures and talks collected here show Elizabeth's ongoing concern with that fundamental – and fundamentally important – struggle.

For Elizabeth, engaging with 'how-the-world-is' required facing up to uncomfortable realities. She wanted theology and theologians to engage with the fact that when she asked twenty-two students what they meant when they said God exists, she received 'about thirteen *substantively* different answers, some of them quite incompatible with one another', indicating that when people say the same thing, they do not always mean the same thing. How do theologians engage with that? Elizabeth wanted them to think about it, to acknowledge this as reality and not pretend that words mean the same to all people in all contexts. She wanted to engage with the truth of doubt, whether expressed within or outwith the Church, and to recognise that apparently secular discourse might be revealing something about God's relationship with the world. These fundamental convictions are expressed in the texts gathered in this section in her powerful reflection on apologetics, which grew out of her own experience of having to rethink, and rediscover, the basis of her faith through her encounter with philosophy, but they also underlie her gloriously imaginative approach to teaching the 1968 Junior Bible class at her church, which ended with the entire congregation talking about theology, and her explorations of the assumption of faith with a group of counsellors. In 1992, they inspired her to found Threshold, the theological drop-in centre that she ran at Tollcross, Edinburgh, until 1999.

Elizabeth was deeply aware of the way in which the theological landscape was changing, but she was aware too of the even more radical changes to the intellectual landscape, and she worried that theology was failing to respond to these. In an unpublished essay on 'Truth, Authority and Freedom', Elizabeth affirmed her position of 'gratitude to all those who point out the ways in which we are culturally conditioned in thought, feeling and conduct, both individually and as a society'. However, she said:

> I am not convinced that that awareness makes it necessary to give up all confidence that some things are true and others false. What it does force us to recognise is that there may be, in our seeing, all kinds of blinkeredness, and that we need one another to have any hope of corrigibility. But it is a long step further (and a *non sequitur* to boot, I suspect), to argue that there is nothing at all to see.

There are important insights here for our current age of 'fake news'. Elizabeth was deeply aware of the danger that postmodernism 'merely nurtures a culture of separate, non-communicating worlds' serving 'to increase the sense of fragmentation and disintegration which characterises so much of contemporary life'. But she also saw opportunities: could postmodernity herald 'a global advance in the renunciation of dogma and the recognition of how belief shifts, depending on all sorts of local, cultural, linguistic, political factors'? Elizabeth hoped it could, and that through these developments, both theology and scripture might 'become living and dynamic protagonists in present life-decisions'.

For Elizabeth, 'how-the-world-is' also meant looking at the natural world and its realities. These could be inspirational, as her vignette on the lake and the sand-dove (drawn from her paper on 'Truth, Authority and Freedom') illustrates, but the realities of the world also brought her to ask some difficult questions about the relationship between good and evil. Here too, Elizabeth wanted language to be anchored in reality. How do young people actually understand the terminology of 'evil', she asked: what do they – and indeed we – actually count as evil? How does this vary between, and within, religious traditions? And how can these questions speak into a context which has become profoundly 'sceptical of truth claims'? These were questions she felt should be being asked by all students of Religious Studies, at whatever level.

Elizabeth's deep sense of the connectedness of the world brought her to reject much theological discourse about evil. She insisted: 'I do not want my soul made, thank you very much, at the cost of my neighbour's pain and misery and death. Nor do I believe that God wants souls made at that cost.' The natural processes of ageing, which, she recognised, bring maturity, also bring 'obscene senility where communication breaks down'. Her own home-life showed her that. Elizabeth's sense that 'our involvement in the cosmos is, existentially speaking, bitter-sweet' acquires a new and urgent resonance in the face of the deepening realisation of the true and terrifying implications of climate change. We need to hear her words:

> There is a sense in which it seems to me merely a sophisticated sort of selfishness even to want ourselves or those we love healed or raised or specially helped a moment sooner than the whole cosmos is transformed; to want this lump of cosmos made malleable while the intractable rocks stand firm elsewhere; to want the unviolated communion with our nearest and dearest, while existentially, the rest of the world is treated as dispensable.

In the cosmic context of spiralling global warming in which we find ourselves, we might do well to heed Elizabeth's recognition that 'it is God who entitles us to yearn beyond articulation for a new earth as well as new selves'.

These brief pieces show us Elizabeth as a deeply challenging and in many ways prescient theological thinker, whose insistence that theology must be approached through an honest assessment of the realities of our lives continues to speak into the challenges of the world in which we live.

I

*What Is the Church's Task in Apologetics?**

We are handling this topic not as a matter of cool academic interest, but as a matter of passion, in which we wrestle with a deep malaise about the communication of faith.

Many of you may have gone to seminary in a day when apologetics was a subject on the timetable! The dogmaticians were there to say: 'This is the truth the Christian Church stands for.' And the apologetics people were there to defend that truth, preferably rationally: to explain it in ways which were persuasive to those who did not believe, and to face and deal with the kinds of critical stances which come at Christian faith from other perspectives, from the natural sciences, from history, psychology, sociology, Marxism and so on.

Traditionally, apologetics has dealt with the arguments for God's existence, the problem of evil, belief in the immortality of the soul, or of life after death. The truths defended by apologetics were those accessible to all normally functioning reasonable people. It may be that places still exist which have apologetics on the curriculum in that form. But I will be assuming in this context that we're on about something deeper, much less bland and much harder. For I think we live in a world where the existence of God is no longer an axiom among reasonable people, but a matter of widespread scepticism, vast perplexity or, perhaps most sinister of all, laissez-faire indifference. (OK, so you believe in God; I go for aromatherapy myself!)

Shortly after Christmas, the bishop sent me some batches of answers to questions I had posed from a number of groups, seminarians on course and being examined for ordination, members of the Diocesan

---

* This address was one of four given in February 1992 to a conference of Anglican diocesan clergy in Connecticut, USA.

Standing Committee and the panel of examiners from your Commission on Ministry. Both to my relief and to my dismay, the answers confirmed my sense that apologetics today is a big problem: to my relief, for the selfish reason that I did not have to tear up and rewrite what I had been writing. But dismay, because what emerged from these forty-one replies was a real sense of crisis. Every major doctrine in the book seemed to someone problematic in terms of communication or credibility:

The existence of God
The doctrine of the Trinity
Incarnation
Resurrection
Providence (though no one used the word)
Salvation (sin/forgiveness)
Eschatology.

The sense of pain, of disturbance, of loss of clear identity, of knowing that street-credibility had gone was almost universal. So, I assume that we are handling this topic not as a matter of cool academic interest, but as a matter of passion, in which we wrestle with a deep malaise about the communication of faith.

Since I am inviting you to risk the intimacy of theology which involves gut as well as head, I should perhaps say a little bit by way of personal introduction or autobiography. I grew up in a securely religious family: churchgoing but unstrident, with bedtime prayers as part of the day's rhythm, but grace said only when the minister came to tea! I was lucky in having a parish minister who took seriously that loving God was a matter of heart and soul and mind and strength, and who exposed his congregation to moral, political, spiritual and intellectual challenge steadily and unobtrusively, and to ecumenical issues. So, by the time I was sixteen, I'd been through many of the classics of European mysticism, John of the Cross, *The Cloud of Unknowing*, Julian of Norwich, von Hugel, Evelyn Underhill. This sounds precocious, but it was done, I assure you, with no straining, as gently as breathing.

When I went to university to do English Literature and Philosophy in the mid-1960s, British philosophy was still deeply empiricist, and though I had known in a vague way that lots of people didn't believe in God, I had never really met disbelief on the offensive. And this was not dismissible disbelief. It was voiced by men whose integrity and thoughtfulness were beyond question, yet who were convinced, many of them from

Christian backgrounds themselves, that to be a Christian you had to be either a fool or a knave: intellectually dishonest or culpably naive.

Gradually, but steadily, they pushed the questions. How would you know a God if there was one? How was the idea of infinite being not a contradiction in terms? If there was no palpable difference to the world which made it clear that God was there in some public way, was belief not just a confused hangover? Did psychology, sociology and anthropology not combine to give enough explanation of why people believed, without there being any need to postulate God as a ground of belief?

Gradually, but steadily, my self-doubt grew. Or rather, it was not self-doubt, but conviction that they were right both to put such questions and to answer them as they did. I didn't *want* them to be right, but I could see no way they were wrong. In the face of that, life in the Christian community became very strange: prayer was impossible, since I had no longer any confidence that there was anyone to address, or to hear. The Creed, which in those days Presbyterians heard a few Sundays a year, bounced off the walls as a series of incredible affirmations I could not make. And I really did toy with the question of whether churchgoing was, in this context, an immoral act.

My teenage reading, of course, gave me a glimmer of hope, because the loss of any articulate faith was almost a standard stage for my mystics – and with hindsight they all looked back on their dark nights of the soul from the vantage point of coming through them. But I had no hindsight: I had only this exposure of not finding belief possible or credible, and doubting whether it was even desirable! Yet I desired it. Most of the people I loved were there, and the sensation of distance from their conviction was a little bit like feeling deaf in a world of speaking people. But I knew I could not let my desire make it true if it was not true.

Going to do theology was, then, for me, an act of agnostic desire to discover how people who were presumably neither fools nor knaves articulated and defended faith. In other words, I wanted apologetics like insomniacs want sleep. But I didn't get it! Of course, we cantered round the proofs of divine existence, the theodicy question via John Hick, the relationship between Christianity and Humanism, Marxism, science, history, psychology and so on. But nothing began to touch the levels of agnosticism I felt about it all. And even more distressing than the specific arguments was the apparent inability of everyone around to be *disturbed* by the inconclusiveness. Well, of course, you couldn't expect to prove God: it was a matter of faith!

I won't at this point embark on the saga of how, after about seven years of almost unflagging agnosticism, the Christian thing began to gel again for me towards credibility. But I want to suggest that we do not *begin* to do apologetics until we have stood, actually or empathetically, in the shoes of those who find belief impossible, and have heard in our bones as well as in our minds what they are saying about the incredibility of faith. Let me just signal and illustrate briefly four convictions about the apologetic task:

- It involves listening at a level of accuracy and attentiveness which is very, very rare in church life. I remember once when I was teaching a class of divinity students, beginning a lecture by asking how many of them believed that God existed. All of the twenty-two hands went up. I then gave out postcards and asked them to write the closest paraphrase they could for the sentence 'God exists'. When we looked at the results, there were about thirteen *substantively* different answers, some of them quite incompatible with one another. The surface language, which seemed to express consensus, in fact was masking quite significant divergence.

- Secondly, I think apologetics today has to be done in genuine mutuality, and not in patronising superiority. It actually seems to me to be a betrayal of faith in the generosity of God and the surprisingness of the Holy Spirit to assume that we have a monopoly of God's self-disclosure. Unless our engagement with another faith, with secular atheism, with New Age, with psychoanalysis, begins with genuine openness to learning something of the truth of God, we neither will be, nor will deserve to be taken seriously by our interlocutors. If, in effect, we say, or think without saying it, 'I really can do without you and what you think as part of this conversation', we underestimate the ecumenism of God.

- I think that we have to do apologetics not just for the sake of the outsider but for the sake of ourselves. A few years ago, I took part in a Probationers' Conference in Scotland at which a mixture of Presbyterians, Episcopalians, Congregationalists and Roman Catholics were present, all with one or two years of experience in parish ministry. The question I began with to them was: on the basis of your experience of ministry so far, do you expect to be able to go on with your ministry with theological integrity? Ninety-five percent said 'No' – and I had this sense of a roomful of people dooming themselves to a life of clandestine thought, which would be likely to end up by simply smothering the questions. Some was to do with the gap between doctrine they thought they believed but found spinning loose and disengaged in relation to the life of the parish. And much was to do with a convention of silence about such matters once you were in the job: that once you're 'in', 'ordained', 'inducted', you're supposed to have everything sewn up. This seems to me like a disease: for how can we expect to live theologically with so pervasive a malaise and have our people taste anything of the freedom and delight of loving God with all their minds?

- Finally, I think the apologetic task involves a confidence which for me is part of the doctrine of creation, that people can bear anything. We all know what T.S. Eliot meant when he said: 'Humankind cannot bear very much reality.' But in the deepest sense, I think he was wrong. We are made to bear reality, no holds barred! As those of you will know who have children, the sharpness of questions, the demand for reasons for believing one thing rather than another is native to them.

Certainly, as a culture, people are often on the surface afraid of thinking. But I am convinced that that is overlay, albeit often hard to penetrate. We are disinherited if we miss out on that exploration of the big basic questions as to what's true about the world, the cosmos, ourselves, one another.

Apologetics, then, seems to me a task to be done from two ends simultaneously. We have to do a major job of decoding, which involves detecting what people think they're saying when they use the language, and what people think they are hearing when they hear it from outside. It also involves a careful and attentive conversation between past and future: seeing tradition not as a lump of intact dogma, but a process of grappling with truth which we bring into our engagement with the future we do not know and are busy discovering as we live in the immediate world around us.

But, as well as the decoding of our given language, we must, in this post-Christian culture, do something bolder. We must look for signs of God and of Christ in idioms which are not recognisably Christian at all and have no surface resemblance to the doctrine of Christianity at all. That exercise in detection, in recognition, in discernment, seems to me even more vital if our mission as apologists is to be adventurous in faith and not merely propagandists for a verbal belief system. That means exploring that: looking for what Peter Berger called 'rumours of angels'.

Theology as a Tool for Transformation[*]

Everyone who wrestles with the questions of life and death, identity and belonging, tragedy and hope is a theologian.

The Polish poet Zbigniew Herbert, who died a couple of years ago, has a little prose poem called 'The Paradise of the Theologians':

> Alleys, long alleys bordered by trees which are as carefully trimmed as in an English park. Sometimes an angel passes there. His hair is carefully curled, his wings rustle with Latin. He holds in his hands a neat instrument called a syllogism. He walks quickly without stirring the air or sand. He passes in silence by the stony symbols of virtues, the pure qualities, the ideas of objects and many other completely unimaginable things. He never disappears from sight because here there are no perspectives. Orchestras and choirs keep silent, yet music is present. The place is empty. The theologians talk spaciously. This also is supposed to be a proof.

Not just outside but also inside the Churches, the image of theology is pretty negative. Harold Wilson, the British Prime Minister, famously used the word to mean mere vaporising, connected with nothing. If you were to brainstorm any bunch of people at a bus stop, there would, I suspect, be a complete, conversation-stopping blankness on the part of some, and a high level of association with words such as academic, sterile, authoritarian, boring, abstract. It's quite cool these days to be into spirituality, but 'coming out' as a theologian in normal mixed company has people edging away along their seats!

---

[*] This talk was given to a conference in Sheffield in October 2004 sponsored by the St Mark's Centre for Radical Christianity and by the Progressive Christianity Network. The informal, interactive flavour of the address has been retained.

I'm starting from the assumption that everyone who wrestles with the questions of life and death, identity and belonging, tragedy and hope is a theologian. I want to start anecdotally, with three episodes where I gained confidence that theology was actually something which could energise people, give them new insights, start them chasing new questions, and move them to communicating in new ways.

Opening up theology

It was 1968. I was a theology student, having gone to study the subject in sheer despair because my wonderful, honest philosophy tutors had virtually convinced me that to be a Christian you had to be either a fool or a knave. And I was in a trough of deep agnosticism which was to last a good few years.

As part of my practical training, I had to help with a Junior Bible Class in Chalmers-Lauriston congregation in Edinburgh, thirteen to sixteen year olds who were neither academic kids nor very Bible-literate or pious. I'm going to try, I thought to myself, to get at something I care about with these kids.

At the time, one of my most gnawing questions was whether there was any way of decoding religious language into non-religious. I began by asking the teenagers if there were any words they could think of that they heard or said or thought about on Sundays. Back came a huge list: God, Jesus, salvation, sin, heaven, hell . . . Then I asked them: suppose you could ask the adults in the church any question, what would you ask them? Back came wonderful, searching questions:

Does God speak to you?

If you believe in God, why do you think other people don't?

Did Jesus really never do anything wrong?

What is the Holy Spirit?

Do you expect to be alive after your death?

Has God changed his mind about the Jews being his chosen people?

Do you think God is against the Russians? (It was the height of the Cold War.)

In all, we gathered sixty-one questions and distributed them to the congregation. They were to be answered anonymously. About eighty answer-sheets were returned, each of which must have taken at least an hour to fill in. No question was answered unanimously. Again, for a non-academic congregation, the answers were amazing:

What do you think is the cause of sin? – *Living life*

Does God live in heaven, or just in your head? – *Everywhere – Nowhere – Here and now*

Where is Jesus now? – *God only knows.*

The Bible Class was hooked. For several weeks, we collated replies and discussed the questions. I could spot almost every theological heresy in the book, but it was wonderful to see the energy that had been unleashed.

We then devised a belief game, a sort of Snakes and Ladders. We drew up boards of one hundred squares, the last square being marked 'heaven'. You threw the dice, and if you landed on hate, fear or despair, this stopped you in your tracks. Sixteen other squares were marked crisis of belief: e.g. Scientists have disproved life after death. Each crisis square had the following options:

Ask the minister

Leave the church

Refuse to believe it.

One Sunday evening, we invited the congregation to play the game, with one young person at each table and three adults. Throughout the evening, people who would have run a mile from anything billed as a discussion talked with animation about whether God would send anyone to Hell, or whether it would be good to speak in tongues. Conviviality and merriment was evident as well as serious exchanges.

This depth of discussion was possible because the questions came from the young people, and because the responses were anonymous. There were resources enough there for months and months of creative teaching, preaching and study!

Theology and counselling

Here is my second example of an exploration of theology, this time with an adult group of professionals. Participants in this training programme of the Pastoral Foundation for counsellors exhibited the most varied beliefs: from pagan, to Jewish, to Christian, to agnostic or atheist. I was told by the supervisor that the levels of nervousness about this theological training day had been very high. We started by asking them to fill in questionnaires anonymously. They were to answer the following questions with Yes, No or Not Sure:

God can help mend broken relationships.

God can help mend broken legs.

God can't do anything about death.

God is an idea that stops people facing reality.

Prayer promotes psychological recovery.

On the spot, people were asked to shuttle around and read the responses of another person. A flipchart listed the thirty-six possible responses to twelve questions, each with three possible answers.

The aim was to tease out why people believed as they did. The process raised the question of how it would affect the counselling encounter if clients came with these attitudes. By the end of the day, the room was bursting with issues.

Counselling, of course, is meant to be non-judgemental – but what if one is privately convinced that someone's beliefs are primeval, or neurotic, or superstitious, or heretical? Participants had also begun to see the possible connections between their or clients' theological convictions and professional counselling attitudes. Initial anxieties about the process were replaced with excitement and absorption.

A theological drop-in centre

This project was born of years of frustration that congregations were being deprived of their adulthood, and that there was an unhelpful collusion between trained clergy: 'I mustn't disturb my people' and the laity: 'I can't say this out loud to the minister/priest.'

A year's planning and fundraising preceded the project. Preconditions for success included a relaxing lounge area, good coffee and reading resources!

We gathered together twenty-six volunteers of all ages and denominations, including students, two retired bishops, housewives, a counsellor and a journalist. People with a specific expertise in, say, religion and science, mysticism, other religions and so on were available when required.

People came to browse, talk or link up with groups at the following drop-in times:

10 a.m. to 4 p.m., Monday to Friday

10 a.m. to 12 noon on Saturday.

Then there were monthly forums, with themes being suggested by the audience.

Forum members with different perspectives were chosen. Some of these forums sparked off follow-up sessions. After the Moderator of the Church of Scotland suggested that belief in the Virgin Birth need not be taken literally, four hundred people turned up on a bleak winter's night.

Interest focused on themes such as a credible faith for today, the use and abuse of Bible, gender and sexuality, inter-faith dialogue, and being the church 'outside the Church'.

Care was taken to respect all views, whether conservative or radical. People came for a while, then left. It was mainly a middle-class constituency. It was intended to be a fluid, remedial operation to give people better access to the tools for theological reflection, but not to be a para-church or to pursue any activist agenda. It was called *Threshold* and ran from 1992 to 1999.

Since theological disagreement is not primarily 'of the head', but relates to life commitments and to one's sense of identity, it involves deep vulnerability. It responds to the cry: 'I am not yet made; make me.' A series about the historic creeds, for example, had people in tears and in rage, for theology is about passion, pain, risk and desire. Some people saw the creeds as part of their lifeblood, while others found them almost the biggest obstacle to faith. Theology, though, is also about hope and trust and fearlessness, the openness to be surprised.

Personal transformation

My own reason for deciding to study theology was that I could believe none of it, and I wanted to ask the people who could believe it how they did! Since then, my journey, which has certainly transformed me, has gone through strange places. My most significant single, personal running conversation has been with a then unknown Greek Orthodox theologian, John Zizioulas, who loved the Cappadocian Fathers, writing between the fourth and seventh century CE. Not a likely inspiration, you would think, for a keynote speaker at a conference of 'Radical Christians'! This man, though, and the Eastern sense of God and human person-hood, has opened for me horizons of theological possibility which, I think, transcend the wearisome Western debates between fundamental-ists and radicals, traditionalists and modernists, which are so life-sapping. We live in a culture so aware of subtexts and spin that there is a dominant ethos of distrust, so that it is often necessary to dismantle or unravel false stories claiming to be true, such as the Church as the community of love.

Theological conversation, in the deepest sense, involves the transfor-mation from meeting the other in distrust, with a sense of the superior truth of one's own position and thinking that we have 'them' taped, to a meeting which is a real dialogue of questions, not a ping-pong game of answers. The dialogue aims at transparency, at giving and receiving. This has nothing to do, though, with the avoidance of conflict, or laissez-faire permissiveness, as if a theological position was like having a preference for tea or coffee.

We are not islands: your theology may threaten me as a matter of life and death, and mine may threaten you. But we need to find out! 'Oh, now I see. What you mean by God is what I mean by the devil.'

Presumably you have all come here with some kind of sense of the transformation you would like to see, in the world, in the Church, in yourself. As the day progresses, we are hoping to do detailed work on how theology might be a tool for transformation in each of these areas, and by the end to share some signals. I hope we will all have a taste of what it means to glimpse the potential of theology as a resource for depth-exploration, and that from that exhilaration and circulation of energy, you will feel empowered to do more. Go for it!

3

*Contemporary Trends in Theology**

The Holocaust was the event which seared all subsequent sensibility.

It is no exaggeration to say that theology today is hugely transformed from what it was like thirty years ago when I was doing my initial training in Edinburgh. In those days, at least in Protestant Scotland, and pretty well anywhere else in Western Europe or North America, the central divide was between the Neo-Orthodox, marshalled around the giant figure of Karl Barth, and the Neo-Liberals clustering in the other corner around Rudolf Bultmann. How much of the New Testament was mythology? Was God's revelation direct from above and quite different from the religious traditions of mankind? (Feminist consciousness had not yet identified mankind as exclusive language, at least not in our faculty!) Was God objectively knowable? These were the big questions.

The fact that they now seem curiously dated, or that Barth and Bultmann are often mentioned in the same footnote nowadays as more alike than different, may simply be the telescopic effect of time, and of settling dust. It is not, of course, that these questions have gone away or been answered conclusively. But the focus of theological concern and interest, as manifested in the titles which pour into the libraries month by month, is so very different that it feels as if we live in a different world.

Today, on the whole, I am going to concentrate on two areas: one which is called, technically, hermeneutics, which is the big scary word for how anyone interprets anything, and what people believe about their route to understanding. The other is a fascinating shift in New Testament studies from philology and dogma to what might be called a sociological approach to the Bible. That explores what can actually be known, not so

---

* This quite comprehensive account of the shifts in recent theology was offered to religious educationists in Preston in June 1998.

much about Jesus as about the kind of people who were attracted to the early Jesus-movement, and therefore responsible for all the pre-written traditions, as well as for the Gospels. It documents a shift from the idealised pictures many of us grew up with of this pastoral carpenter, spending his time on Galilean hillsides, to a movement located largely in cities and among artisans and small-business people living in a complex and pluralist society.

What I hope will be strengthened by today's experience is the sense that Christianity, then and now, has never been an agreed set of doctrines, a happy-clappy band of enthusiasts or a Moral Rearmament Group. Rather, since the start, the Christian movement has lived with tensions, dilemmas and crises which reflect basic issues about how we choose and manage to be human.

First, I want to offer you a kind of backcloth – a thumbnail sketch, a whistlestop tour of the theological cosmos and how it has changed most significantly in recent decades.

One major factor has been the globalisation of theological discourse as a result of the Ecumenical Movement. Largely due to the work of the World Council of Churches, with its sensitivity to local and indigenous forms of Christian belonging, and to the Second Vatican Council, which paid significant attention to the diverse and decentralised expressions of Catholic faith, there has been a huge recognition that Europe can no longer regard itself as the heartland of Christianity. Partly, this is a matter of numbers: in Europe, almost all the mainstream denominations are shrinking. Century-long practices of church-tax in Scandinavia and Germany are being challenged, with significant losses in adult Christian education as a result. In the UK, the only growing Churches are the Eastern Orthodox, the black-led indigenous Churches (often Pentecostal) and the fundamentalist sects. Strange bedfellows! But it is more than a matter of numbers. Deep in the processes of ecumenical conversation has been a recognition, painful and difficult to acknowledge, that the Europe which has so proudly exported Christianity for centuries to the rest of the world is, itself, parochial, restricted and, many would say, significantly diseased.

Certainly, that was a major component in the atmosphere and dynamic of the General Assembly of the World Council of Churches in Canberra in 1991. Growing representation of African, Asian and Latin American Christians, many of them confident and mature spokespeople for forms of faith and worship, drawing more on pre-Christian native culture than on European orthodoxy, challenged all our European complacency that we were, par excellence, custodians of the faith. This confidence, which will, I believe, transform Christian theology in the next millennium, has been nourished by different levels of theological activity, one academic and one grassroots.

The academic one has emerged via the increased communication, both personal and technological, which comes from the recognition that the universities of Asia, Africa and Latin America are dialogue partners in any academic conversation. Writers of the stature of C.S. Song or Raimon Panikkar, for years wrestling to articulate cross-cultural dialogue, are at last recognised as vital to the health and integrity of the Western academic enterprise. They testify not just to the more crude and obvious imperialisms of land-grabbing and renaming (who called Hinduism 'Hinduism'?), but also to the much subtler failures to attend to custom or language. What do you do, preaching individual salvation in a culture which has no singular noun for person, no verb for 'have' except 'be with', no word for 'homeless' except being far away from where you belong? How, as Panikkar put it in lectures given in Edinburgh, do you make sense of the Jewish–Christian–Muslim story of time and salvation in Bangkok, where the word for the day before yesterday is the same as the word for the day after tomorrow?

The more grassroots end of the transformation has been brought about by the mushrooming confidence expressed in what have come to be called Liberation Theologies, rooted largely in the two-thirds worlds of the South – Latin America, Asia and, to a lesser extent so far, Africa. There has been in recent decades a global explosion of voices claiming the right to speak from below. No longer are the dictates of scholars, theologians, Church assemblies, the Vatican, the official guardians of the tradition, to be received as normative. Rather, the people – the poor, the excluded, the little ones – are to be given a voice, allowed to wrestle with the scriptures in their own idiom, and to hold the people at the top to account. What are you doing for us? What bearing has your Gospel on us? How are your words about peace, reconciliation, the Kingdom of God and so on reflected in your lives, in your commitment, in your financial arrangements, in your partnership plans?

While some of the political energy for these theologies of liberation came from Marxist-inspired analyses of the human condition, as much came from the recovery of biblical themes in the Old and New Testaments, the Exodus, Jubilee, the Magnificat, the sense of the Jesus-movement as an empowering of the weak. The educational methods of writers such as Paulo Freire, with his process of conscientisation, have proved hugely enabling, and the tools for contemporary communication mean that there is mutual strengthening among peoples of very different backgrounds. It was very striking at Canberra, for instance, how Aboriginal Australians could be identified with by South Koreans, or by Canadian Inuit people.

One function of teaching Religious and Moral Education is to give young people the gift of attention: to help them register, notice, appreciate those aspects of a culture which give people their deepest sense of identity, to let them explore who they are and where they belong, and to let them have sensitive and intelligent recognition of others who are different.

On the edge of the third millennium, in Christian terms, it is clear that if the world is to survive, the differences have to be wrestled with, enjoyed or overcome in non-destructive modes. For the potential we have to blow everything up, in Kosovo, in Kashmir, in Belfast, even – heaven help us – in Marseille, shows that we stand on the precarious edge of irreparable self-destruction.

Theology today inhabits that awareness, and cannot escape it without becoming pietist self-indulgence. But, as many young people are aware, theology has also created or significantly contributed to the destruction by supporting boundaries, defining categories of friend and enemy, invoking divine wrath on outsiders and inciting ideological hatred.

The recognition that stories are told from vantage points is the linking theme in what I want to focus on. For I think that informs all recent developments both in what used to be called Systematic Theology (does anyone now believe such a subject exists?) and in Biblical Studies. What I hope to do is to outline this self-consciousness about story.

One of the disputed questions of our time in Europe (and the ex-colonies) is whether we have entered a quite new age, comparable, say, to the shift from medieval to renaissance life, or from pre-industrial to post-industrial society. Think, for a moment, of some signals. Sons and daughters whose response to any stated position is likely to be: 'Well, that's just your point of view.' Journalists or media commentators, whose report of a diplomatic encounter is likely to contain words like: 'The subtext of this meeting was . . .' Adverts, where all direct allusion to the shape, size, cost and virtue of the product are scrupulously avoided, and hosts of associated images of speed, energy, sexiness or achievement bombard the viewer. All of this is part of what many would see as the biggest cultural shift in recent decades in Western Europe, that from the modern period to postmodernism. This shift, and what it means for how theology is done, is central to what I want to explore with you.

When I was training, 'modern' or 'modernist' were words either of approval or of reproach. If they were words of approval, they were being notionally contrasted with words like medieval, out of date, primitive; whereas if they were accusations they were being contrasted with traditional, orthodox, classical and the like. The picture, in both cases, was of two substantial worlds, one, for better or worse, modern, the other premodern.

What characterises the shift from modernity to postmodernity is complex and elusive. I myself find it significant and more than coincidental that many of the writers most associated with creating postmodern consciousness, Derrida or Foucault for example, have a European Jewish heritage. For I think that the Holocaust experience was the event which seared all subsequent sensibility.

For the modern world, emerging gradually from Renaissance and Reformation, maturity came with the confident rise of the scientific and technological worlds and with the political and intellectual axioms of the Enlightenment. These axioms most significantly included the confidence that reason was universal, that there was a moral consensus among sane and mature people about the basic virtues such as respect for liberty, tolerance and human rights. The alleged objectivity and reliability of the natural sciences offered the normative way to know the world, and in principle such methods were transferable to human society, to historical research and so on. There was huge epistemological optimism. Even in the sphere of religion (though some moderns saw that as a vestigial premodern hangover), there was a Kantian framework for reasonable religion, with sober wonder at both the cosmic and the moral orders.

Traces of resistance to such secure confidence existed of course within modernity itself. In the theological, philosophical field, one can think of both Kierkegaard and Nietzsche in their different ways. It is in Nietzsche, however, that we find the proto-postmodernist, with his sense of language as power, and of the vested interests which so often lie behind apparently innocent myth-making or story-telling. This is a central theme of postmodernist interpretation. There is, in a sense, no objective world, no way things actually are. There are only fictions, constructs. And the first question to ask is: 'Who is served by this fiction?'

In recent years, many people have had access to this hermeneutic of distrust, both from the widely available feminist theologies with their critique of patriarchal narratives, and from the Latin American writers like Sobrino or Gutierrez, whose theologies of the poor document how selective and loaded theological doctrines have been on behalf of bourgeois and individualistic interests.

One fascinating thing about the current theological scene is that the acknowledgement of the postmodern predicament has in itself generated both radical and conservative responses. Probably best known as a populariser of radical scepticism in the UK is Don Cupitt, in a series of books going back to *The Sea of Faith* and *Long-legged Fly*. Cupitt's theological invitation is to embrace non-realism, the recognition that the old, objective God is a fiction, a construct, and that we humans have to accept our ultimate responsibility for defining moral value, for making commitments to create a certain kind of world. The story Cupitt chooses is unashamedly that of post-Enlightenment Europe, though in his more recent writings he is increasingly drawn to Buddhist philosophy, with its deep reluctance to engage in metaphysics, and its profound ethical and pragmatic wisdom. For Cupitt, the refusal of a meta-narrative, a cosmic story, is the challenging, liberating adventure for the contemporary spirit, and the only creative future for the Church.

At the opposite pole, many conservative theologians have embraced the postmodernist account as a way of deflecting menacing questions from outside. If you can only tell your form of the story, there can be no legitimate questions asked of it from outside. You inhabit a certain world of narrative. It is alien to raise questions from history or philosophy. Not only that, it may be intellectually inappropriate. Belonging in the community means being the person who shares this story.

I recently encountered this stance personally while being engaged over the last two years on our Church of Scotland Panel on Doctrine, where I was introduced for the first time to the body of New Testament scholarship which has come to be known as Canon Criticism. Associated most closely with the name of the American scholar Brevard Childes, this is a school of interpretation which believes that any part of scripture is best interpreted by the cross-referencing of other parts of the canon.

It is therefore deeply suspicious of and hostile to the methods of historical criticism which have tried to isolate and document scriptural passages in their own initial context. A key example of this would be the principle that you read the prophecies of Isaiah not in Christological terms, but in terms of contemporary Jewish Messianic understanding as far as that can be reconstructed. The common New Testament practice of raiding the Jewish scriptures to vindicate Messianic claims for Jesus is by historical-critical scholars acknowledged as a kind of distortion, easily understandable in the light of early Christian hope and conviction, but something quite distinct from the original meaning of the text.

For Canon Criticism, this distinction is blurred or even denied. The key question about a passage's meaning is precisely 'What does the whole Canon make of it?', and the accumulated retrospective story is more important by far than the strata which can be identified by historical-critical methods. Indeed, one Old Testament scholar on our panel went so far as to say that he thought it served no purpose for the Church to have ministers trained to think in historical-critical terms.

What is at stake in all this for the world of Religious and Moral Education?

The explicit philosophy of the current practice in schools and colleges is that the different religious stories are to be laid out side by side for the appreciation of the student, each in its integrity – that those who are sufficiently interested, or who already inhabit one faith-tradition, may learn to relate their own personal journey to some of the stories told by all the religious communities, growing in understanding and awareness of the contribution all make to the human enterprise.

What contribution does the postmodernist analysis have to make? Many see it as a cause for panic, a corrosive destroyer of every ideal of truth, the ultimate laissez-faire ideology: 'You tell your story, I'll tell mine.'

Certainly, if it merely nurtures a culture of separate, non-communicating worlds, it is going to increase the sense of fragmentation and disintegration which characterises so much of contemporary life. My hope, however, is that postmodern consciousness can be a more creative tool in the processes of exploration we are all involved in, namely:

- The awareness of how thinking is embedded in lived desires, assumptions and power structures is a valuable one, provided we are willing to include our own thinking whenever its locus is in any of the variables which contextual theology recognises: class, geography, wealth, gender, sexual orientation and so on.
- The potential for distance from the claims and counter-claims of rival fundamentalisms could be a gift. This depends on whether the postmodernist hermeneutic can be seen, not as a withdrawal from all commitment, but as a way of purifying commitment: by screening it, scrutinising it for traces of blinkered self-interest. Here, I believe, the fundamental study of languages and religious traditions which I alluded to earlier is vital.

- The Scriptures of the Old and New Testament become living and dynamic protagonists in present life decisions, rather than being encased classics.

The disturbing and potentially creative element in this seems to me to be facing the question of whether students really believe that everything is so relative and subjective, or whether they want to defend any standard of, for example, appropriate justice and freedom which they regard as universal. If the latter is true, they are immediately involved in the question of how to negotiate and defend such standards. Is postmodernism merely a necessary stage in European cultural contrition, or is it a global advance in the renunciation of dogma and the recognition of how belief shifts, depending on all sorts of local, cultural, linguistic and political factors? Is it, seen much more negatively, as the ideology of a bankrupt culture where individualism, scepticism and careless relativism rule? Or is it an implication of a Gospel where people have been told that there are things they cannot yet bear, but will be able to learn in God's generous providence?

Nothing can be done, in churches, in other faith communities, in schools, without encountering this question. As we approach the constructed Christian millennium, such issues of identity, purpose and the interpretation of past, present and future will intensify. We owe it to our students to help them grapple with such questions.

4

Gifted Knowing[*]

God was deeper than the lake, and our knowing of him drained his depth less than the sip of a sand-dove.

We spent last summer in Connecticut, and a few hundred yards from our house was a lake, long, narrow, fringed by pines and maples rising steeply from the shore to the skyline so that the whole visible world was the water and sky surrounded by these dense woods.

Often in the morning I went and swam there, preferring the early warmth to the scorching midday; and since the nearby campers were not usually up that early, I had the rare experience of feeling like some kind of prelapsarian Eve in a world of complete beauty, still, full of light, warm, unmarred.

One particular morning, as I turned in my swimming, there was a tiny sand-dove, about six inches long, standing just at the edge of the lake, maybe forty yards away, sipping. I had the fear that somehow my seeing it would disturb it; but it seemed unaware, or unaffected by my watching, and went on drinking. I don't quite know how to name the impact of that moment, or what elements of thought, feeling or fantasy went into it. But I had a quite overwhelming and simultaneous sense of gifted knowing: that there was such room for this little bird and me to be tasting the lake in our quite different ways, that there was so much other room, the length and depth of the seemingly untenanted water, with

---

[*] In a paper given in Leeds in March 1994 to the SCM Press Trust, Elizabeth argued that truth, authority and freedom can never be played off against one another. She dedicated her talk to the memory of the Cambridge scholar Donald MacKinnon, who personified for her the intrinsic connection between the defence of freedom and dignity and the struggle for intellectual integrity. In the course of an address which cited the Ardnamurchan poet Alasdair Maclean, and *Scented Gardens for the Blind* by the New Zealand novelist Janet Frame, she offered this little vignette.

goodness knows what other forms of life being sustained by it. That there were a million lakes on the earth, each such a world, and all of a common water. That God was deeper than the lake, and our knowing of him drained his depth less than the sip of a sand-dove. That I could not share the sand-dove's life, that if I went too close it would be frightened and fly away. Yet that we were somehow blessed by each other's being there. That if 10,000 sand-doves drank and 10,000 people swam in the lake in the course of time, it wouldn't be exhausted.

Of course, the moment may be dismissed as a trick of the fusion of light, unaccustomed physical and emotional relaxation and the absence of an earth-anchoring breakfast! But I have found it enduring; and several weeks later, in the different heat and light of Santiago de Compostela, as the Fifth World Conference of Faith and Order struggled with the obstacles to communion, it comforted me.

5

Dealing with the Dark Side:
*The Problem of Evil**

*Who is evil? What is evil? Does the term identify something which
transcends merely ethical identification?*

To address such a topic in the presence or even in the wake of Professor
Hick gives me all the confidence of a pond-minnow chasing an Atlantic
salmon. For his book *Evil and the God of Love* is still, thirty years and
more on, a classic text for students engaging with theodicy issues in
Christian terms.

When I chose 'Dealing with the Dark Side' as my title, however, it was
partly because I wanted to widen the agenda. Only some faiths find
anything akin to theodicy either necessary or possible, and one of the
most important things for advanced students to recognise is that there is
no one problem of evil: that the terms of reference in which one religion
deals with the dark side of human experience cannot necessarily be
translated or, in any meaningful sense, compared.

This, I think, emerges clearly from that other scholarly classic, John
Bowker's *Problems of Suffering in Religions of the World* (1970). Here,
where human beings seek insight, control and comfort in relation to all
that afflicts us, we face the fact that, alongside some manifest overlaps
and parallels, there are yawning, seismic differences of feeling, perception and understanding of the human condition. A-level students
mapping this area need to have a nose for strange territory.

What I want to try to do is some highlighting, drawing attention to
issues which cannot be taken for granted as we grapple with the dark
side, not just as a piece of intellectual archaeology, but as contributors to
the human enterprise of 'making sense of things'.

* This talk was given to Religious Education teachers on 3 January 1998.

When my seventeen-year-old daughter heard my title, she insisted that I watched with her *The Empire Strikes Back*. That was one thing I had not registered: that, for many in her age group, the first association of the dark side comes from this Star Wars melodrama culture, with its grotesquely 'other baddies', its unremitting dualism and its vulgarity of imagination. Our young people have been nurtured in such a culture, which is manifest not only in the mythic form of popular film but also in much of the pre-millennial moralising which is exploding all around us, and in tabloids thundering about 'evil monsters'!

Meanwhile, our young people also belong to a generation with a public access to forms of pain which were not present to their parents. They grow up with the knowledge that sex is linked to the risks of HIV and AIDS. They see their peers sitting on pavements begging. They watch a world and a political culture which, with all the resources of the late twentieth century, is letting the gap between rich and poor widen. Their media expose them to almost daily images of the human capacity to destroy other humans, whether in the surreal melodramas of James Bulger (a Merseyside boy murdered in February 1993), the film *Little Monsters*, the Wests (husband-and-wife serial killers in the 1970s and 1980s), or the massacre of sixteen children and their teacher in 1996 in Dunblane. Then, of course, the slower-running atrocities of war, famine and neglect.

How is the A-level teacher going to relate the classic traditions of identifying and dealing with the dark side to this very specific context?

In the first instance, it seems to me, there needs to be some open exploration of whether, and how, the word 'evil', for example, actually has a locus within the young person's vocabulary. Who is evil? What is evil? Are certain people evil? Is everyone a mixture of good and evil? Is evil the attribute of certain kinds of actions rather than of people, so that, in an almost karmic sense, one becomes evil by accumulating evil actions? What is being said beyond the normal moral categories of good and bad when a word such as 'evil' is introduced? Does the term identify a kind of darkness which transcends merely ethical identification?

This clarification will be a necessary preliminary to any discussion of whether there are also non-moral evils, those traditionally classed as natural evils in some religious traditions, for instance, disease, death and the various forms of disaster which afflict human beings.

To many brought up in the naturalisms of biology, geography and physics, it can be quaint to think of such things as evil. They are merely there, part of the natural order of things. Subjectively, humans may encounter them negatively under certain conditions, but I think it is extremely difficult for someone reared in our post-Enlightenment culture, with its evolutionary biological insights, to enter imaginatively the axiomatic recognition of the Greek Fathers, for example, that death was a metaphysical outrage, an attack on the world's integrity, empirical evidence of the Fall, or the fallenness of things at a cosmic level.

Religious myths of paradise, primordial or ultimate, are obviously the places where faith-traditions explore the sense that we can conceive of better worlds than this, and the pull of these myths on the religious imagination is potent. At the very least, one might argue, they articulate a distress at the way things are which is not necessarily limited to the morally culpable. You can't blame lions for eating lambs! But you can dream of a world where they don't, or where the chain of cause and effect is broken, where karma loses its grip.

This then, is the first major issue contemporary people have to revisit. What are they, or anyone else, counting as evil? Only when that has been explored can one do more than a formulaic account, for example, of monistic or dualistic religious imagination; or an appraisal and critique of Augustine's account of the Fall; or grapple with the dynamic of *moksha* in Hinduism. And the recognition that there are very different starting points here is one which needs delicate cultural awareness.

I still, for example, find it almost metaphysically shocking, as one who grew up with the Psalms, the Book of Job and Gethsemane, to realise that, if I understand it aright, unjust suffering is not a possible category, though unnecessary suffering may be, for a devout Hindu. For all suffering is precisely correlated with the karma of previous and present lives. This is axiomatic, part of the ABC of learning Hinduism. Yet it exposes fascinatingly, hauntingly even, how huge existential chasms yawn as we deal with the dark side.

John Hick's later work is marked by the sense that through our 'epistemic distance', i.e. the degree of autonomy granted us in creation, God invites and beckons us. His key argument is that this epistemic distance is ultimately constructive, a space of freedom for us to grow in. Students exploring in depth how any given faith deals with its darkness need to explore the plausibility of that. How does it help us deal with the dark side that the formulation of questions which seem to some profoundly important, questions of identity or injustice for example, seem to others pointless, or not to arise?

Certainly, to many wistfully outside faith, like Ronald Hepburn, for example, a philosophical peer of John Hick's, the epistemic distance is precisely the major crux of the problem of evil. It is too great for any revelation claim to be plausible, too great even for the discernment of a coherent reality to be claimed in outline.

This is the second clear task for the grappler with the darkness: to artic-ulate the relationship between what is identified as evil and the other central categories within a faith. (Depending on given syllabuses, this will for some be done primarily in Christian terms, and sometimes with refer-ence to more than one faith. But in both cases, the skill is to be able to make the structural connections.) Of course, as *Evil and the God of Love* so brilliantly demonstrates, it is a crass oversimplification to suggest that any faith has only one way of dealing with the Dark Side. The Calvinist strand of Christianity, which sees it as a matter of God's specific provi-dence that one mother has enough milk for her newborn infant and another has not, shares a closer resemblance to many Islamic views of God's control of history than it does with the whole minority tradition Hick classifies as Irenaean. The Theravadan traditions of the *Dhammapada*, advocating the wise man's detachment from the suffering crowd below, are very different from the later Bodhisattva development, which seems to have much more striking similarity to Jesus weeping over Jerusalem in yearning and desire.

Particularly when one looks at the practical or operational aspects of the response to suffering and evil, the devotional classics of the ages present many echoes of one another: in the advocacy of patient resigna-tion; in the commitment to solidarity with the pain of others; in the sense of the soul being smelted by adversity into more imperishable strength.

Where the obvious significant differences arise is at the theoretical level – perhaps why the Buddhist traditions distrust speculative meta-physics – where there are widely different perceptions of the reality of evil, and of its relationship to the power and goodness of God. These are well documented in the standard texts, which have continued to generate ongoing debate. Stephen Davis's *Encountering Evil: Live Options in Theodicy* (1981), for example, is a fascinating running conversation, largely in Christian terms, on how one does theology post-Auschwitz, in which six philosophers and theologians, again including John Hick, develop responses which range from a form of the traditional free-will defence to a Process Theology response which disclaims omnipotence in anything like the traditional terms of that word. What I mean by recog-nising structural connections is that the form the question takes in, say, the Psalms or the Book of Job or the writings of Karl Barth, depends on a doctrine of God who is a creator, unconstrained by anything which limits his creative freedom. It also depends, structurally, on the recognition that the presence of evil or suffering is real and is not sufficiently justified as punishment, as moral tuition or as testing. There must then be some sense of God as one who has personal initiatives in relation to events in history. Pantheism, for instance, excludes this.

That is certainly the presupposition of most biblical writings and of the Koranic tradition, but it is not a presupposition of modern European consciousness, insofar as that has been shaped by the Enlightenment project of naming the world *etsi deus non daretur* – as if God were not given. Whereas for Job the axiom of God's being was unshakeable, so that rage and protest were his natural responses, for the last two centuries at least, the presence of, or at least the extent of, evil in the world seems to many people to threaten not God's claim to be just but human claims that any God exists. If, as Hume argued, you could not infer a good or a competent deity from the way the world is, we now, after Auschwitz, face a steelier postmodernist challenge that every meta-narrative is to be treated with distrust – or rather, to be scrutinised from the vested interest which lies behind it. If 'work makes free' could be the legend over the gate of Auschwitz, what is to be made of 'King of the Jews' or 'eternal dharma' or even of eschatological verification? Who is kidding whom? Why?

What I am suggesting is that the climate in which Europe hears theological utterance today is sceptical of truth claims at a level which had penetrated only a few bones thirty years ago. My impression, though, is that the major tradition in English-speaking Philosophy of Religion, to which John Hick's account of theodicy certainly belongs, is still innocent of this deep postmodern scepticism. It believes you can argue from the idea of a historical Fall; it presupposes that there is a reasonable appeal to the moral consensus of good people that, in the end, only a universalist solution is compatible with the goodness of God. And it actually uses such arguments to critique elements of the traditional teachings which seem incompatible with the broad liberal theism which Hick himself profoundly believes.

So far as I can see, the setters of exam papers also still inhabit that world, assuming you can juggle with a formal concept of omnipotence (being able to do anything you can in order to bring about a state of affairs at the point when you want to) and a broadly utilitarian account of benevolence (bringing about the maximum good for the maximum number of people by your deliberate intent) and give some argued case for preferring some accounts of God to others.

What I am basically saying is that we have to grapple, in our context, social, cultural and political, with the recognition that time and place deeply affect how we think, what we can respond to. And I wonder if we need to take on board the way in which many inside and outside the Christian tradition find the discourse of traditional Western Anglo-Saxon philosophy of religion parochial, dated and increasingly abstract.

I have great misgivings about this judgement, partly because I want to give no hostage to fortune on behalf of those who want to return to authoritarian modes of handling scripture and/or tradition. On the other hand, I think we can no longer take seriously this somewhat Olympian God of omnipotent benevolence with infinite time at his disposal to bring the world to perfection.

The celebrated Ivan question in *The Brothers Karamazov* is well rehearsed. Would the greatest outcome be worth it, if it cost one child's tears? For Bonhoeffer, it was clear that, from the vantage point of a Nazi prison, only a suffering God would do. For the feminists and liberation theologians, the omnipotence of Western classical theism is specifically the projection of oriental despot models onto God, not the character of the one who stands in solidarity with the pain and oppression of those who struggle for life.

Curiously, scandalously almost, radical Christians find that they can't do theism divorced from Christology in some form, which identifies God's ability to deal with evil with God's willingness to be overwhelmed by it. Evil is nailed, centrally, not in some calculated reversal of past or present ill fortune, but in the willingness of God to enter the dereliction of God.

I doubt whether we actually map the options for students to consider, to reject, to be amazed at, if we do not give them the feel of these post-Auschwitz theologies of silence, where God does not speak, promise to put things right – what the Japanese writer Kazoh Kitamori called *The Theology of the Pain of God* (1965). I actually think myself that that is more deeply there in Eastern Christian spirituality and theology than in Western, though in a very different form. There seems to me no way of reading Irenaeus as suggesting a global universalism without that being related to the conviction of Christ's willingness to share our human death and disintegration in total solidarity.

I find this a particularly subversive suggestion to introduce to people whose political culture – the only one they have known – believes that, rather like *The Empire Strikes Back*, goodies and baddies are different sub-species and should have as little to do with each other as possible.

How axiomatic is it for them that you deal with the wicked, the evil, the feckless, the nasty by excluding it?

I think we have to be aware, and help our pupils be aware, that their culture, who we are, may prejudice our ability to hear a lot. We have also to help them be aware that to be who they are, where they are, when they are, gives them a particular gift, that only they can contribute to the human script of how people deal with the dark side. We are not simply reading the scripts of history, fascinating as that can be.

If I were a Religious Studies teacher, I think I would have several hopes for maturing or eventual outcomes.

- We would recognise something of the perennial structural shapes of different attempts to grapple with suffering and evil, both theoretical and practical, in various religious and non-religious traditions.
- We would wonder at the strangeness, possibly the pain of the non-translatability of different thought and feeling worlds – sensitised to the difficulty of entering someone else's country.
- We would scrutinise our individual and collective images of evil, about what it is to be human, about the presence, absence or action of God, about time, about power.
- We would register something about the current fault-lines in philosophical thought between modernist and postmodernist ways of handling the world, and check where we felt at home.
- We would face the specific nightmares, terrors and memories of the late twentieth and early twenty-first centuries and discover something about contemporary theological responses to those, and consider whether they modify the traditional debate.
- We would gain tools, intellectual, moral and spiritual, to walk the tightrope between being overwhelmed and afraid of the vulnerability of the human condition, and being complacent and dissociated from it.

Impossible! Can't be done in *n* weeks, with kids who have absolutely no starting blocks in historical, philosophical, religious awareness. Some of what I heard yesterday makes me realise what gifts of courage, imagination, zest and sensitivity it takes to teach in present conditions, under present pressures.

Still, it's my tested conviction that, on the whole, we understretch and patronise children and adults rather than overstretching them. I believe that there is continuity between the conversations you might have with a four-year-old child, a sixteen-year-old adolescent and a professor of philosophy, more than discontinuity. And I'm sure that the engagement with the dark side is one of the agendas of the human spirit which is the human birthright, long before and long after the A-levels are a twinkle in the eye!

After all, as Browning very nearly said:

A teacher's reach should exceed his grasp
Or what's a heaven for?

6

*Critique of the Reformed Position on the Problem of Evil**

We cannot think of ourselves rescued from evil without the cosmos being rescued.

Every time that I re-read John Calvin on the problem of evil, I wonder whether anything in the world can justify anyone in the world remaining a Presbyterian. Let me remind you of the key themes. The mystery of the Fall lies firmly in the context of the mystery of God's election, and

> There could be no election without its opposite, reprobation . . . Those, therefore, whom God passes by he reprobates, and that for no other cause but because he is pleased to exclude them from the inheritance which he predestines to his children . . . The will of God is the supreme rule of his righteousness, so that everything he wills must be held to be righteous by the mere fact of his willing it. Therefore, when it is asked why the Lord did so, we must answer, Because he pleased . . . By the will of God, all the sons of Adam fell into that state of wretchedness in which they are now involved: and this is just what I said at the first, that we must always return to the mere pleasure of the divine will . . . I will not hesitate, therefore, simply to confess with Augustine that the will of God is necessity, and that everything is necessary which he has willed: just as those things will certainly happen which he has foreseen . . . The first man fell because the Lord deemed it meet that he should: why he deemed it meet, we know not. It is certain, however, that it was just, because he saw that his own glory would thereby be displayed.
>
> (*Institutes of the Christian Religion*, III.23.1, 2, 4, 8)

* The occasion and the date of this address is not known.

Now, let me not malign the *intention* of Calvin. I am sure that he was overwhelmed by a desire to witness to the transcendence of God, and to the unshakeable security of salvation for those who were saved, and that for him the reprobation of the fallen was a mere minor corollary. Nevertheless, the theology he actually suggests to articulate that vision seems to me to be so ugly as to be blasphemous, unless one merely psychologises it as a piece of spiritual pathology, and avoids a theological punch-up.

I am not really concerned to give you a historical account of the developments of theodicy within Reformed theological traditions. It is extraordinarily difficult to identify any single mainline continuity. The variations run from the immense effort of Barth to draw Calvin's sting by making election in Christ universal in its intention, to the gentle liberalism of Baillie's *The Sense of the Presence of God* with its virtual minimising of evil as a provisional impediment to the global realisation of that presence. One might, however, risk the judgement that everyone who writes with any level of Reformed self-consciousness is somehow or other squirming to get off the hook on which Calvin has impaled them.

What I would like to try to do here is to dismantle that hook by trying to refute the central axiom in Calvin's thinking about God's relation to the world. The sentence which contains that axiom slips in quietly among the more colourful ones about God displaying his glory through reprobation. But it carries lethal potential.

> I will not hesitate, therefore, simply to confess with Augustine that the will of God is necessity, and that everything is necessary which he has willed.

Now, in going for that sentence, I am returning to the 'omnipotence' horn of the dilemma about God's goodness, God's power and the reality of evil. That is not necessarily because I accept the philosophers' setting-up of 'If God is good, he does not want evil, / If he is omnipotent he need not have it' as the best way in to theodicy; but it is because I think the most grotesque misrepresentations which bind popular imagination and theological intelligence in our culture are to do with the sense of God's power in relation to the cosmos. When people frame their apparently spontaneous cry of outrage, 'Why did God let it happen?', there lie behind that generations of teaching, of imagery, of piety in which God is Supercause. Our funeral liturgy is explicit that death is an instrument of

God's providence; and popular consolation in distress frequently takes the form, 'It must have been meant for you'!

All this seems to me more worthy of Islamic monotheism than of Christian theology, and I suspect that it has a double rooting in the massive determinism of Calvinism and the blander general causality of Deism, with its watch-winding God, and the Newtonian Enlightenment.

Yet in its highly distorted form, I think it witnesses to one significantly truthful intuition. Unless you have some frame of reference for understanding God's relation to the cosmos, his relation to the human becomes an abstraction.

The pervasiveness of the abstraction is again manifest at all levels, from that of sophisticated theology to popular piety. In the work of so influential a theologian as Rudolf Bultmann, 'cosmological' is used as equivalent to 'mythological', and contrasted with 'real' or 'existential'. It is for Bultmann a basically pagan, magical view of God to suppose that he interacts directly with the material world; rather, he challenges and inspires human decisions, which may in turn affect the material world. And I suspect that, for many ordinary Christians, God is thought of almost entirely in terms of moral influence or disembodied spiritual support.

If the alternative to that is a deist Supercause, or a post-Newtonian 'God of the gaps', it is not of course surprising that a cosmologically active God has fallen into disrepute. For the gaps have steadily closed; and the very notion of a God who now and then intervenes in particular situations leads to its own moral problems! If God occasionally acts in some specially providential way, say to heal or to transform a situation of despair, how can one understand his so often leaving the insolubly defeating situations unsolved? It is, again, often to vindicate God from charges of capriciousness or arbitrariness that people have found it easier to believe that he doesn't interfere with nature at all, than to suggest that he sometimes does.

Nevertheless, unless we can somehow include an account of God's relation to the cosmos in any exploration of his relation to evil, we cannot begin to talk convincingly about his relation to persons through their experience of evil or of good; for the 'I' to whom God is alleged to relate cannot be detached, except by fantasy, from the physical, concrete world. The interrelation between mind and body, nerve and sinew, the form we take, the embeddedness in contexts of space, time and material concreteness are what give us our identity, as we well know in our most truthful moments of love and grief. It is the expression of an eye, the tone of a voice, the possibility of touch which mediates our relating to one another as persons. And that body we are is continuous with a wider cosmos. Part of the nightmare of envisaging post-nuclear life in the official images of civil defence is that we would be asked to exist, if we still existed at all, without access to natural air, earth, fire and water. The medieval astrologers did a kind of physiology which we now find quaint, but they were not wrong about our inter-involvement with the elements of the cosmos. Whatever dabbling Christianity has done with Spiritualism and Gnosticism, I take it to be an implication both of the incarnation and of the doctrine of creation that we are inalienably made as bodies.

Zbigniew Herbert, the post-war Polish poet, puts this protest against religious etherialism tellingly in a little poem, 'Anything rather than an angel':

> If, after our deaths, they want to transform us into a tiny
> withered flame that walks along the paths of winds, we
> have to rebel. What good is an eternal leisure on the bosom
> of air, in the shade of a yellow halo, amid the murmur of
> two-dimensional choirs?
> One should enter rock, wood, water, the cracks of a
> gate. Better to be the creaking of a floor than shrilly
> transparent perfection.

If he is right, we cannot think of ourselves rescued from evil without the cosmos being rescued, just as we cannot consider our free fallenness without considering the cosmic aspects of the problem of evil. Now, various theologians try to suggest that so-called 'natural evil' is not in fact 'evil' at all, but mere misfortune. Barth at times comes near it, in his account of the 'shadow side of creation', where sickness and health, autumn and spring, light and darkness are part of a marvellous complementarity, a richness of being which is, seen as a whole, a matter for celebration. When he comes to death, however, on the whole, Barth, fortunately, finds himself unable quite to domesticate this within the natural rhythms of a provident creation (though many contemporary pastoral counsellors do it!). Here, he admits, we lurch into something more awful; we see disclosed an actual threat to the whole of creation, light and shadow; the encroaching menace of what he calls 'nothingness – Das Nichtige': that which God does not will.

Yet even Barth, whose existential and political sensitivity towards actual good and evil is so fine, seems to me at this point to be trapped in a conceptual tie-up between God and necessity. Just as what God positively wills has to be, so what God does not will, what he wills against, has to be, with a negativity corresponding in reality to the good he positively wills. Now, if this is not simply a logical muddle, like some of *Alice in Wonderland*'s playfulness about 'nothing' and 'nobody' being something and somebody, then it is a disastrous vision of God, so to speak, as the victim of his own cancelled imagination. God is like King Midas. Whatever he thinks, whatever he unthinks, turns to gold. We are back to Supercause, and in this case Supercause impotent against the ontological force of even his own negated conceptions.

But this is, in any case, surely a wild anthropomorphism for Barth, the exponent of God's otherness. We may find ourselves presented with alternative images, possibilities, options, between which we choose, but God does not choose good. God is good: evil does not occur to him or in him even potentially. He cannot but be love and freedom: that is not constrained externally, nor is it a chosen option. It is his mode of being himself.

We glimpse that, fleetingly perhaps, in the purity of love we rarely encounter. We do not find then that loving those we love is an option. We do not, on the other hand, find it constrained or necessitated from outside. Yet, in that quality of love which is simply our being most ourselves, we find our freedom realised. This is where we are, humanly speaking, most liberated into our true selves. (It need not be the person-to-person situation of 'being in love' – and even that paradigm case must be qualified by the recognition of how much necessity the erotic component carries. One can see the same quality of relation between the artist and his creativity or about any vocational response to the world. In some sense, in the freedom which we are called to taste with God, choice disappears – one reason why I am unhappy about the glorification of free will as the core of our image of God.)

Now, that was in parenthesis. To return to Barth's account of evil, it will not do, I think, to suggest that it is what must correspond to God's negative will. And it certainly will not do, as Barth himself recognises, to aestheticise evil into some cosmic tapestry, where light and shade interpenetrate for the good of the whole. We are talking of things which destroy living beings, destroy the love in them, destroy their freedom to be in community.

Even John Hick, who agrees that an aesthetic theodicy is gruesomely impersonal, puts the weight of justifying 'cosmic evil' on the moral and spiritual effect it has. Only in a world where we have to grapple with the unyielding constancy of scientific cause and effect, only in a world where disease, death and shortage of resources tease our souls into loving the good disinterestedly, can we mature morally, can we undergo the process of soul-making. The obstacles in the environment, precisely because we are not responsible for them ethically, test our mettle. They are, as it were, spiritual hurdles.

'The very irrationality and lack of ethical meaning contribute to the character of the world as a place in which true human goodness can occur, and in which loving sympathy and compassionate self-sacrifice can take place.' The incentive to hurdle would be lost if you knew that for the good people, the hurdles would evaporate.

Well, for my money, a theodicy of aesthetics is not much worse than one couched in terms of moral or spiritual athletics. I do not want my soul made, thank you very much, at the cost of my neighbour's pain and misery and death. Nor do I believe that God wants souls made at that cost, for that already ploughs into a kind of Gnosticism in which the vulnerable flesh may go to hell, and the really important thing is the detachable soul. If that is so, we must insist that anything is evil which frustrates the fullness of communion in freedom which is God's invitation to the flesh of the cosmos. And that means not only the appalling violence and carelessness of man to man, but also many aspects of the so-called natural world. The bone structure which carries our embodied presence to one another is liable to mind-twisting arthritic pain and disintegration. The same space across which a look or a gesture may communicate love can also be a desperate agent of separation. Time, which transforms us towards maturity, carries the process through to obscene senility where communication breaks down. Our involvement in the cosmos is, existentially speaking, bitter-sweet. Spiritualism, moralism, any religiosity which makes 'the real us' independent of such contextualisation, abolishes the bitter in the end. But it does it at too high a price, by vaporising the sweet concreteness of our existence.

This for us, surely, must be a central issue in exploring the mystery of evil as we live it – and particularly as we live it with the historical and scientific consciousness of the twentieth century. For we cannot actually affirm – or at least I cannot – that there was a historical time before man when the cosmos had a significantly different causal structure. Lambs and lions have been enjoying unreciprocal relationships since long before human beings appeared. Mountains were not skipping a few millennia before *homo sapiens* emerged. Drought and glacial erosion, the silicon galaxies, the cholera germs, the ozone layer, the genetic code which ultimately programmes the human brain – all of that is there before persons, chronologically speaking.

We are not morally responsible for that, fallen or unfallen. Yet that conditions our identity and our capacities as human beings, and destructively as well as creatively. Little wonder then that, at least in cosmology, a latent determinism rules. For, if we did not create our environment, and if we are not Gnostic dualists, then it must have been God. And since God cannot create evil, the only cosmic evil must be our mishandling. Whatever the protest of screaming flesh, cosmological Toryism prevails: 'Whatever is, is right.' God or nature rules. Supercause rides again.

Is there an alternative?

There is at least some hint in the New Testament, some would say an overwhelming insistence, that the proper place to look to see God's creation is not the past or the present, but the eschatological future, anticipated in the prototype of that new creation, Christ. We are, in our contemporary world, properly embarrassed about the nature miracles of the New Testament. I use the 'royal we', to mean 'I and my theological friends'. The embarrassment has to do in part with the conviction about the regularity of nature, and the arbitrariness of God or Christ as super counter-cause this time apparently switching off the traffic lights and redirecting things by hand. Still he is shunting the cosmos about, and selectively at that. For every Lazarus raised, a generation dies.

If we could learn to reread the biblical imagery in a non-causal way, I suspect it would transform both our embarrassment and our evasiveness about God's relationship to the cosmos. I am, frankly, agnostic about what publicly observable events lie behind the Gospels. If we could resurrect Mark and take him through the intellectual history of the West in a crash course, and then say 'Now look, Mark, what I mean by historical fact is this. Mrs Thatcher was at Wimbledon yesterday. Now, Mark, was it a historical fact that Jesus raised Jairus's daughter, and stilled a storm on the Sea of Galilee?' I tend to think he would say 'Of course not. That's not the sort of story I was telling.' But he might say 'Yes, he did', but only as a foretaste of a common transformation.

What I think he would mean, in either case, is this: 'Eikonographically, we, the Church, affirm that the cosmos is invited to share the purposes of love and freedom.' When this is done by a representative person who is holding the world with himself in the direction of God's future, new things can happen, physically new things. Maybe they have not empirically happened yet, even with Jesus. (We are not writing biography – an eikon is not a life-portrait.) But the world is now transparent to that hope of transfiguration. It is not a matter of counter-causal instances which are notched-up evidence for God. There is a sense in which it seems to me merely a sophisticated sort of selfishness even to want ourselves or those we love healed or raised or specially helped a moment sooner than the whole cosmos is transformed; to want this lump of cosmos made malleable while the intractable rocks stand firm elsewhere; to want the unviolated communion with our nearest and dearest, while existentially the rest of the world is treated as dispensable.

Of course, psychologically, imaginatively, we cannot do everything; but there is all the difference in the world spiritually between an invest-ment in the transformation of the world which is selective, and one which is representative. There is a point at which one has to fall silent, go *apophatic*, fail to speak categorically. This is mine. I do not know how to 'cash' biblical images/eikons/affirmations about skipping mountains and a reconciled animal world; about a risen body which has recognisable form but not substantial solidity; about a sacramental presence defying empirical absence, about a world where there will be no loss of particu-larity, but no possibility of isolation. I am, however, convinced that they warrant some resistance to equating the present, natural structures of the world with the creative intention of God.

Let me try to explore that resistance, before I stop, in a Kierkegaardian sort of story. It is not a causal, chronological, quasi-scientific account of how our human freedom relates to the bondage of the cosmos; it is the kind of identification made by the strange logic of the Sermon on the Mount between scorning and killing. Causally, these are quite different. Existentially, they are both elimination from the significant world.

Once upon a time, God wanted to make a world, and he wanted it to share his own delight and freedom of love which knew no bounds. But with the delicacy of someone who loves the other's otherness, he did not want in any way to coerce the world into being related to him, to programme it into communion, nor even to put it under any pressure of need or habit. (For communion constrained by need and habit is not free.) Yet if he loved the world into being, he could not make it less than be. He could not unlove it out of existence again. How then could he safeguard its freedom? So, when he came to love it into being rather than camping there as a constant presence on it, he made himself a significant absence. He created a world of apparently natural self-sufficiency, which ran according to fairly discoverable rules, had a discernible order. And he waited for the eventual emergence of a being who would belong physically to that self-sufficient world, and yet would be able to recognise his significant absence. For only then, if someone who was a free and representative person could find his freedom enlarged in holding up the world towards that significant absence, could God show the possibilities of his presence without overriding or manipulating things. So, God waited. But when man emerged from the cosmos, able to glimpse the freedom and love of God through his significant absence, he panicked. As he was, he was able to manage the world, to have it taped, to define the boundaries of things, even if the last boundary was death. He knew where he was, who he was. From this significantly absent God came hints of chaos. 'Love's function is to fabricate un-knownness.' You couldn't organise a world in which nature was liable to be invited to freedom. You couldn't be efficient, you couldn't even know who you were if causality wasn't going to be predictable. You couldn't even identify yourself adequately if you responded to the invitation of the absent God. For he suggested that really, in his freedom, you were as close to the beggar at the door as you were to your wife. In his freedom, you would not esteem people in terms of their past achievements, but in terms of the future your love hoped for them. In his freedom you would be naked, for the need of protective coverings would be gone.

Such glory sounded appallingly dangerous, disruptive of rank, order, moral responsibility or social stability, so man settled for managerial competence. Only occasionally, when he was made temporarily vulnerable by love or death, did he wonder what the other way might have meant. Then, when his administrative capacity broke down, he almost saw the point of the significant absence. If only he could move now to batter down the terrible otherness of space and time which separated him from his loved one. If only he could resist the predictable isolation of death, gather the other from this last definition as a body subject to normal causal processes. But then common sense would reassert itself. Two or three pastoral counsellors would remind him that he must accept the universe, and back he settled to cope with normal finitude, dismissing his other instinct as deranged.

We have not, chronologically, causally, made the cosmos as it is – but, in some existentially meaningful sense, I am suggesting we reinforce 'the Fall' every time we dismiss that other instinct. Whenever we cherish necessitating causality as the definition of our identity, we are somehow pulling against the process of salvation, not with it. When, like Calvin, we build necessitating causality into that very salvation, we blaspheme.

Of course, the causality is empirical, apparent, pervasive. When I say we must resist it, I do not mean pretend that it is not the status quo. Jump off the Empire State Building and you will be in smithereens. But I believe we are invited, called, free to resist the finality, the ultimacy of that self-identification. The modes are multiple: we may resist it by play, by longing, by art, by dream, by fantasy, by rage, by sacrament, by suffering it as appalling pain.

If we could by any means break the equation between the state of the non-human cosmos and God's provident creative intention, then I believe that our Christian co-existence, and certainly our pastoral care, would be revolutionised. At present, psychologically aware counsellors know that, for psychic health, people must be allowed to vent grief or rage, say at death. But they cannot give that human recognition the deepest theological backing while the suspicion lingers that God is behind the causality which causes death, endorsing it. We come near schizophrenia if we are sensible to all the moral obscenities which blotch our universe, but are reconciled to the physical features of the world which converge towards our un-freedom and lovelessness. We may indeed be impotent, but let us not be blandly well adjusted towards the cosmic status quo any more than we are to the ethical one.

For it is God who entitles us to yearn beyond articulation for a new earth as well as new selves; he who calls us to look at the very basic physical structures of the cosmos as well as at our human failure, and to resist their finality; he whose freedom in incarnation and *epiclesis*, invoking the Holy Spirit, defies our cosmic complacency.

I hope this doesn't appear to you as speculative, abstract, ideological comment on theodicy. I offer it as a contribution to the exploring of the lived question, one which, sadly, I have not found the resources for in my own Protestant tradition, but which is, I hope, not unfaithful to a wider ecumenical vision of how we grapple with evil in the name of Christ.

PART 3

THE COMMON LIFE

Introduction

Tim Duffy

In the 1970s, the Jesuit Bernard Lonergan's book *Method in Theology* caused something of a stir across the theological spectrum. An ecumenical seminar was arranged, at New College I think, and Elizabeth was one of the speakers. Also attending was a priest I knew. He was speaking to a group of friends later and said: 'That Liz McLaren's awfy good-looking to be a theologian. What really worries me, though, is I studied under Lonergan in Rome, and I think she knows him better than I do.'

Elizabeth addressed a particular Christian *Zeitgeist* which produced differing responses. There is the 'melancholy, long, withdrawing roar': the nearly empty churches of nostalgic greyhairs singing the old hymns. There is the certitude of the rising swell of fundamentalism elsewhere, and its counterbalance in an atheistic scientism. Elizabeth was trained in the mid-twentieth-century tradition of analytic philosophy – the linguistic turn – which believed that if the nature of philosophical language could be clarified and made more exact, many supposed problems would simply evaporate. Her own approach to language was more expansive and took as a guide Wittgenstein's statement that 'if we had to name anything which is the life of the sign, we should have to say that it was its *use*' (*Philosophical Investigations*). At a stroke, a rigid and dogmatic theory of meaning becomes not only unworkable but also counter-productive. On the sea of faith, it is useful to know whether one is just drifting with the current or getting somewhere. A hermeneutic of suspicion was transposed by her into a hermeneutic of discovery.

At one point, Elizabeth admits that 'the actual phrase "Christian ethics" is one that I deeply distrust and would never willingly use with sympathy or ease. That is partly because I think ethics is about the morally manageable, while I take Christian faith to be about the unmanageable.' This is the quandary of Christian living: as she says elsewhere, 'we live muddily at all levels'.

Before actually looking at the contents of the following pieces, it is worth considering the various audiences being addressed: parliamentarians, international students and church groups as well as the conferences of theological peers. Circumstances led Elizabeth to become freelance – 'underpaid', as she glossed it. Yet it also released her from the curriculum of academia, where, as she notes, 'Minding one's business academically is almost certainly walking by on the other side of a road some human being is lying on.' Her focus could shift to interpreting the faith response of all manner of people to their own situations.

She once said to me: 'It's interesting to work on the margins and at the boundaries, because you're not so constrained by the agenda at the centre – and you meet a greater variety of people.' This required more than ticking the boxes of classic theological agendas. There are echoes of Lonergan's view of theology mediating religion in diverse cultural situations without dissolving into mere subjectivity. Religious formation requires not only an intellectual conversion, but a moral and spiritual conversion as well. If then Elizabeth often showed a preference for the margins rather than the mainstream, we are the beneficiaries. The bookshelves may not groan with a bulky systematic theology. From her work on the various margins, however, we have inherited an inspiring set of marginalia.

These pieces span a period of over thirty years and are often prescient. They are remarkably consistent in their undogmatic approach, which attempts to understand other points of view without feeling any need for endorsement or refutation. This in turn draws the reader in as a significant part of the conversation.

Indeed, Elizabeth more than once refers to the 'running conversation' from the early 1970s with her friend, colleague and mentor John Zizioulas, an Orthodox theologian and subsequently titular Metropolitan of Pergamon. This approach was exemplified by Elizabeth's intervention at the World Council of Churches Assembly in Canberra in 1991. There was serious disagreement between Reformed and Orthodox on intercommunion and criticism of the exclusive ecclesiology of the Orthodox. Elizabeth comments: 'The brokenness of the eucharist is not your problem. It's all our problem. I take seriously what is being said by the refusal – that I am not of the Church. But I don't believe it . . .' This goes way beyond apologetics, which always run the risk of making a fetish of truth. Elizabeth states her position clearly: 'Truth is not contemplation/detachment/objectivity, but it is communion.' At the conclusion of his poem 'The Common Life', W.H. Auden says that although truth and love should coincide, on those occasions when they appear not to, 'the subaltern should be truth'.

Elizabeth invites us on a journey at once challenging and inspiring. Moving beyond stereotypes to make contact with those who are different is another way of saying love your neighbour, discover the common life at the heart of humanity. In one of his *Adagia*, Wallace Stevens remarks that 'reality is a cliché from which we escape by metaphor' (cliché originally meant the clicking sound accompanying printing from stereotypes). And if metaphor is the assertion of the identity of different things, then the greatest example is surely the Incarnation.

I

Scottish Parliament: Time for Reflection[*]

Beginnings are both wonderful and stressful. They are wonderful because they introduce new possibilities and the chance of a fresh start. They are also times that can burden us, because we know how many new beginnings end up ploughing the same old weary furrows as before.

Scotland's annual ritual of making New Year resolutions is followed by peaks in the counselling profession's agendas as people fail to do whatever it was: give up smoking, spend more time with their wives and children, keep up their piano practice, or find out more about how their colleagues tick.

I imagine that the start of a parliamentary year manifests similar ambivalence. Can the hopes and opportunities of this still infant Parliament be sustained, not only in public expectation, which is so ignorant of the graft of political life and so quick to judge – bad media leads to cynicism and scapegoating – but, more important, in your own sense of the balance between realism and vision? Politicians who cannot dream out loud have lost something, but politicians who can only dream without the disciplines of a detailed economic, sociological and political expertise will dream in vain.

Last week, I was involved in a conference of teachers of religious education from all over Europe. Some were Christian, a few were Muslim, and an unexpected number were humanist, agnostic or atheist. At one point, we were invited to play a values game. On a pyramid-shaped board, there was a range of options which ran from 'of absolute value' at the top through 'earth-shatteringly valuable', 'extremely valuable', 'valuable', 'fairly valuable', 'not entirely worthless' and then, below the base of the pyramid, a dustbin. In groups of six, we worked through a pile of cards: justice, wealth, success, freedom, love, beauty, self-satisfaction, tolerance

[*] Wednesday, 5 September 2001.

and many more. We took turns to place the card in our hand somewhere on the pyramid, but if another card was already in that space, we had to take two turns – one to demote the value that was there, and the other to replace it with the one that we valued more.

Perhaps that is a game worth playing. Which three values would be at the top of your pyramid of this Parliament's political life? Honesty? Peace? Power? Hope? Which other values would you demote to prioritise those? Should humility have a place in public life? Is integrity compatible with the pressures of presentability? Is there a way of resisting the corporate image of professional politicians, as one dictionary definition sadly puts it, as 'men' (*sic*) 'of artifice and cunning'?

Pericles would turn in his grave, and most of us who know anyone in the world of professional politics find that stereotype to be an unworthy caricature. I suspect that the clash of such values is what lies behind much nitty-gritty political debate. Perhaps that deserves a moment of reflection.

Even within my Christian tradition, there is no consensus about the top values. Faith, hope and charity are big words, but can be code to many people. At the beginning of a new session, I wish you the energy to keep asking such basic questions of one another, self-forgiveness for being part of the compromised human condition, and the ability to refuse to accept that how things are is how they are bound to be.

Towards the Realisation of Common Life*

We need to engage with the deep scepticism about the methods and processes of formal ecumenical theology, most specifically when that means doctrinal exchange and ecclesiastical negotiation about mutual recognition.

Common life is about birth and death and all that goes on between. It is about living under the sky, with sun and rain sustaining or destroying. It is about desire fulfilled and frustrated; about the pain and joy of child-rearing; the responsibility of finding bread; the mellowness or bitterness of old age; about war, land, exile, the use and abuse of power.

Common life is about tiredness and singing songs, about making money and playing with children and washing socks. It involves all the concrete diversity of existence summed up by Sartre as 'the glory, the horror and the boredom of being human'.

We belong to a common world, not just in the accelerated twentieth-century sense of the global village, touched by the winds of Chernobyl, spanned by telecommunications, faced by ecological menace and orphaned by escalating AIDS – but in the deeper sense that in the human-ness of any of us we have to recognise the humanness of each. As Shylock voiced it, against his anti-Semitic environment: 'Hath not a Jew eyes? Hath not a Jew hands, organs, dimensions, senses, affections, passions, fed with the same food, hurt with the same weapons, subject to the same diseases, healed by the same means, warmed and cooled by the same winter and summer as a Christian is?' (Shakespeare, *The Merchant of Venice*, Act III, Scene 1).

---

* Address to the World Council of Churches Faith and Order Conference at Santiago de Compostela, 1993.

If Faith and Order has a contribution to make to the life of the world, it is by articulating how this common life is not accident or mere human construct, but gift and invitation, grounded in the communion of God's own life as it reaches out to touch and welcome all that is created, nourished by its access to that life, and finally, we hope, transfigured and purged into inalienable belonging in that context of freedom and love which, clumsily, we name as the Kingdom of God.

Deep in the vision and documentation of Faith and Order is the sense that the existence of the Church, the vitality of the sacraments and the specificity of apostolic order is about making this affirmation palpable, about tasting, and giving to be tasted, the consummation of all things in the strangeness of God's future, earthed by Christ in the very stuff of the cosmos, and made present to us in the dynamic gift of his Spirit, who opens into their eschatological possibilities all the patternings of being which space and time and culture and history throw up for us.

Nothing much less than such a vision could sustain people through the hours of blood and sweat and toil and tears which go into the construction of ecumenical paragraphs! Nothing else could vindicate the centuries and decades of wrestling, across massive gulfs of tradition and language, to achieve the recapitulation of past divisions in shared ecumenical documents like baptism, eucharist and ministry, or Church and world.

The jet-polluted air and the despoiled forests on which we produce our pre-millennial utterances demand contrition, unless our work contributes to the real credibility of that hope. But does it?

The present situation: a challenge to Faith and Order

My experience of the dedication and passion of ecumenical encounter at all the levels I have been privileged to share makes clear to me that cynicism is an unworthy response. The easy criticism that ecumaniacs fiddle while multiple Romes burn recognises nothing of the depth of desire for a manifest earthing of the *koinonia* of God, and of commitment to that.

Yet not necessarily in cynicism, but in sadness and sometimes in desperation, the world in which our common life is lived asks us how on earth what we are doing can be seen as constructive of a shared future. Where is the touchdown, what French airline notices call *atterrissage*?

For we live in a world where dogma, faith and religious identity are bound up with some of the most dehumanising situations of our planet; where Christians kill and rape Muslims in the former Yugoslavia, apparently only because they are Muslims; where the Middle East and Ireland and the Sudan and countless other places seem to fragment because of self-identifications which are in part religiously partisan. To many who watch this from the outside, and even to some who live inside the hope that the Church exists to heal creation, this is an almost unbearable irony. For, de facto, our actual ecclesiastical institutions and traditions manifest themselves as obstacles to the unity of peoples rather than as signal of it.

De facto, the sacramental practice we observe, instead of anchoring the whole earth in the communion of God, seems to reserve his generosity for a part of it, conditional upon right belief, right practice or right discipline. Even the trinitarian horizon of Christian faith, instead of meeting and challenging the world's yearning with its own immeasurable enlargement, becomes, as heard, a cramping dogma, a shibboleth, an elitist Christian password to which most of the earth has no access.

To suggest therefore that baptism, eucharist and ministry, if it could only find a way to resolve the remaining internal questions documented in the volumes of responses, would thereby have elucidated the form of our common life, seems to me to underestimate the credibility – and communication gap we have to bridge, those of us who invest energy and hope in the Faith and Order process.

I am not speaking merely about the obvious and perennial gaps between theory and practice which blot Church history. Most adults who live in the world with their eyes open know that we live, institutionally as well as individually, as justified sinners – *simul iustus et peccator* – that vision and aspiration often exceed capacity to sustain; and that we walk a knife-edge between proper self-forgiveness and the exploitation of cheap grace.

So, the challenge to Faith and Order is not just the challenge of a naive utopianism, nor the impatience of a mortally foreshortened perspective on the things of eternity. (Though some, indeed, might be tempted to retort that professional ecumenicals are temperamentally disposed to overestimate the patience of God and are loath to hear the urgency of one who was hungry for figs on the tree even out of season!)

I overhear a deeper malaise, sometimes among churchmen and women who have devoted lives to ecumenical communication, that they doubt whether, in principle, Faith and Order can deliver the goods for the Church, let alone for the world's common life. It seems to me that we must not brush this critique aside as malicious or superficial, even if, in the long run, we resist it. For, if our documents are to move off the page and out of the conference to vibrate in that shared life, then we have to grapple with several issues in what I would call the apologetics of ecumenism. By that I do not mean the process which our presentation-conscious world calls packaging. I mean engagement with the deep scepticism there is about the methods and processes of formal ecumenical theology, most specifically when that means doctrinal exchange and ecclesiastical negotiation about mutual recognition.

The search for new methods
The very structuring of this conference title ('Towards *Koinonia* in Faith, Life and Witness') expresses the traditional priorities: first faith, then life, and then witness. And faith is elaborated doctrinally, certainly with constant reference to the cries of the world for peace and justice, and in commitment to spelling out the shared faith in *diakonia* and lives of costly reconciliation. But still, whether we share the same faith is tested by whether we can use the same sentences to affirm what we believe.

I think there is a great risk in this – that we commit, albeit at a more sophisticated level, the error of all fundamentalism, and perhaps all confessionalism, of confusing our statements about God with God himself. Supposing the whole world were struck dumb tomorrow. Would our common life cease? Of course not! Would we be incapable of worship? Of course not! Would we be less vulnerable to the splits in human community which arise because of difference of endowment or greed or competition or fear or diverse aesthetic sensibilities or the absence of a sense of humour?

I doubt it! Would we be further from a common faith? I suspect not! Even in a speaking world, we register often enough that it is easier to share deep life with those who do not share our credal or confessional positions than with some who do. It was a poet, a lover of words, who registered the pathos of our speaking:

> . . . Words strain,
> Crack and sometimes break, under the burden,
> Under the tension, slip, slide, perish,
> Decay with imprecision, will not stay in place,
> Will not stay still.
> T.S. Eliot, *Four Quartets*, Burnt Norton, V

This is not to argue that words are to be reckoned a handicap – an irony that would be indeed for a faith which has 'word' as a central category!

But it is a real question whether, when words get in the way of life, they become demonic. And I think we have not yet articulated in a way which is convincing to the outside world why it matters tuppence whether or not you believe in the *filioque*, or whether you think that churches need bishops or can admit women into the apostolic succession of clerical priesthood.

When people overhear such debates, they think, more or less sympathetically: 'There goes a group of human beings defending its identity against violation.' If they are one kind of person, they think that it's important to have such boundaries defined in black and white, so that people know where they are with one another and with God. If they're another kind of person, they wish the boundaries weren't there, or believe them to be a regressive tendency in human beings, inimical to the openness of God and unfaithful to his inclusiveness.

Certainly, within all our Churches, both responses are found, complicated of course by the fact that some identify the separating creeds and confessions and practices of sacramental life with God's self-revelation, while others find that idolatrous. This division does not align denomination against denomination, but marks a more subtle and, I suspect, a more problematic fault-line which cuts through all our communities of faith.

This fault-line has on the one side people who believe that, whatever disputes remain about doctrine, order or praxis, they are trivial in the light of the confidence that we are one in Christ, and that we could and should be already exploring that confidence in sacramental life, exchangeable ministry and common service. On the other side are those who find it a mere pious or sentimental fiction that we are all one, until we can wrestle into concrete agreed articulation what we believe, how we structure our discipline and liturgical life, and sanction our practice in the light of God's self-disclosure. None of the affirmations about rich and legitimate diversity clarifies what it is, but the hidden fault-line is not far below the theological crust.

It must be a major part of Faith and Order's agenda to expose, explain and, if possible, close this fault-line. For, unless it can be closed, common ecclesiological life in this pre-eschatological world seems impossible. Yet I have a niggling fear that the more successful Faith and Order is in producing celebrated texts like BEM or *Confessing the One Faith*, the more the fault-line is going to be masked rather like the twigs and grass which cover the hole in the ground from the unsuspecting boar, but cannot bear the weight of his charge! For who, longing for unity, and knowing anything of the delicate, painful, dedicated work, not to speak of the time and money that go into ecumenical dialogue, is going to abandon hope that the next document might just close the fault-line by a millimetre, until, millimetre by slow millimetre, we stand on common ground?

And yet there are yawning distances in perception and reception of the faith we share which will not be closed by these carefully negotiated texts until we can fill in more of the holes from the bottom up.

Some specific challenges

Let me, in closing, name some of the 'holes' about which we have to be candid if we are to find that there is solid ground for us to walk on together. And I hope they are named not in a spirit of destructiveness, but so that we may face the challenge which the French call *reculer pour mieux sauter*.

There is the hole identified by the liberation theologians, among others, that theological method is distorted if it works from exegesis and authoritative tradition to praxis, and not the other way round. Our working document for this conference clearly takes on board the rich lesson of that voice, demanding that all true doctrine must have a palpable bearing on how we stand in solidarity with the poor, the marginalised, the unloved.

But it does not quite hear the sharpness of it, the conviction of many who live each day with the slenderest hold on life, that it doesn't matter a fig whether you subscribe to the doctrine of the Trinity, or affirm the hypostatic union, provided that you give yourself to the struggle for justice, peace and a sustainable future for the whole earth.

Nor does it grasp the nettle of the conspicuous fact that most of the traditional Faith and Order issues have been tabled by the relatively powerful presence of those who are predominantly male, predominantly clerical, predominantly European in thought form, predominantly with most control of and most investment in the disintegrating structures of Christendom. I have little time for conspiracy theories of theology; and it is part of my hope against hope that ecumenism involves us in so entering one another's being and life that representation is redefined, not in these disgusting terms of quota allocations per category – male, female, young, old, lay, clerical – but in terms of the learning of each, from whatever place, to make his or her very own the humanness of the other, so that to make any decision which excludes or constrains them is like losing one's own life. (It is, for example, in this context that we properly carry together the ecclesiological question about women's ordination into the threefold ministry, not in terms of a power struggle between winners and losers on that issue.)

Yet, while the intentionality of the Faith and Order movement is, at its best, i.e. at its most free and loving, not to do with power, but with truth and fidelity responsive to God's initiative, we do all have considerable skill at spotting other people's specks of ecumenical manipulation while ignoring our own domestic planks. We must face the kind of culture shocks which so rocked the Canberra Assembly, the outrageous questions to our own cultural presuppositions which arise from letting people speak in their own idiom, especially if that relativises idioms about which we have become complacent.

Most specifically, I think that the Montreal recognition of the area of hermeneutics as one demanding more attention has not yet been boldly enough addressed, though everyone is aware of it, and hit-and-run references pepper the BEM text and the work on the Nicene Creed. But there is a long way to go here. I suspect it is still unintelligible to some Christians why others believe that what is called the historical-critical method should be taken seriously. It is unintelligible to others how it can be dismissed. And to yet others, that whole debate is as irrelevant as the angels-on-pinheads controversy. Until we not only understand, but also can stand in one another's shoes on that deep procedural question, I wonder if our substantial doctrinal consensus can bear much pressure.

In all this, of course, I have to acknowledge and can only offer the perspective of my own theological training and ecclesiastical formation: European, academic and Reformed, though I have had enough ecumenical benediction to know that I owe my survival in Christian life to more exuberant explorations of the love and freedom of God.

It is because we do sometimes taste in theological encounter the quickening of love and enlargement of imagination which are the real *raison d'être* of Faith and Order that we must resist both the abuse of doctrine as an ecclesiastical straitjacket for our common life and the dismissal of it as a footnote to ethics. We are wrestling together with the mystery of the Church as a vehicle of life for the world, and of dogma and concrete form as vehicles of life for the Church. But these are not self-evident truths, and they often look like falsehoods. To test their reality in the teeth of the world's pain, in the complex opening of inter-faith engagement, and in the robust suspicion of those who think, inside and beyond the Church, that theology is a menace, is a

Elizabeth and her brother Peter on holiday. As children they had a very secure existence, not rich materially but without any sense of being deprived of anything. They lived in Govan, in Glasgow. Summer holidays were spent 'doon the watter' in Rothesay, Arran, St Monans, Nairn, Grange-over-Sands and St Anne's-on-the-Sea.

As a pupil at Hutchesons' Girls' Grammar School in Glasgow, Elizabeth embraced the competitive and academic culture of the school and earned the accolade of school Dux in 1963.

She joined the English Speaking Union Debating Society and was invited to the ESU headquarters in Edinburgh on the occasion of its opening by the Duke of Edinburgh. *The Scotsman* featured this photograph of her in school uniform under the headline, 'Talkative Schoolgirl meets Duke'.

Elizabeth Anne McLaren, as she was then, at her graduation at Glasgow University in 1967 with a First Class Honours Degree in Philosophy and English Literature. Professor Keith Ward, then lecturer in Logic at Glasgow, recalled that she was the brightest student he had ever taught.

Being greeted by Pope John Paul II. Elizabeth was the only woman member of a British Council of Churches delegation to the Vatican in April 1983, returning the Pope's visit to the UK the year before. The delegation was led by Bishop Alastair Haggart, Primus of the Scottish Episcopal Church.

Douglas and Elizabeth with Kirsten and Alan on the beach at Southend, Mull of Kintyre, where the Templeton family had a house.

Elizabeth with Kirsten, Alan and Calum (on her knee) and their friend Catherine Hepburn in 1984.

In Perthshire, early 2000.
Elizabeth and her friend Catriona
Matheson from Dunedin,
New Zealand.

Elizabeth and Douglas with
Alan at his graduation from
Aberystwyth University in July
2003.

With their friend Ute Fleming
and her two children, and their
dog Donald.

In 2006 Alan disappeared. He was 25. It was not until 2012 that his remains were found. Throughout that dreadful time of searching and waiting there was always the hope that he might be alive. Meanwhile, Liz was active in the charity Missing People.

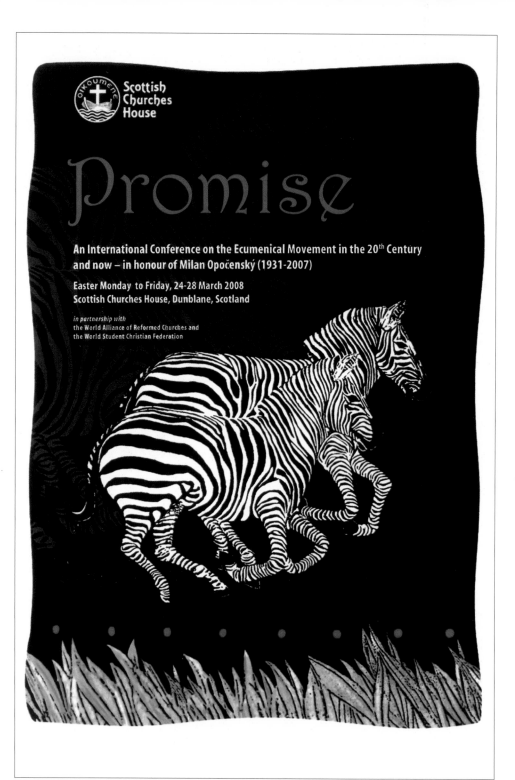

The *Promise* conference, at which Elizabeth delivered the address, *Angels in the Trees? A Theology for Today.*

Elizabeth was a key member of the planning group which organised two very successful International Theological Summer Schools at Scottish Churches House. The first of these, with twenty participants of different ages from five continents, was held in 2007.

The Interim Management Group of Scottish Churches House in 2005. From left, Alastair Hulbert, Andy Bews, Danus Skene (Convener), John Lackie, Jim Lugton, Caroline Butterfield, Iona McCullagh, Alison Elliot, Elizabeth Templeton. Elizabeth had particular responsibility for programme and theology.

Elizabeth and Donald Smith, Director of the Scottish Storytelling Centre in Edinburgh, leading a workshop in the Centre library about 2005.

On holiday on the Isle of Gigha.

With friends Heinke and Peter Matheson during a visit to New Zealand in 1991.

Elizabeth and Douglas outside their house at Milton of Pitgur near Pitlochry.

Throughout her life Liz was an indefatigable campaigner on behalf of institutions of learning threatened by secular or Church authorities.

task to keep Faith and Order in business. But not, I hope, with a sense of leisure. For our own redundancy might be a signal of the Kingdom's imminence, at least if it meant that we had discovered the unconditionality of the common life we are charged with as stewards of God's future.

3

Self and Word[*]

*When I recommend that theology reconnects with existence, I do not
mean with a theory of existence which may in its way be as doctrinaire and arbitrary as other philosophical systems. I mean that must
start by paying attention again to how life is.*

I suspect that in our culture theology is very nearly dead because it has
nothing to do with existence. I do not mean by that that it isn't relevant to
daily ethical dilemmas, for I don't think it is theology's job to resolve our
ethical dilemmas. I mean that it has taken off from the common ground of
what life is like into a stratosphere of special 'religious experience'.

What I want to do in these lectures is to try one way of bringing it
back to the earth we all inhabit, whether we are awake or asleep, pre-
conceptual children or literate adults, mentally defective or fully rational.
For I am suspicious of any theology which only works for, or with, the
small percentage of people who deliberately and consciously think religious thoughts. So, I want to invite you to forget that you belong to a
religious community, and to ask you to reflect a little on what it means
that you exist as a human person.

Then I want to argue a fairly strong case for the provisional abolition of
religious language with non-initiates, and a stronger one for a retraining
programme for insiders. Finally, I want to try to define what is distinctive
about maintaining a theological identity. For, if a special language can't
sustain our existence, and specifically 'religious' experience is suspect, it
might seem at first sight as if we should pack our bags, shut up shop and
go home. In what sense then does, or could, our existence present any sort
of crisis for the world? What makes us who we are as Church if it isn't
having a special vocabulary and a special subsection of experience?

* Church of Ireland Clergy Refresher Course, sometime before 1989.

I don't know whether or not it has been shown recently in Northern Ireland, but the BBC has just been showing a series called *Life on Earth* in which David Attenborough traced the lines of evolution from the first primitive soup to the present day. In the last programme, he asked how unique or distinctive among the life on earth man was. Traditional religion of course might leap to defend itself by talking of souls: those entities undetectable by camera or scalpel which allegedly only man has. But the programme never discussed souls. Rather, it pointed out that man was the only symbol-user – the only one who could represent the world, who could communicate without being physically present.

Let us concentrate for a little on this capacity to represent the world, and its implications. Animals are characteristically bound in their environment, and their highest possibilities are of adaptation to the givenness of things which makes their survival surer. They live instinctively, belonging to the cosmos as far as we can judge without the possibility of question, manifesting the rich complexities of biological development.

The poet W.H. Auden, in a chorus from *The Dog Beneath the Skin*, muses on the point:

> Happy the hare at morning, for she cannot read
> The hunter's waking thoughts. Lucky the leaf
> Unable to predict the fall. Lucky indeed
> The rampant suffering suffocating jelly
> Burgeoning in pools, lapping the grits of the desert
> Or best of all the mineral stars disintegrating quietly into light
> But what shall man do, who can whistle tunes by heart,
> know to the bar when death shall cut him short,
> like the cry of the shearwater?

This, according to the existentialists, is sufficient reason for not defining man in terms of the continuities of nature. He can make the future be present. He can bring the not-there before him representatively in paint or word. He can rescue what has been from forgottenness or the threat of perpetual obscurity, as the sonneteers remind us who battle with time for the beauty of their loves.

This ability to generate and suggest alternative worlds is, I suggest, a key starting point for a theological analysis of existence, whether it be a child's saying 'this shoebox is an elephant', or a Lascaux cave painting, or even a lie.

The critic and philosopher George Steiner has a fascinating book called *After Babel* in which he explores the multiplicity of natural languages and tries to explain it, since it seems to serve no obvious biological purpose. In that book, his third chapter is called 'Word against object', and he spends a great deal of it contending that the possibility of falsehood is a positive and significant aspect of human freedom, even of human transcendence:

> When did falsity begin, when did man grasp the power of speech to 'alternate' on reality, to 'say otherwise'? There is of course no evidence, no palaeontological trace of the moment or locale of transition – it may have been the most important in the history of the species – from the stimulus-and-response confines of truth to the freedom of fiction. There is experimental evidence, derived from the measurement of fossil skulls, that Neanderthal man, like the newborn child, did not have a vocal apparatus capable of emitting complex speech sounds. Thus it may be that the evolution of conceptual and vocalised 'alternity' came fairly late. It may have induced, and at the same time resulted from, a dynamic interaction between the new functions of unlettered, dictive language and the development of speech areas in the frontal and temporal lobes. There may be correlations between the 'excessive' volume and innovation of the human cortex and man's ability to conceive and state realities 'which are not'.

We literally carry inside us, in the organised spaces and involutions of the brain, worlds other than the world, and their fabric is preponderantly, though by no means exclusively or uniformly, verbal. The decisive step from ostensive nomination and tautology – if I say that the waterhole is where it is, I am, in a sense, stating a tautology – to invention and 'alternity' may also relate to the discovery of tools and to the formation of social modes which that discovery entails. But, whatever their biosociological origin, the uses of language for 'alternity' for misconstruction, for illusion and play, are the greatest of man's tools so far. With this stick, he has reached out of the cage of instinct to touch the boundaries of the universe and of time.

But while man, through speech and symbol, has a way of expressing resistance to how things are, still, they are in certain ways, and a great deal of this century's Existentialist philosophy has tried to plot man's existence between the givenness of his context and the freedom of his possibilities.

Heidegger's word for the facticity of existence was 'thrownness', finding yourself launched in an existence you didn't ask for, in a specific space and time and set of relations you had no part in choosing. There seems no cosmic necessity about your being-there-in-the-world. It just happens to be so. And the sheer contingency of it provokes in man the teasing question, 'Why is there something and not nothing?' Why is there me, and not no-me?

This contingency, however, is not merely passively encountered as a fait accompli, for man not only exists in thrownness but as possibility. He is not fixed and complete in his being, simply unwinding with the necessity of a coiled spring, or blossoming like a plant specimen. He has, at least to some extent, the making of himself, the responsibility for his future. He is charged with care for who he becomes. The question 'Who will I be tomorrow?' is not simply an enquiry. It is a decision. Man is burdened, as no other creature seems to be, by life-options.

And yet the options have a fixed parameter, for all his possibilities are in the shadow of death. He is, from his birth, a dying being, and his contingency is marked as clearly by his ending as by his beginning. It is in the face of his sure death that he has to ask who he is, who he will be.

For Existentialism, the characteristic human dilemma is whether to face the question truthfully, or to take one of the many ways there are of evading it. One can, for instance, so immerse oneself in business that one never lets it be raised, until of course a colleague at the next desk collapses over his lunchtime soup. Or one may formally admit it as an issue, but see its settlement as an automatic thing. 'I've lived here since my childhood; my roots are here; I can't move anywhere else.' 'I'm a good son. I must go into the family business.' 'I'm bound to fail: see what an emotionally deprived childhood I had.' 'I'm a Scot. You don't get Scots showing their feelings.'

Any kind of unquestioning assumption of a role, particularly one defined for one by others – any collectivism in which I am willing to have myself exhaustively defined in terms of a class's behaviour standards – any determinism which I regard as fixing me absolutely: such acts of 'bad faith' are to the existentialist the marks of fallenness. For it is, in the eyes of most such philosophers, a world with a tendency towards in-authenticity, pressurising people out of genuine selfhood towards conventional being. As Sartre says in *Being and Nothingness*, 'A grocer who dreams is offensive to the buyer, because such a grocer is not wholly a grocer. Society demands that he limit himself to his function as a grocer.'

It is not that the past must necessarily be renounced; it may, of course, be positively affirmed. The point is that an active stance must be taken in relation to it: one must not just slide into a ready-made slot. And the dangers of simply letting oneself be conditioned into being are so great in relation to the past that for most existentialists the future presents a better visual aid to what 'becoming a self' is about. The act of responsibility involved in 'taking a grip' on one's selfhood is clearer when no possibilities are ready-made.

There are caricatures of Existentialism, sometimes warranted by some of the statements such philosophers have made, which suggest that by will-power man can do anything, from defeating the common cold to renouncing his entire past. This seems to me an absurdly unrealistic notion in view of our common experience, and I suspect that it is a subtle modern form of Gnosticism, in which the real self is detached from the concrete material world in which it lives, and from the external facts of its history.

When I recommend that theology reconnects with existence, I do not mean with a theory of existence which may in its way be as doctrinaire and arbitrary as other philosophical systems. I mean that it must start by paying attention again to how life is.

Now, that is so big a question that it seems virtually impossible to know where to start. 'How life is' is how all the novelists and dramatists in the world portray its quirks and particularities. It is how I find the raggedness of my day-to-day activity. It is what the economists and the politicians and the psychologists and the sociologists say. It is how the new bulletins report it. It is so complex and elusive as to effectively exclude definition.

We may however identify a skeleton, which, however fleshed out it is in concrete distinctiveness, nevertheless forms the underlying structure of our existence. In the first place, we exist within the limits of space-time. The co-ordinates of space and time are for all of us, as for all things, constitutive of our identity. I am a twentieth-century British-born version of *homo sapiens* which has taken a certain form in the world for a certain length of time. That fact also isolates me to some extent. I am incapable of immediate direct communion with, say, a person in Tokyo, or my great-great-grandfather. If two people I love need me, and they live in different places, I have to decide between them. I cannot be with both at once. I am embedded in a spatio-temporal territory.

Secondly, there are limits about which I can do nothing, or at least very little, in my psycho-somatic constitution. I fall asleep, I wear out, I can only cope psychically with so much of certain people. And this is true even when I am, so to speak, at my moral best. It isn't an ethical limit, but an ontological one.

Thirdly, there are limits which I face because of the very structure of moral alternatives and choices which arise from the physical limits. Given the world's finite resources, and the vulnerabilities of flesh and blood, I find that my existence is at the expense of others. As a white twentieth-century Britisher, I live off a lot of people in the Third World, killing them slowly by ongoing economic attrition. My taxes go into a defence budget liable to be used against Russians I don't hate. My education and my present job are available to me because money was made available for cleverish children which was not spent on backward starters in the same primary-school class. The resources of energy we are now using mean that our great-great-grandchildren will have less.

None of these are things I have consciously or individually chosen, but they are facts which involve me – and, if I set about altering them, I face other dilemmas. If I cannot help being a white British twentieth-century middle-class intellectual, what if I at least 'act out of character'? Suppose I stop paying taxes, or I become socially or politically disruptive, either by quiet subversion or overt revolution? Still I am faced and perplexed by limits. There is a whole galaxy of people opposed now to my policies: existentially, that is to say, I have created new enemies. What will I do about them? Eliminate them if I can? Suppress them? Tolerate them? Welcome them? The former two mean I menace their existence and freedom, the latter two probably that they menace mine. By acting against the standard conventions of my family, my tribe, my race, my class, my peers, I am bound to alienate or distress or come into conflict with someone. And by accepting them, I am already surreptitiously alienating others.

Similarly, we are caught in all sorts of common dilemmas which are characteristically agonising. I want to speak the truth, yet if I do it in situation x I will certainly make life significantly harder for my friend y, who is already under considerable pressure. I want to endorse maximum freedom of speech – but, if I do that, my neighbour will spread his poisonous racist policies. Over and over again, what the moral philosophers classify as justice, truth, freedom and love clash with one another, or generate frightening ironies, whether in the individual or the socio-political realm.

Now, there is obviously a common usage of the word 'freedom' in which such cosmic limitations are not taken into the reckoning at all. A person is regarded as free precisely because he has options and no one is stopping him choosing. To say you are not free because you can't help dying, or you can't be in two places at once, seems bizarre to most users of the English language. It is, however, I am suggesting, one of the most significant aspects of our existence from the point of view of theological analysis, because it is ultimately such factors, and not just our ethical failures, which frustrate our personal being. We are incapable of sustaining communion with one another because such elements isolate and separate us (and I am taking it as an axiom that freedom of communion is the essential thing which makes us distinctively personal).

So far, I have been trying to avoid technical theological vocabulary, because I think it so important that the religious community learns to pinpoint and identify the salient features of common existence which presuppose no special, esoteric experience. But I am convinced, in fact, that when classical Christian tradition, particularly Eastern tradition, talked about the world as fallen, it was referring to such features of the world.

We in our Western tradition have learned, I think, a rather different theological placing of 'the way things are'. Partly because God was identified with Aristotle's 'First Cause' in the Thomist tradition after Aquinas; partly because of the immense impact of Calvinism with its predestination emphasis; and partly because of a pervasive Enlightenment deism which saw God as the great watch-winder, it has gone oozing into our religious subconscious that how things are is how God must want them to be. God is directly behind the order of things.

Allied to this goes a whole strategy of counselling and pastoral care which recommends acceptance, the coming to terms with the cosmos. People are told, or half-told, that their bereavement is part of God's providential dispensation, and that once their natural distress has had some expression they must reconcile themselves to what must clearly be the will of God. They are encouraged to see their limits and moral dilemmas as the stretching obstacle course of a wise creator, or as proper reminders of the humility of the creature. Resistance, challenging, is a sort of Adamic pride. Faith accepts the harmony of how God fits things together. The rhythms of life and death.

Against this view, the Christian philosopher Nicolas Berdyaev launches in all his writings:

> a world harmony is a false and an enslaving idea. One must get free from it for the sake of the dignity of personality. This world harmony costs too much. Dostoevsky everywhere hunts down this world harmony, and that is the most Christian thing about him. Rational theology establishes not only a false theodicy, which in actual fact

justifies not God but godlessness; it also sets up a false doctrine of divine providence in the world. The world is not in such a state as justifies an optimistic doctrine of the action of divine providence in it. If everything is from God, and everything is directed by God towards happiness, if God acts in the plague and in cholera and in tortures, in wars and enslavements alike, the consequence, when thought out, must be to lead to the denial of the existence of evil and injustice in the world.

But God is not world providence, that is to say not a ruler and sovereign of the universe, not *pantocrator*. God is freedom and meaning, love and sacrifice: he is struggle against the objectivised world order. Freedom from servitude is freedom from the crushing idea of world order which is the outcome of objectivisation, that is to say, of the Fall. The good news of the approach of the Kingdom of God is set in opposition to the world order.

If there is any truth in this, then the existentialists' resistance to defining man in terms of his given nature is not an impious blasphemy, as it has sometimes been presented as being. It is rather a legitimated dissatisfaction, a hopeful sign that man, for all his manifest fallenness, is not simply able and willing to settle for it. The violence of Dylan Thomas's protest against even an old man's death,

> Do not go gentle into that good night,
> Old age should burn and rave at close of day;
> Rage, rage against the dying of the light.

is no longer met by outraged and decorous piety, but celebrated by a faith that God also is against the dying of the light: that he is an ally in the battle to free things from their restrictedness and perishability, and not a limit to that struggle.

More significantly, if this is anything like an account of what theology is about, it is perhaps possible to take the subject out of closed circles of esoteric religious experiences, and to replace it in whatever marketplace you happen to find yourself in. The question of interest is no longer whether people encounter the supernatural, or have extraordinary psychic glows and tingles. It is not even what doctrines they subscribe to, or what words they use about God, salvation, eschatology and so on. Rather, one starts with such questions or test situations as: 'What is their attitude to death? Do they accept it as a reconcilable limit, or are they outraged by it? Can they take delight in the world's representation through play or art or any other mode? What is their attitude to the outsider, the non-conformist, the abnormal? Is he met as a bearer of creative possibilities or as a threat to safe identity? Are they complacent about their ethical systems, or disturbed by them and restless at their defects?' and so on.

Theological questions, put in such a form, immediately bite on any existence, since no human being avoids the situations they probe. People may have no self-consciousness that they are implicitly giving answers already to such questions, but it ought to be possible for the recognition to be made. In some cases, that might take the form of culture shock, of presenting a real way of doing it differently, practised elsewhere and exposing the parochialism of one's axioms. In others, it might more gently be done by exploration of alternatives through story or play. There is a vast number of books, none of them explicitly theological or abstractly conceptual, which might start people thinking, e.g. Saint-Exupéry's *The Little Prince*; or Adrian Mitchell's *Friday*, which retells the story of Robinson Crusoe from Man Friday's point of view; or Virginia Axline's account *Dibs in Search of Self*, which describes the psychotherapy of a child wrecked by an emotionally sterile home. Certainly, it seems to me to be the main demand which formal theology has conspicuously failed to meet on the whole, that people should be teased and imaginatively quickened into restlessness at the existential status quo, and at cultural complacency about it.

All this has been an attempt to articulate the conviction that man is invited towards freedom and communion, towards ecstasy if you like, in terms of unconstrained outgoing towards the other. Whatever he finds in his existence to frustrate that is evil, and he is only really human in his resistance to or dismay at such limitation. While people may balk at such a general description of themselves, or not recognise it, I suspect that their concrete longings in the identifying situations of love and death actually mark that conviction as central to their being. If it were not so, I would, I think, give up theology. This then is the context in which I am suggesting that we discuss specifically religious language and specifically Christian identity – and, if you don't like the account of that context, you may immediately want to go home. But perhaps before that, some clarificatory discussion might take place!

4

Intellectuals Between
Power and Resignation*

You do not know anything properly in neutrality. Knowing is an intimate, delicate, delighted willingness that 'the other' should disclose itself to you as you invite it to emerge. In Christian imagery, the freedom of the new creation is not restricted to human beings, but it is to be extended to the created world. For this to be explored, we need a recognition of the passion of knowing.

It is an extraordinary and teasing assertion to be told: 'You are the salt of the earth.' It is intolerable to say or think: 'We are the salt of the earth.' The grammar of faith does not allow the one to be translated into the other. Salt, and saviours, are without Messianic self-consciousness. It is at the outset a handicap for us that we want to claim that as our banner, if we do. For the characteristic irony of the salty Christian God is that when you have most consciousness of doing his will, you may least be doing it, and when you have no consciousness of your significant mission, you may have one.

First there was a god of night and tempest, a black idol without eyes, before whom they leaped, naked and smeared with blood. Later on, in the times of the republic, there were many gods with wives, children, creaking beds, and harmlessly exploding thunderbolts. At the end, only superstitious neurotics carried in their pockets little statues of salt, representing the god of irony. There was no greater god at that time.

Then came the barbarians. They too valued highly the little god of irony. They would crush it under their heels and add it to their dishes.
– Zbigniew Herbert, 'Mythology'

* Address to the World Student Christian Federation (WSCF) European Students Conference, *Salt of the Earth*, in El Escorial, Spain, April 1981.

I suppose that, for most men and women now in our European culture, questions of survival, birth, death, sex, war, money, safety, power and identity have to do with no gods. For gods are absolute, commanding nakedness and blood, but the genius of European civilisation has been to relativise the gods. Gods are portable options, carried by some as a matter of superstitious neurosis or of temperament. Cosmic sanctions have dwindled to the mappable laws of cause and effect. Man/woman is the measure of things in law, science, historiography and art. We are responsible. All the dimensions of joy, pathos, failure and hope are human.

That situation is often said to be the outcome of a tradition which is distinctively European and conspicuously intellectual. It is the culmination of a history anchored by such names as Plato, Aristotle, Dante, Bacon, Galileo, Leonardo, Shakespeare, Descartes, Erasmus, Cervantes, Racine, Grotius, Newton, Voltaire, Goethe, Kant, Darwin. What has characterised that tradition has been a momentum towards self-sufficient humanism, even if some of the particular contributors were also Christian. Their significant, cumulative, unplanned power as intellectuals was to suggest and sustain a world of self-images capable of supporting Europe's existence, able to provide a massive confidence that even if the gods were domestic creations with harmlessly exploding thunderbolts, truth, goodness and beauty were real, and people could know them.

Now, some forms of Marxism must of course read any intellectual traditions as an epiphenomenon. The spurious by-product of exploitation, the fantasy world of an illicitly powerful elite, immune from fluctuations in the price of fish. Worlds are sustained by the sweat of hands, not by ideas.

It seems to me, however, that if we are to understand our own powerlessness, it must be in the context of taking seriously what power that European tradition has had. We must recognise that it could generate centuries of confident physical and mental exploration, ethical systems, art, music. And we must believe, hard as it seems, that it was not just 'idealism', with a Marxist curl of the lip, but a potent conviction about the real, actual world. How society was structured or restructured; how social roles were specialised and divided; how intellectual culture gained prestige over peasant or artisan. All of this was, I believe, powerfully sanctioned by the sense that the grain of the universe was penetrable and reflected in these values.

Now there are, of course, residual outcrops of that European humane tradition: those who believe for instance that the most intelligent people should carry the burden of legislation for the good of all; that the division of labour between head-thinkers and hand-workers is appropriate and beneficial; that there are absolute moral values, independent of cultural change or context; that the essence of man is good and realisable by education.

I take it, I hope not unfairly, that few wistful Platonists frequent WSCF conferences, and that that tradition seems to most of us a quaint or sinister survival, depending on how much power we think it still has. But it is not dismissible if we want to explain the present situation of the European intellectual. He is, of course, beleaguered by all sorts of external pressures, financial constraints, shifts in the social power bases, vocal 'barbarian' demands for direct social utility, government blackmail. But the inwardness of his loss of nerve, his loss of self-confidence is, I suspect, to do with the vacuum left by the substantial disintegration of Platonism.

In a post-Platonist world, it is no longer possible to be confident that thinking gives anyone privileged access to truth. Indeed, the only serious candidate for a globally alternative ideology, Marxism, suggests the reverse. The person who does not sweat, who is professionally removed from the direct productive transformation of the world, or at least not accountable to the producers, is bound not to see the truth. Thinking, far from being pure penetration of reality, is a dislocated activity – the spinning of a disengaged cog. The intellectual is by definition alienated. But it is not just Marxism which generates cynicism or pessimism about ideas. Common speech, even common Tory Party speech, can count on sympathy for cuts in university budgets by contrasting 'the university' and 'the real world'. At a more sophisticated level the recognition of relativism, the cultural conditioning of any perception, *any outlook*, makes it seem a prerogative of fools or rogues to claim knowledge of the truth.

So we live, characteristically, as intellectuals of radical sympathy in a sort of endemic schizophrenia that we inhabit an unreal world. The unambiguously real world is the world where neutron bombs lurk in Arizona deserts, where Ugandans starve, where unemployment divides the West into two worlds, where baby-food manufacturers campaign against breastfeeding in the Third World. The real world is the world facing death, the world in pain.

Over against that, there are empirically actual 'unreal' worlds, where women spend pounds a week on diets or hairdressing, where parents clap proudly at prize-giving ceremonies, where couturiers fabricate costume designs, where executives do deals over whiskies, where double agents penetrate spy networks.

And the universities, we fear, are another empirically unreal world, fitting people for unreal existence. They do not, with a few departmental or individual exceptions, ask questions about the poor, the oppressed, the exploited. They function as if such people did not exist, were not at any rate their business. Normally they depend on financial resources which are disposable national or private capital. Normally they reinforce the isolation of thinking, study, controlled experiment, from socially or politically engaged action. They promote the stratification of the community, there being a recognisable gulf of culture, language, self-confidence and often salary between those with and those without higher education. Minding one's business academically is almost certainly walking by on the other side of a road some human being is lying on.

So, what are we to do? My brief for this paper was to address myself to 'The question of ethics as it confronts students and young intellectuals, Christians in modern Europe, in a world with no sound values, where unemployment threatens, where the positive contribution of "socialist" ideology has failed, where the "great helmsmen" have all died or been killed off, where the Third World is not our affair . . . where the New Religious Movements and Conservative Evangelicals of all sorts come swooping in with their certainties to fill the gaps . . . How, the question ran, do we construct a lay Christian ethics today in such a context?'

Now, the actual phrase 'Christian ethics' is one that I deeply distrust and would never willingly use with sympathy or ease. That is partly because I think ethics is about the morally manageable, while I take Christian faith to be about the unmanageable. It is also because the indispensable category for ethics seems to me to be 'obligation', while the central category for Christianity is 'freedom' or 'possibility', and I find them unhappily yoked. But I don't want to get stuck on the word 'ethics'. It is a real, specific question, 'What *are* we to do?', and behind it another one: 'Can we make any coherent sense of our doing in the light of the Gospel we believe, or is our action simply random if good-hearted, under specific pressures of demand or frustration or panic or outrage?' If I prefer to talk in terms of 'the lifestyle of the Kingdom of God' rather than of Christian ethics, you will, I hope, trust that I am addressing myself to those questions all the same.

I should, I suppose, before going further, give you some indication of what I mean by 'freedom' and 'unmanageability', since they lie behind all the rest I think. Roughly – by 'freedom', I mean a condition of transformed existence which seems to me the ultimate Christian affirmation for the world. Its ultimate context is the destruction of death and of the structures of causality which mediate death; and its centre is a re-creation in which people will not know themselves as isolable individuals, but irreplaceably as members of another identity. No one (and, incidentally, nothing) can in that condition of existence be a mere thing for another: no one can be himself or herself apart from his relatedness to whatever other. And the mutuality of that community will be uncoerced.

When I say that such freedom is 'unmanageable', I mean that there is no organisational strategy, no legislation, no influence even which will make it inevitable or even probable. One cannot *cause* a transformation of existence, or not that one, by any means/ends programme. That I take to be the meaning of some New Testament categories about the elusiveness of the Kingdom, or about justification being by grace, not words, or of the suggestion that the Church (don't laugh – the prototype of the Kingdom!) is only a creation of the Spirit. Whatever the power of God is, it is not the operation of some predictable determinism of input and outcome: certainly not the conditioned result of human endeavour.

But when I say that the freedom of the Kingdom of God is not manageable, I do not mean that it lies in a world of utopian fantasy, a mental hope to be tucked in a corner of the mind while we live in resigned acceptance of the status quo. The freedom *is* signalled, anticipated in all sorts of concrete ways in human flesh and bones, and in inviting us, both as glimpsed presence and as significant, potent absence. I still think the most clarifying image is that of loving someone so that you would die for them: that is freedom. It implies the irreplaceability of the other, the intolerableness of his not being there, the lack of coercion, the mutuality of your identities, the disappearance of self-preoccupation. But it is not, of course, confined to, or even at all guaranteed by, contexts of sexual intimacy. I take it that Camus or Einstein or Britten had that quality of encounter in their artistic creativity, that Dag Hammarskjöld had it in his political commitment, Archbishop Romero in his priesthood, and that many parents glimpse it representatively with their children. Certainly, I think it is what is recognised or celebrated by the many small groups of globally insignificant Christians who discover that they do not need to own or possess or protect what they thought they did; that they need not live behind locked doors; that they can discover a richer identity through dispossession and vulnerability, in saying to 'the other', 'Give me myself.'

But if that *is* intelligible as an account of Christian hope, what follows? I find it obviously impossible to move from that description to any prescription for anyone, let alone a generalised prescription.

Nevertheless, there do seem to me to be several implications which might be worth registering, though they will not have the form of ethical directives.

1. To live out of, or towards, the Kingdom of God in the world will always generate tension between two lifestyles. Biological instinct, social prudence and political stability converge towards a lifestyle of self-preservation, towards the demarcation of 'kinship groups'; the definition of friends and enemies. I think we lose the cutting edge of faith by talking as if the distinctively Christian question was: 'How are your life and mine to be sustainable in just co-existence?' Of course we could, with will and directed resources, achieve something much more like distributive justice in relation to wealth, education and leisure – but we kid ourselves if we think this takes us out of the structures of existence in which we threaten one another. Whatever the equity of distribution, what I eat or use in my life is unavailable to you or some child a generation ahead.

2. It follows from this that the life of a Christian in the world is always ironic. We must recognise, between humour and melancholy, that we are compromised, and that it is utopian to expect purity of existence. We live muddily at all levels. This understood must make for forgiveness and self-forgiveness as the modes of Christian existence rather than judgement and self-judgement – though, of course, forgiveness is not saying 'There, there, everything is all right as it is.'

3. There are, it seems to me, a number of ways of enacting faithfully the hope that transformation of the structure of things is the world's future. Each will have its specific irony, its particular visible or invisible pain, its own absurdity. One particular job for the 'Christian' intellectual – and I become increasingly uneasy as I use the phrase throughout this paper – might be to register and document the variety of ways in which people might be enacting their hope, faithfully.

Various options

- Pure, lunatic, unsustainable prophetic action
  This, most often, has the character of protest, of some acted question to the values and assumptions the world makes. It is not rationally viable, not aiming to be rationally viable. In the tragic mode, it might include such acts as Jan Palach burning himself, hunger strikes to the death, living as a hermit – or, in the comic mode, 'streaking' (who are all you people behind your clothes?), 'punk', 'flower-power'.

- Direct identification with 'the poor'
  This may share characteristics of the 'prophetic lunacy' mode, e.g. when Simone Weil goes to work in a factory, or when graduates choose to spend their lives as labourers in a gesture of solidarity. Or it may be a more 'rational' and intentionally 'exemplary' involvement. For example, when one puts professional skills, as a doctor, teacher, economist or agriculturist, entirely at the disposal of 'the poor', normally forfeiting status, prestige and the 'privilege' of one's profession. This too has characteristic ironies. You are already different from your community in choosing to be there when you needn't be. You forfeit much of your apparent power at the decision-making levels, and suffer (with or without resignation) the impotence of those 'at the bottom'.

- Critical presence in the structures of 'the rich'
  One may remain manifestly and confessingly unjust. The irony here is that one is liable to be rationalising one's own inertia and comfort. (I am most suspicious of this one, because I actually live here, existentially speaking.) That is, one may recognise the structures of the top government, education, Church, medicine, etc. as diseased, but think it worth trying conscientisation within these structures, or alternative modes of operation.

- Direct political action
  This may range from 'legitimately warranted' influence, lobbying MPs, writing, speaking or attempting penetration of media to 'passive resistance', techniques regarded as 'breaching the peace', or to guerrilla action, urban terrorism and so on. The characteristic ironies here are that (i) such action may well be counter-productive in terms of provoking realignment of stances and attitudes in the rest of the community, and (ii) the effectiveness when it does occur is almost certainly in terms of coercion, e.g. when a government yields to political demands through some sort of fear. And that is

the supreme irony for any group claiming to represent 'uncoerced mutuality'.

There may be other modes which we could explore together, but the above seem to me to be those which cover most of the options I can envisage. They are of course not absolute alternatives, though it may be that, as a matter of temperament or vocation, people find one or other their most convincing mode, or that in terms of time or energy doing one well precludes most of the others. What I think we must overcome is the distrust and self-distrust which makes, say, the person working within the structures guilt-ridden, and the person standing over against them self-righteous, or vice versa.

None of the above modes specifies a particular responsibility for the 'intellectual' as such, nor indeed for the Christian as such. Let me try, for the rest of the time, to address the question of the particular responsibility Christians might have in that context.

At the moment, in our culture, though there is, I think, the possibility that the intellectual will become a despised marginal, he is not yet there. For all that money and power are dissociated from thoughtfulness, it is still the case that intellectuals are 'the rich' in terms of social prestige, apparent authority in the media (though carefully selected) and public envy. I, however, having put myself in the Nicodemite category of critical presence in the structures of the rich, should perhaps say more about the job I see for those who stay within touching distance of the intellectual milieu.

Still, I have a sense that there is something else worth doing which is somehow not in competition with feeding the poor, though it may seem to be.

I said earlier that we were suffering as a culture from the collapse of Platonism. Personally, I am glad that it has collapsed at last, not because it 'had ideas' but because it generated, expressed and ratified an existence which was deadly: it represented man to himself in ways which were ultimately disintegrating. Its ideas were, from my point of view, dehumanising.

But I am not glad of the vacuum, because I believe people need ideas as they need bread: that ideas are not a pastime of an odd minority, any more than art or music properly are, but the articulation of self-images, ways of exploring convictions, hopes, identity. The fact that dictatorships characteristically go for the intellectuals as well as the gunpowder gives me some hope that this is true.

I do think that in the pluralism of our foreseeable future, and in the universities of that future, there is a Christian epistemology worth exploring, over against both Platonism and Marxism, an epistemology which suggests an alternative worth inviting a world to. In a post-Constantinian situation where I hope we will soon join the East European Churches, that can only be manifested and presented as a strangeness, not as a norm. It will make the following central suggestion:

Truth is not contemplation/detachment/objectivity, but it is communion.

This is not just the fairly obvious fact, documented by 'scholarship', that you need a team of people to explore the diversity and complexity of the real world. It is the more polemical suggestion that you do not know anything properly in neutrality. Knowing is an intimate, delicate, delighted willingness that 'the other' should disclose itself to you as you invite it to emerge. In Christian imagery, the freedom of the new creation is not restricted to human beings, but it is to be extended to the created world (ecology not as the prolongation of usefulness). For this to be explored, we need a recognition of the passion of knowing.

• The passion of fragmentation

If, as we have said, the partisan of the Kingdom of God knows himself to be unidentified without 'the other', then universities and other academic structures are a nightmare. We need to enact, to confess, to brandish the absurdity of psychologists working without historians, scientists without philosophers, theologians without artists, 'natural sciences' without 'human sciences'. We need to pilot alternatives, formally or informally.

• The passion of time

It is a proper and lovely urgency in human beings to want the world saved in foreseeable time, before the bombs drop, before this generation starves. It is obscene of God, if he has power, to have let so many people rot already. What on earth justifies the time of history, with its weight of disaster? Have we any Christian understanding of that? Is it conceivably to do with freedom?

The painstakingly tiny attentiveness of intellectuals raises the question in an acute form. If it needs thirty years of one man's concentrated energy to find one answer in crystallography, or to reconstruct one aspect of life in Confucian China, how do we measure that against the number who meanwhile die prematurely? Is it callous indifference to dare spend time on such things, or is it an evangelical modesty to believe that one's part in doing the truth may have no measurable results, no calculable relevance?

- The passion of 'alienness'

There are paradigms of alienating irrelevance on intellectual existence, the study of twelfth-century verb forms or artificial logics, or Celtic
art. They offend even the moderately liberal conscience as conspicuous
failures to improve anyone's quality of life. At least there is a possibility
of domesticating science, sociology, economics, geology or medicine in
the agenda for significant action. I suspect this response as sinister, the
thin end of a utilitarian wedge which will eventually define art, music,
fantasy and fiction as somehow unnecessary for human beings. I believe,
on the other hand, that we *need* as a community people who will do
apparently 'irrelevant things', 'licensed fools', who, as children will, for
delight and in fascination, pick up stones. This is partly because I think
that if we begin to monitor and censor delight, we may eventually deny
the most Christian exploration of creation, where nothing is irrelevant
or undeserving of attention. More pragmatically, as any marriage or
cultural exchange reveals, it is often by concentration on what seems
most alien and strange in the other that understanding emerges. There
may be an analogous 'prophetic lunacy' in making room for people to
engage in 'alien activities' (cf. the importance of quite uncensored art in
a community).

It may, however, be tested by conversation, if that is not reduced to the
exchange of words. That is why I suspect that the primary immediate
task of the Christian intellectual is to facilitate real conversation between
like and unlike, real hearing and understanding. This may be on the
small scale of breaking down the barricades of specialisation within the
intellectual community (a one-talent sort of operation), or it may be in
penetrating the impenetrabilities of ideological difference, or the unmeet-
ing worlds of rich/poor, exploiter/exploited.

I am not naive (I think) about education being salvation: I think that
when the situation is clear to people, that may polarise into even more
defensive attitudes towards what they have against the claims of the
have-nots. But I find it an irony that students who have, on the whole,
been somehow or other radicalised over five, ten, fifteen years of education should be so massively pessimistic about the possibilities of consci-
entising 'the bourgeoisie'. That I find an unwarranted resignation. And
if Platonism had the power to inform all levels of culture to the extent
that it did, have we really begun to explore the imaginative communication of alternatives?

When, if we do, the alternative will not be in terms of verbal commu-
niqués, printed harangues, stated theories. It will somehow be through

the offering of new self-images: images in which people can discover themselves to be neither individuals nor collectives, neither impotent nor omnipotent, neither demons nor angels, neither the sum of what they own nor the sum of what they achieve; images which will sustain art and music and liturgy, and not simply propaganda; images which will generate commonplace but fresh metaphors for people; images which will be roomy enough for all that human beings need to do, eat, love, hate, kill, rest, play, invent and explore. I think that has almost not begun to happen in the shrivelled concerns of our intellectual cosmos at the present moment.

5

The Churches' Mission
in a Secularised Europe*

What makes the Church matter even as a local community is that it addresses the world with questions of its life and death, its freedom and hope, its catholicity.

Dorothee Sölle has a poem somewhere called 'On being accused of being a Marxist', in which she comments: 'I use the telephone daily, but no one calls me a Bellite.' That is, the Churches' primary relation to secularisation in Europe or elsewhere is not 'having an opinion about it', but being inextricably involved with it. It is not an option, not a dilemma for the Churches to be for it or against it.

'Could Europe have been Europe unsecularised?' and 'Would it have been better unsecularised?' are abstractly hypothetical questions, inviting facilely speculative reconstruction and dangerous nostalgia for a seamlessly 'religious' world in which God, heaven, hell and so on were axiomatic parts of the frame of reference.

The analysis of secularisation is a delicate business. It is usually done from a medieval-to-modern perspective, which concentrates on Reformation and Enlightenment and underestimates the effective secularity of classical pre-Christian humanism. There is also a tendency in some contemporary Christian writing (e.g. Newbigin, *The Other Side of 1984*) to regret the rise of our post-Enlightenment axioms with their liberal optimism, their laissez-faire individualism and their cultural arrogance. It is of course true that we are heirs of a plundered cosmos in which Europe has been a primary plunderer; that the capacity for exploitation has been in part linked to

* Address to the Conference of European Churches, Switzerland, 16–20 November 1987.

technological prowess; and that technology is in part a spin-off from secularising science.

Nevertheless, I think we underestimate the sociological, historical, social, geographical and philosophical complexity of 'secularisation' as a phenomenon if we think we can chart it in six easy moves. I also think we have lost our theological nerve if we long to reverse it or to have reversed it. The work of Barth, Bultmann, Bonhoeffer and Gregor Smith should have got the Churches past the secular/sacred polarisation and wistfulness for a more 'religious' past.

The more important critical/prophetic question seems to me to be whether Europe, as such, has a future or is culturally, socially, politically and spiritually bankrupt, in part because of its religious history. A former colleague of mine in Edinburgh, having worked for five years in New Zealand, and having returned to Britain and Germany for six months' sabbatical, wrote recently of 'Europe's disintegrating culture'. To many Third World observers, the present surge of right-wing monetarist, laissez-faire governments, appealing to crude selfishness with the rhetoric of freedom, prolonging 'enemy' mentalities because the interests vested in these prevail against a world's starvation and hunger for peace, and continuing to treat Europe as the economic and cultural centre of the world, manifests a damnable bankruptcy.

Superficially, the West is portrayed as having accepted or responded to secularisation, while the East has resisted it. This account seems to me to miss several complexities of the actual situation. On the whole, the Western Churches, while reluctantly yielding the secular entitlement to be itself, are in fact increasingly paralysed by people just being human without reference to religion. The identity and self-consciousness of the Churches depend on being somehow or other different from the world, in moral achievement, in God-consciousness, in social concern, in doctrinal allegiance. This Church/world polarisation has, of course, some biblical precursors but is, in my judgement, at odds with the Gospel.

Eastern tradition, on the other hand, has in some ways a more worldly and less 'gathered' ecclesiology. The Church is the world, but the-world-represented-in-the-fullness-of-its-future, which is to be a sharer in the life of God. It is a cosmological fact because of Christ's relationship to humanity and cosmos, not an option for people to be persuaded into. The interpenetration of our humanness, whereby any of us represents the human condition, and all are represented in the new Adam, breaks down the boundaries between holy and unholy, saints and sinners, religious and unreligious. It is suggested for instance in the whole fictional world created by Dostoevsky; or empirically in the solidarities of a Greek village which accepts the prostitute as a member, not an alien; or in the liturgical act of sharing the blessed bread outside the church. (This of course produces other practical and pastoral problems, e.g. about theocracy and dissent, or about the distance between eschatological and empirical existence.)

It does not depend for its existence on a more or less growing club committed to a certain kind of piety, the achievement of a certain standard of moral or social concern, the practice of a special religious system. What makes the Church matter even as a local community is that it addresses the world with questions of its life and death, its freedom and hope, its catholicity. Of course the Orthodox Churches, in practice, fail too, but their normative ecclesiology seems to me potentially more open to the secular norm than many Western traditions.

I hope we are capable of recognising how much our marginalisation within Europe is deserved, because of our recurrent panic in the face of what we identify as secular opposition. We have not heard Bonhoeffer's challenge to explore the faith non-religiously, and that forty years on. We have not yet listened undefensively and eagerly to the bearers of our secularised culture and its values, to the artists, to the psychotherapists, to the media. If we are to share in the healing of our world's common future even, let alone to pioneer it, we must reverse our perception of 'us' as givers to needy 'them'.

In Scotland, certainly, to illustrate the case I know best, the most critical and yet cherishing appraisal of our cultural handicaps comes from poets and novelists who are explicitly atheist or agnostic and certainly outside the Church. Or, to cite a recent embarrassing example, the people deserving celebration as imaginative, compassionate, humanly open in a recent debate on AIDS were not the Church spokesmen but the not-Christianly aligned members of the Terrence Higgins Trust, a recently established body for the support and care of AIDS-sufferers.

What then of 'mission' in this Europe? My sense of the present and the past makes me think that any account of the Churches' mission in Europe must purge itself of the de facto claim to be the bearer of the Gospel. I think we may be having the Gospel borne to us, in part from other continents and contexts, in part from our own secularised world, and in part from some of the Churches (but only some) who within Eastern Europe have engaged in mutual exploration with Marxist partners of the human predicament. But I wonder if we are capable of receiving it.

This sense of mutuality, of dialogue, is well established in some areas of Church life, largely where ecumenical co-existence is well rooted, or where some special pressure to deal with a given 'other' is recognised. It is, for instance, central to the methodology of the Vatican's Secretariat for Non-Christian Religions, which explores with brain and gut the conviction that Christ is already ahead of his Christian Church in the humanness of Buddhist Sri Lanka, or Muslim Sudan or whatever (and sometimes even in their religious life). The mutuality of the truth in encounter as given and received is not a diplomatic courtesy but a fact of Christian experience. It has occasionally been articulated in the theology of various Churches: Ricci and de Nobili in the Jesuit missions, Karl Barth on Christian responses to life in a Marxist state; but it has rarely been explored in our everyday churchmanship. I would guess that most grassroots Christians either retain latent assumptions about converting pagans, or are simply embarrassed by common decent liberal assumptions about individual 'rights to believe'.

We are not, I think, in a fit state to evangelise anyone (and when we are we won't want to) until we learn or relearn the delight that Christ is in the other for us more than we 'take him to them'. This applies as much to 'secularised Europe' as to people of other religious traditions. It is not in their religiosity but in their humanness that persons 'bear' Christ. And the need for dialogue is neither defensive nor political, but Christological and exploratory of God. Not only may Christianity have become, or be in the process of becoming, a minority faith in Europe; more significantly, one might ask whether it has become a minority faith within the Churches. Have we so steadily and subtly aligned ourselves with national or state concerns, with sectarian interpretations of the faith, with exclusivist ethics and piety that we are incapable of manifesting the generosity of God to anyone? Perhaps the radical dismantling of the cultural Christianity of our post-Constantine era should be celebrated. It may re-expose widely, for the first time in centuries, the nerve of the evangelical question about what it means to be charged to be 'the salt of the earth'. What passion and costliness is involved in European churchmanship (cf. Latin America or South-East Asia)? Can we anticipate the Kingdom of God by *de iure* representation on education committees and hospital appointment boards? Are we entitled to land, to property, to broadcasting time? Should we really be battling for such rights?

Given this malaise within European Christianity, I find traditional aspirations to proselytise inept and offensive. If, however, we recovered in our Churches the truth of being Church, then I think proselytising would be unnecessary, for the very existence of such an 'institution' (an embodied anti-institution, refusing boundaries, refusing to outlaw sinners, resisting the bullying of the powers that be, even with its life) would generate for the surrounding community the amazement, horror, delight and crisis which are the dynamic of mission.

There are, I believe, some signals of such Church struggling to emerge from the cocoon of our European Christendom, but that already produces a problem for most of our 'Churches', confronted by the need to renounce all their pride and power.

PART 4

ECUMENISM

Introduction

Alastair Hulbert

Elizabeth liked the distinction between representative and participative ecumenism: she herself was active on both fronts. Representative ecumenism involves inter-Church dialogue and co-operation at an official level – assemblies, conferences, commissions – while participative ecumenism is the people's work, unofficial and self-motivated. Representative ecumenism is the basis of organisations like the World Council of Churches, regional and national councils. Participative ecumenism happens usually at a local level and arises out of personal interest rather than institution, commitment to a cause rather than the established agendas of Faith and Order, or Life and Work.

This book illustrates Elizabeth's ecumenical involvement at both levels. The six papers chosen for Part 4 are diverse: a sermon reporting to her local church in Edinburgh on the WCC Assembly in Canberra; her hard-hitting address as one of the main speakers there; two sermons for Action of Churches Together in Scotland, one for its inauguration and the other when they sold Scottish Churches House; a talk in which she subjects identity and authority to a critique founded on the love of God and his openness to the other; and finally a little piece which enlarges the scope of ecumenism to include the whole world.

'The Church's Task in Reconciliation', Elizabeth's address to the WCC Assembly in Canberra in 1991, is vintage Templeton. Here she gives us 'as truthful an account as I can manage of how I find the doctrine of reconciliation biting on all my instinctive alignments and partisan belongings'. It was the beginning of the Decade of Evangelism; and with a luminous integrity she challenges the ecumenical movement to be a counter-culture to all forms of division and exclusion.

She insists that eucharistic openness – shared communion – is essential for the Churches, and anything less is denominational tribalism. God's generosity is offered to everyone and is not dependent upon right belief or right practice or right discipline. So, the whole earth is anchored in communion, and for us to judge that we may eat while others can't means scorning God. She takes her cue from the parable of the Prodigal Son where the elder brother, when invited to the celebration of the Prodigal's return, has no grounds for refusing his father's welcome. 'We cannot begin to address a broken world creatively unless we can handle our own brokenness,' she says, referring to the mission of Churches which don't share a common eucharist or fully recognise each other's ministries.

In 'Identity and Authority in the Anglican Communion', she shares with a high-level Anglican theological commission in the USA her struggle to overcome the malaise about identity and authority in the Churches and to demythologise what she calls the monolith of scripture and tradition so as to articulate Christian faith in an inclusive way. She calls it being 'un-boundaried people', resisting every community of exclusion – all the classifications of dogma, ethics and piety: this for her is the most significant evangelical counter-culture we can imagine. And she goes on to ask what it means to say 'You are accepted: just as you are' to a delinquent world. Can the Church find an idiom for that which is an enactment of what we say about reconciliation? With typical aplomb, she asks: 'Is it not the offence of the Gospel that this awful God loves these bastards too?'

Elizabeth was always a conscientious servant of the institutions of the ecumenical movement at home and abroad. As well as her grassroots work with Threshold, Scottish Churches House, Missing People and others, she convened committees and commissions for the British Council of Churches, ACTS and different Churches dealing with both Faith and Order and Life and Work. I sometimes questioned the time and commitment she gave to the structures of ACTS, as I did the huge amount of work she put in as a non-stipendiary minister in the Presbytery of Dunkeld and Meigle during the last twelve years of her life.

Let us remember that this is a woman speaking, a lay theologian, unordained, neither a hierarch nor a professor of divinity. They kept inviting her to address their gatherings and genuinely appreciated what she had to say. But what difference did it make? Was she any more than an alibi for the ecumenical movement, for their Church assemblies and councils, one who gave them a comfortable feeling of being in the right place, theologically and ethically active, while in reality nothing changed?

It has only been since her death and my discovery of the body of work published in this anthology, most of which I was not acquainted with, that I have come to recognise her full brilliance – her modesty too, and her glimpse of 'love-knowledge' as the way God interacts with creation.

But Elizabeth's patience with ACTS was running out by the time she was invited to preach at the ACTS Members' Meeting (general assembly) in October 2011. She had been a leading campaigner in the effort to keep Scottish Churches House open, and this was the meeting at which ACTS decided to sell the house. Her sermon gives a brief account of the Interchurch Process, 'Not Strangers but Pilgrims', which culminated in the Swanwick Declaration of 1987 and led to the formation of new ecumenical instruments across the UK and Ireland to include the Roman Catholics. It was the high point of ecumenism in the British Isles, and it involved the promise that 'our Churches must move from co-operation to clear commitment to each other'.

She sent me a copy of the sermon, which is included here, along with a card in which she admitted: 'I sweated for it, and felt very ambivalent. Mario [Archbishop Mario Conti] was not ambivalent! He was pure dead outraged, and told me so in no uncertain terms . . . Have you heard that the buggers are now selling Leighton House [the Annexe of Scottish Churches House] as well?!' In the light of that, I'd say that the question she posed in her sermon at the inauguration of ACTS, 'How then, will we test whether the wounds of God's people in this corner of the earth are being mended by this act of creating ACTS?', remains unanswered.

'The Stillness of the Heart', the final paper under this theme, is about an ecumenism which is larger than the Churches and their co-operation or lack of it. It is about the whole inhabited world, the *oikumene*, a world which Elizabeth describes as 'depth-charged with love'. Her encounter with some of the classics of mystical spirituality and Catholic devotion as a teenager had meant that throughout her life she had an understanding of life as shared not just by Christians of different denominations but also by people of all faiths and none. She describes how she came to realise that loss of faith and the collapse of ideas, dogmas and even creeds could be a gift, a form of speechlessness on the journey into what the mystics called the Cloud of Unknowing – the depth of God's darkness. And she rejoices in the fact that artists and writers express their faith not in so many words but in creative ways of seeing and reflecting on the world in their art. For her, that points to the transcendence of God, or, as Raimon Panikkar puts it in his Gifford lectures, *The Rhythm of Being*, which Elizabeth knew and refers to more than once: 'The Divine Mystery is the ultimate *am* of everything.'

I

From Canberra to Jerusalem[*]

*Canberra was a place where the Church recognises and shoulders its
passion, its brokenness, its need for Pentecost.*

If I'd managed it in the almost total deluge of meetings, plenaries,
sections, groups, papers to read, my own paper to write, people to see
before the paper could be written, I'd have sent you a postcard. 'Wish you
were here!' I could have said, smelling the Canberra air, pungent with
gum trees. 'Wish you were here', feeling the rising sun prick your back in
the morning as you stood in the great worship tent singing, with the
condensation dripping onto the hymn sheets. Wish you could share the
colour, the diversity of faces, of costumes, of languages. Wish you could
watch people singing as if the hymns grew out of their bodies. Wish you
could see the change from Sydney airport on arrival day, when people
arrived from all corners of the globe, nervously peering around for someone who'd recognise the WCC sticker on their suitcase; and the departure day when we practically took over the Sydney terminal building,
talking, laughing, hugging across check-in queues, turned into friends
through the shared experience of two weeks. Wish you could have
enjoyed eating on the verandah of the student union, with white cocka-
toos instead of pigeons screeching around the roofs. Wish you could
have been there!

But, as well as being an exhilarating and privileged experience, it was
also a very painful and disturbing experience, and rather than going
through a factual account of topics and themes and statements, I'd like
to try to tell you why. Partly that's because there are much better ways of

[*] Sermon delivered at St Bernard's Church, Stockbridge, Edinburgh, at Easter 1991
following the Seventh Assembly of the World Council of Churches in Canberra, 7–20
February 1991.

digesting the information about what went on than the hit-and-run minutes of a sermon. If you're interested, there'll be books, tapes, videos, articles, follow-up meetings, available all through next autumn. And partly it's because I want to make one connection clear. That from Canberra 1991 to Jerusalem 30-ish AD, to St Bernard's, Stockbridge, is not a very big journey. 'Wish you were here!'

The overall theme of the Assembly was 'Come, Holy Spirit, renew your whole creation', and for me the key image was that of the move from Babel to Pentecost: the confusion of tongues that frustrated communication on the one hand; and on the other, diverse tongues making sense to each other as if they spoke one common language.

At times, Canberra was breathtakingly like Babel! I was terribly glad that the last sermon I'd heard before leaving was Jim Wilkie's strong plea that we learn how to listen to how it looks from somewhere else. Because there was no hiding the pain and anger of voices we, in Scotland, don't often hear from. There was the voice of Australian Aboriginal people, forcing us to acknowledge the shame of our white northern 'civilisation', which arrived at a country full (well, relatively full) of black peoples, and declared it 'no-man's land', *terra nullius*. There were Pacific Islanders saying that now, this year, they can no longer fish safely: the climate changes caused by global warming are causing such awful cyclonic storms that boats are constantly wrecked. What used to be high tide is now low tide. And pollution, nuclear fallout and the pressures to make money from sex-tourism are all present threats to their islands. These things are not acts of God: they arise directly from the acts of our governments in the north-west industrial world, and of our commercial interests. 'How', said the people from the Pacific Islands, 'if you are our brothers and sisters in Christ, do you stand by and let us suffer these things?' The passion of Christ. 'Wish you were here?'

Similar anger was, of course, almost universal about the Gulf War. The position of the majority of English Churches that it was a just war to defend freedom seemed quite obscene to most other delegates, especially as news came in about the hitting of the shelter-bunker full of women and children. And of burning oilwells. To many, this was simply, yet again, a First World power battering a Third World country flat for utterly hypocritical and self-interested reasons.

The accusations of white, European, American imperialism went deeper. Not just guns and pollution and commercial exploitation were our exports, but also ideas, ways of thinking and talking religiously. You may have seen some glimpse on film of the young Korean female theologian who sparked off (quite literally!) a great rumpus. She made a presentation in which she invoked the wandering angry spirits of Korean folk religion, the Han spirits, and burned a paper invoking the spirits of the martyrs for peace and justice. Her claim that these spirits were one with the Holy Spirit raised various roofs in Canberra. Many felt it was paganism. Orthodox and Evangelicals combined to say that unless the Spirit was the Spirit of the Lord Jesus Christ, it was not the Holy Spirit. There were great cries of 'Syncretism!', the Church's official boo-word for the uncritical mixing of Christianity with other faith-traditions. But, on the whole, the Third World came back saying: 'Stuff your criticisms! It's OK if it's your cultural habits – Christmas trees and Christmas consumerism and Easter eggs and trousers and knives and forks, but not if it's ours. Get off our backs! We'll discover our Christ where we discover him. Your creeds and confessions which you tell us judge our religion have nothing to do with us. They belong to your funny old European ways of thinking. You can't export them and impose them on us, any more than we'll take your Marks and Spencer sense of "decent dress" or your account of table manners!'

Of course, many of you, like me, will have known in your heads that such debates go on. But it was quite scary to see the force and fierceness of it which doesn't often enter our living rooms or our churches. Or the force of world feminism, which is here still a subject for cartoonists on the whole, but in the world church is a passionate, painful debate about whether women can live at all within the language and ritual of traditional Christianity. And scary to feel the real scorching of the question: Are there as many Christs as there are cultures and peoples? Or is there one Christ, and if so, how do we find him, know him, speak him? What is creative diversity, and when does it become destructive of any possible sharing of life, of vision, of energy?

Now, all of that may seem terribly far away from Stockbridge, where you can go a week without seeing a black person; and certainly in church circles around us, not many ripples of, say, feminist liberation theology rock our snug wee ecclesiastical boat. But the passion of the ecumenical movement is that it is committed to saying to all these voices: 'You too belong. This Babel can become Pentecost. We live and pray together, or we do not live and pray at all.' 'Wish you were here!'

Do we really wish to be involved in the pain of all that wrestling? Are we at all willing, from our wee corner of familiar Scottish Christianity which for many of us comes from the cradle, to listen to these shouts of anger and pain from other parts of the world?

If not, there is no point in saying 'Wish we were there' about that other passion which is the theme of our scripture readings today. Wish we'd been eye-witnesses. Wish we'd actually heard Jesus. Wish we could have said 'Yes, Lord, we'll suffer with you.'

Today's Gospel faces us with a real warning about phoneyness (Mark 10:37)! These daft disciples, learning hard lessons each day, think that in one breath they can eat and drink with Jesus in his pain, and at the same time put in bids for the best seats in the Kingdom; they still live with their untransformed ambitions, their competitive desires, their natural instincts for status, prestige, security; their human longing to have it all taped. But you can't, says Jesus. You can't go through my passion with me and stay inside that mindset. 'Wish you were there' in relation to me means the opposite. You shoulder the pain, the other person's pain. You care about their life as your own. You even take the weight of their enmity instead of protecting yourself against it.

Still wish you were there? Not at Canberra as a great jamboree, but as a place where the Church, the present body of Christ in the world, recognises and shoulders its passion, its brokenness, its need for a Pentecost. Not at Jerusalem as an Easter pageant, full of daffodils and choirs, but as the place where hate and greed and malice and power-seeking have to be confronted by being suffered.

Really? 'Wish we were there?' We are there. That is what it means that we are members of this church. This smallish congregation, not too confident about its membership, its money, its impact on the parish. It means that we are baptised with the same baptism as the Pacific Islander whose fishing boat can't fish now, the Aborigine Christian living in his demoralised, culturally uprooted remnants of community; with the Korean folk church; with the black American feminist Baptists; with the Greek Orthodox; even with the protesters who stood outside the tent carrying banners saying 'Dialogue is sin'. We stand with them all, or we don't stand at all. Exploring in our small comer, from our small angle of vision, what that means will stretch us until we nearly burst.

And all that stops that being totally terrifying is that the risen Christ beckons us through that. 'Glad that we're here!'

2

The Church's Task in Reconciliation[*]

Unless the World Council of Churches finds a way of bringing its different organs into real encounter as to what is at stake in believing, theology will remain in its operations an inert gas!

Any truth which hovers six feet above contradiction tends to hover also six feet above reality. When I was given the cosmic title for this presentation, not so many weeks ago, my mind went into shock, then spun in all directions. Part of it went back twenty years ago to a grey-covered notebook in which I kept all my dogmatics lectures. For a whole year, we had studied what is called in some circles 'Atonement Theology', going back to the New Testament, and travelling via patristic and reformation theology to an account of the once-and-for-all, unrepeatable, finished work of Christ, the bridging of the God/man gap (for in those days 'man' unselfconsciously meant 'humanity' in English), and the perfecting of all things, sealed by Resurrection and Ascension.

That was where dogmatics stopped. The Church's task was clear. It had to witness to this Christological achievement, to proclaim it, to be faithful to it. But it was a nasty heresy called Pelagianism to think it could make any contribution to it! God, Father, Son, Spirit, in every aspect of reconciliation acted for us, covering our impotence, standing in our place, representing us before God, being all in all.

A mild technical problem was acknowledged, in that the world was clearly not perfect, empirically speaking. But various images were used to plot the gap between the affirmations of achieved salvation and the palpable mess around. The decisive military victory had been won, for instance, and we were now living through the mopping-up operations.

[*] Address to the World Council of Churches Seventh Assembly, Canberra, Australia, 7–20 February 1991.

Or, through the prism of time, our fragmentation seemed more real than unreal. But, in the undifferentiated light of eternity, the reality was transformed, reconciled, whole.

With ecumenical hindsight, I can see some of this, of course, as a conspicuously Protestant account of things, though it intended to be both Orthodox and Catholic. I remember, even at the time, thinking: 'Why on earth did God bother to create us if only to replace us?' But there was something almost trance-inducing about the totalitarianism of the position. God was everything. Could worship or theology gainsay it? The word 'reconciliation' then triggered in my mind all that body of affirmation, the triumph and confidence of it, the 'nothing can contradict this claim' character.

'But', whirled the other bit of my mind, 'was it also six feet above reality? How could it be said without being a deadly insult to the world's actual brokenness? How could it be said to the poor, watching their children die, to the mentally handicapped, ostracised from much human community, to the Arabs in the Middle East, to the Israelis, to those locked into the multifarious domestic alienations of family life gone poisoned? How indeed could it be said in a church where some cannot eat and drink bread and wine with others? Or where they eat and drink comfortably, but have no pain for the brokenness around them?'

It is, of course, facile to criticise the Church's formal account of reconciliation by pointing to the immediate mess. On the whole, those who have affirmed the presence of the Kingdom through the centuries have not been naive utopians with their eyes shut. Since the Thessalonian Christians were amazed that all the dying was still going on, the Church has, in various ways, adjusted to a kind of bifocal vision, 'yet and not yet', 'saved but not sanctified', 'simultaneous citizens of the Kingdom and inhabitants of the earth'. Faith is skilled in refusing to accept the merely empirical as the standard of the real, the seen as the measure of the actual. It is a virtue, is it not, to have the toughness of spiritual imagination to live from what is not seen?

But when does this become so fantastic that, to those who live it, schizophrenia sets in? And to those outside it, the style of this Christian way of being, instead of inviting amazement, terror and hope, provokes pity and contempt as a feeble-minded evasion of reality? Is the present agenda of the Churches an expression of its confidence that the risen Christ is Lord, that all things are already transformed in him, that reconciliation is, so to speak, behind and around us? Or is it a rather desperate scramble to mask the hollowness of that affirmation, even to many who make it? How would you tell the difference?

The question arises within the world community of Churches in many idioms. From the first decades of this century, there have been subliminal and sometimes explicit tensions between the 'faith and order' and the 'life and work' strands of the ecumenical movement. The former had often seemed to the latter cerebral, detached, unengaged and ultimately self-indulgent. Doctrine does not come first: it emerges from 'doing the will', not from theological discussion. The latter has sometimes seemed to the former ungrounded activism, full of programmes and crusades which are liable to borrow from secular concerns and give them a theological veneer, but which have no specific relation to distinctive Christian insight, and are therefore not our primary business.

Overlapping with that, but not exactly coinciding with it, there has been the running conversation between Orthodox traditions and those deriving from and exported by Western traditions, whether Catholic or Protestant. It would be caricature to polarise these entirely, but it seems accurate enough to say that the Orthodox emphasis has been on the being of the Church rather than on its doing, a fact which has, in the ugly distrusts of our past history, led to Western accusations of eschatological inertia. We in the West, by contrast, have been accused of trivialising the glory of God to frenetic ethical pragmatism, so buried in the mundane that we lose all grasp of God's transcendence.

Now, while suspicions still lurk in many corners, it has, I suspect, been the real gift of the ecumenical movement that there is now hugely enlarged trust and appreciation and commitment to these mutual encounters as clear enrichment. But I think that, at the level of global WCC operation, we do need to face the challenge Dietrich Bonhoeffer has posed. It emerges from the first two sentences in his *Ethics*: 'The knowledge of good and evil seems to be the aim of all ethical reflection. The first task of Christian ethics is to invalidate this knowledge.'

I do not know how to live with this as a twentieth-century Christian living where I live. It repels and fascinates me (which may be one sign that it has to do with God). The repulsion is that I can see it so easily being corrupted into the kind of sentimental liberal neutrality which masquerades as Christian openness but is really laissez-faire indifference. How dare I, full of the guilt of Western European and British exploitation, white, well fed, deeply embedded in structures of oppression, not say 'this is evil stuff' and act accordingly? And yet there is something convincingly suggestive, is there not, about this recognition of God as the one whose judgement is not the withdrawal of love but its unconditional invitation?

Our sense of the therapeutic potential in personal contexts (with delinquents, the mentally ill, abused children and so on) of being able to say 'You are accepted, just as you are' is well documented. But what does it mean to say that to a humanly and politically delinquent world? Can the Church find an idiom for that which is an enactment of what we say Christologically, pneumatologically about reconciliation? And which is not pietist nonsense, but a living participation in God's generosity to sinners, enabling newness of life, not as precondition but as emergent faithfulness? Can we enact the dynamic generosity of God to those who really are known to us in the gut as enemy? Can we do it in ways which distinguish themselves from sentimental 'niceness', from squeamish avoidance of conflict and from inert beatitude?

To me, the most signal failure of the Church is not our divisions but the fact that though we talk of 'scandal', most people outside do not find it at all a scandal. It is to them a predictable, to-be-expected manifestation, in one more social context, of the normal human capacity for separatedness. It is ironic, of course, that words of peace and reconciliation are said over these divisions, but the basic divergences of thought, feeling, commitment and imagination which have created our denominations and our ideological divides really shock very few people outside. If they merit attention at all, it is likely to be a rather bored shrug of the shoulder, half a raised eyebrow.

Now, maybe I am singularly unlucky. In Scotland, there are still several places where to be identified as 'Protestant' or 'Catholic' is to be at once caught in the deepest distrust which exists in a given community – even where to be one sort of Presbyterian rather than another marks you as an automatic enemy. But I am sure that in my culture, the secular world pays no more attention to our broken eucharist than it would to the fact that golfers eat their Sunday lunch in different golf clubs.

The Church's task then, in broad terms, is to recover convincing identity as an inclusive community in which the human race, with whatever else creation contains, lives its co-existent future. But what does that mean, in practice? 'Be concrete', said the organisers of this section. Where do we start? I am very nearly sure, to start at one small point, that we cannot do any convincing reconciliation while our eucharistic openness to one another is restricted and hemmed about with conditions. I am very nearly sure that we do not 'cheapen' the eucharist by inviting to it those we regard as theologically deviant, morally intolerable, politically evil. No one receives this 'worthily'.

I am quite sure that if we go on, in our various traditional ways, 'fencing the tables', we will make ecclesiology unintelligible to the young people of the world for generations, and theology laughable. In some of the theological circles I move in which discuss these matters, people speak with horror and disdain of 'indiscriminate' baptism and 'indiscriminate offering of communion'. But is it not the offence of the Gospel, especially to us who think we are righteous, for peace and justice or whatever, that this awful God loves these bastards too? Is it not the indiscriminateness of God's love which so sickened the elder brother, the good Pharisees, the disciples themselves?

Of course, the very offer of that love pinned everyone to the wall, confronting them as it did with the simultaneous presence of those they hoped to exclude from their existence. The eucharist may damn us. But, for us to judge that we may eat and others not – that seems to me the scorning of God. We are not custodians of the truth and goodness and freedom of the Kingdom. They guard us, dismember us and summon us into new belongings beyond the bounds of what we can bear yet. Yet we are called to bear it.

At the level of the WCC activity, then, I think all kinds of doctrinal and activist heads need to be knocked together over this question, theoretical and practical, of whether and how the Kingdom generates ethics or abolishes them. Abolition is a provocative term, of course. 'Transformation' would sound more attractive.

And I do not want to get bogged down in semantics. But it seems to me that ethics is about the management of the good, by setting out rules of living and constraints for their violation. Whatever the content of the ethical vision, the structure is one in which the community relies on the normal human processes of attempting sanctions, constraint, containment and the diminution of the enemy's freedom.

For me, the sting of the Gospel is that this normal sanity for self-preservation, and for the preserving of those we love, is judged by the terrifying Christological way of passionately, actively bearing the pain of the enemy's hostility. It is not sentimental or careless. But it says: I would rather give you your freedom than exercise mine at your expense. That is my ultimate freedom, to be for your life, though you are my enemy.

Of course, we fail constantly in this, and have to live confessingly. But that seems to me very different from being complacent and even celebratory about our successful management of power which overwhelms our enemies. At the same time, I am not abolishing the category of 'enemy'. There are those who, one way or another, threaten our very life. I have, so far, a curious feeling at this assembly that we swallow camels of alien ideology if it comes in the guise of ethnic religion, while we strain at gnats of Christian liturgical practice. And that, in our proper shame at the abuses of our missionary past, we dodge the existential fact that some visions of reality are incompatible with others.

Unless the WCC finds a way of bringing its different organs into real encounter as to what is at stake in believing, theology will remain in its operations an inert gas! At the level of regional, national, local churches, it means devising ways of communication with whoever is the 'significant other', ways which make it clear that welcome and not ostracism is the mode of our encounter even if we are not at one. That will hurt us. It will doubtless hurt many of the welcomed, if not all. It will, almost certainly, muddy our ethical clarities, compromise our prized integrity, threaten us with defilement. But, until we unlearn our agendas of dissociation from the alien, I suspect we have no living insight into the costliness of the reconciliation we claim in Christ, standing in the image of the bizarre Father, who wants both the elder brother and the prodigal son.

We have, of course, no guarantees of the future. If either son says 'Well, I'm not coming to this party if he's there', the good story collapses. But that is quite different from the father saying 'Because he's here, you're not welcome'. In fact, it's the opposite. It's the father saying 'Because he's here, you are welcome, because he can't be himself without you, or you without him, or I without you both.'

I'm afraid this is not yet any kind of specific agenda for a campaign. But it is as truthful an account as I can manage of how I find the doctrine of reconciliation biting on all my instinctive alignments and partisan belongings – especially the belongings I judge to be righteous. Looked at in my local context, it raises questions about how, for instance, the liberal left of centre deals with all kinds of fundamentalisms; of how feminists express catholicity in women-only contexts; of how activists and scholars stand on two sides of what seems a widening gulf; of how we de-hypocritise our verbal invitations to 'the poor'. You must identify for yourselves what that means locally to you.

I am afraid of this sounding like pietism. I am afraid of it being pietism. But I am more afraid that it is Gospel! To earth it in vulnerable flesh, not utopian, not blind to the urgencies of the world's pain, and yet constant in real catholicity seems to me almost infinitely far from what all our Churches do, or even long to do. But the question will not go away. It undermines so much of our history of excommunication, of heresy-hunting, of skilled partisan belonging. To be a counter-culture to every community of exclusion in every idiom of life and speech we can muster – that to me could be the agenda for a decade, no, for a millennium of evangelism – a belonging to wrestle with as earth and Kingdom engage.

3

*For It Was Not the Season for Figs**

We cannot begin to address a broken world creatively unless we can handle our own brokenness.

Mark never made things easy for himself. Here, somewhere in the developing narratives of the early Christian communities, was a rather odd story about Jesus cursing a fruitless fig tree (Mark 11:13–14). Some think it was, originally, as Luke has it, a parable of Israel's faithlessness, which somehow or other got mistaken for an event in the life of Jesus. Some think it was a rather sub-Christian legend, which grew up around a conspicuous dead tree on the Bethany–Jerusalem road. And almost everyone is embarrassed by it. One bold commentator, a certain W.E. Bundy, writes: 'It is irrational and revolting . . . and lacks any sort of moral motive or justification.'

Not much justice, peace and integrity of creation there, they might say in Geneva! If you read it as a piece of documentary history, what on earth do you make of it? Were Jesus's nerves getting the better of him as he braced himself for the final confrontation with the Jerusalem authorities? Was this a momentary lapse from the renunciation of cheap power declared in the temptation narratives? And if so, could he not at least have magicked figs on to the tree, rather than cursing it into barrenness? Even if it had been the season for figs!

And here Mark tells it: first with the witness-for-the-prosecution aside that it was not the season. And then, with no apparent sense of irony, setting it in a context where it is meant to illustrate the power of prayer, and moreover, where hearers are exhorted to pray forgivingly. He couldn't easily have put more feet in it at once, could he? To show the Prince of

* Sermon at the inaugural service of Action of Churches Together in Scotland (ACTS), Dunblane Cathedral, 1 September 1990.

Reconciliation damning a tree that couldn't possibly bear fruit out of season!

Let us think for a moment where we are. We are on a tiny spinning planet, in oceans of intergalactic space. If we do not wreck the place ahead of schedule, it has a predicted future of some astronomical number of years before it burns or freezes into lifelessness. Long before that, we will all have died.

The first *Children's Britannica*, in its article on 'Earth', has the following poignant sentence:

> Because we live upon the earth, we often think of it as the largest and most important body in the universe, but astronomy shows that the earth is rather small compared with the stars and with some other planets, and is probably not unusual in any way, except that the human race lives on it.

That human race, over its few millennia of recorded time, has lived inside countless stories of gods. Thinking more specifically of this gathering, here in this Scottish cathedral city, most of us have grown up inside the Judaeo–Christian story of Yahweh, who is, for us, God with a capital G; who made everything, and without whom it could not be. And our story tells that the planet is unusual, not just because the human race lives on it, but because God has lived on it, in the person of Jesus who came to be called Christ; and still is among us potently, anticipating the newness of all things in the community of transformation we call church, and in the creativity of his unharnessed spirit.

Outside these walls, in the Scottish autumn, many more people than are here find this, our central story, more difficult than we find the fig tree! Out of all the galaxies and planets, God should have chosen this tiny speck of the cosmos as the place of salvation for all the rest? Come off it! Here – where Catholics have burned Protestants for daring to read scriptures for themselves, and Protestants have hounded Catholics into exile on pain of death? Where, as this service proceeds, one lot of sincere people who also take the name of Christ picket us, because they think we are turning a house of prayer into a den of ecumenical compromises. And where we lay on discreet ecclesiastical vigilantes to exclude them, should they disrupt our ceremonies in their – to us – misguided zeal!

Even to many moderate members of all our denominations, excitement and celebration over this event seem puzzling, so little does it touch their Sunday lives, let alone their Monday-to-Saturday ones. How, then, will we test whether the wounds of God's people in this corner of the earth are being mended by this act of creating ACTS? Can we bear fruit each month of the year, and leaves for the healing of the nations?

A few months ago, our family had a close encounter with an illness called osteomyelitis. What happens with that is that a perfectly common-or-garden bacterium, of the sort our bodies host with impunity all the time, every so often gets trapped, especially in younger children whose bones are not yet joined up, and lodges in the end of a growing bone. There it festers, eventually causing an abscess in the bone marrow.

You know, as well as I do, that if we were all stripped of the ceremonial skin we wear on such occasions as this, we are probably all prey to bacteria of fear about this new venture, as well as properly joyful. We must see that these fears don't get trapped in the bone structure. Some are afraid, for instance, that it's mostly clerical church leaders ganging up against ordinary punters. Some on the Protestant flank secretly share the fear which has kept the Baptist Union of Scotland out, that this dallying with what Archie Craig, that hero of ecumenism, enjoyed calling Episcopalianism was 'the thin end of the Scarlet Woman'. Others, at the Anglo-Catholic pole, worry that proper authority will be debased by alien intrusions of secular democracy. Peace and Justice types worry about too much Faith and Order. Faith and Order types worry about too much Peace and Justice. The young find us, yet again, a male-dominated structure. Hierarchies and bureaucracies find us potentially subversive. The denominationally entrenched find us a menace. The transdenominationally happy fear crushing by our dinosauric institutions.

With so much buried fear around, one might say: 'It is not the season for figs! Please God, don't expect us to be fruitful. Not yet! Not when there is so much preliminary work to be done, handing on, passing over, settling in, explaining ourselves to one another, sorting out the files, interpreting the politics. Not when we're just starting. Our leaves look quite promising. Come back later. You can't expect figs at this time of year.'

But what if God is hungry? What if, like Jeremiah's Yahweh, he sees the woundedness of his people, and is urgent for their healing? What if, like Mark's Jesus, he cannot be doing with our prevaricating failure to make a place where all nations can pray? For Mark again is the only evangelist bold enough in the cleansing-of-the-Temple story not to drop the 'for all nations' from the Isaiah quote. The Temple is not just for those who share our insider cult!

So, how do we test for fruit-bearing? Certainly we must go through the niceness barrier. All those fears which can fester poisonously under the ecclesiastical skin must be faced and explored – some with ecumenical candour. So much effort, labour, prayer and money has gone into getting us here together that it's a big temptation not to rock any boats. But God, if you remember Jonah and Paul, goes in for boat-rocking! And we cannot begin to address a broken world creatively unless we can handle our own brokenness. And we are still broken. This service could not, for instance, be a eucharist.

Many theological cats set all our denominational pigeons flapping. How does God communicate truth to us? What, if any, are the limits of salvation? Can anyone represent Christ? Is there an absolute Christian ethic? More importantly, we need to learn together, better than we have apart, how to listen to the outside world. Most of that batch of burning internal theological questions is not of the slightest interest, at least in that form, to the vast majority of people on the streets of our cities (and not even to many in our pews). And that majority doesn't consist of spectacular atheists, conspicuous sinners or dedicated pagans, but of ordinary nice, sane people of good enough will, going through the ups and downs of life as decently as they can with no sense at all that the Church has the remotest bearing on them.

Most of them know we're there, much as they know the Royal Company of Archers is there. They are not hostile. But we engage with none of their experience. I think we have hardly begun to listen theologically to the actual questions the outside world is interested in asking, because we are too busy scolding and nagging it for not appreciating our pre-packed, vacuum-sealed message; for not filling our pews; for not paying our awful repair bills; for not seeming to need us.

Finally, of course, we will be fruitful when people start saying, without irony:

'Goodness, how these Christians love one another. How free they are. How welcoming. How unafraid. How able to bear truthfulness. How un-self-preoccupied. How healed we feel in their company: not furtive or inferior, but wonderful, wanted, loved, human, alive.'

That will be fruit worth God's eating.

4

*Identity and Authority in the Anglican Communion**

We have to find a way of demolishing the monolith Scripture and Tradition, to articulate different concepts of identity and authority.

I marvel again at the generosity of a communion which invites what, in the Highlands of Scotland, are called 'incomers', to share its intimate conversations. That seems to me already to signal a graceful adventurousness of spirit which is the very opposite of many Church attitudes. (For instance, when a certain Board of my esteemed Church was recently invited to share its in-service training with other denominations via the recently formed ecumenical body ACTS, its reply was: 'Thank you, but no. We must get our own house in order first.')

It has become for me increasingly axiomatic over the last ten years that none of us has the remotest hope of getting our houses in order if we do the reconstruction or the spring cleaning, or even the controlled demolition, in isolation from one another. That is a conviction held partly at the deepest level of my theological vision that we are, in God, part of one another. And partly it is the merest pragmatic recognition that the echoes and resonances of your discussion about identity blur into those which almost every Church in Christendom or post-Christendom emits at present.

Nevertheless, it is a rare privilege, on the level of actual invitation, to be allowed into a company which could so easily go it alone, since your spread of context and capability is a microcosm of the globe's resources! And I have struggled over the months since I was invited to think what on earth I could contribute that would be of any significance.

* Address to the Inter-Anglican Theological and Doctrinal Commission, Virginia Seminary, Alexandria, USA, 8–18 December 1991.

Clearly it is nothing to do with the specifics of your structures: how the episcopal levels of consultation and decision-making relate to others, for instance; or how the influence of the Church of England affects the whole communion for bane or blessing. I am an occasional overhearer of such debates, but I have neither the experience nor the insolence to make any comment on them. Such questions are for you to wrestle with.

I feel no need to apologise for that diffidence; but I fear I may have to beg pardon for a deeper theological inadequacy. The further I get into these ecumenic questions of identity and authority, the more I feel like a rabbit mesmerised by a snake. I know I have theological legs, but I'm blowed if they'll move. I encounter this feeling in all sorts of contexts, from local ecumenical bodies deciding who they'll let in and who they'll keep out, to the Faith and Order operations of the World Council of Churches, struggling against almost impossible odds to articulate what constitutes Christian faith in a way which will satisfy all the member Churches.

What I intend to do for you, or to invite you to do for me, is to attend a little to this paralysis, to diagnose it, if possible as real illness, hypochondria or malingering; and, depending on that diagnosis, to say what needs to be dealt with if cure is to be effected.

Let me then outline what I want to do in this brief paper. First, I want to canter round the track of the ecumenical malaise about authority and identity, and to ask you if you recognise yourself there. Secondly, I want to sketch what are my learned (!) insights into the possibly distinctive and certainly terrifying Christian account of identity and authority. And that should leave you with some probably unanswerable questions about the implications of both for issues of management, power-sharing and the like.

As anyone who was at Canberra will know, the sense of lurching from the Pentecostal aspiration of the main theme into something much more like the Tower of Babel was hard to resist. I must confess that, used as I am to seeing ecclesiastical infighting, and even *odium theologicum*, I found the levels of anger and bitterness and distrust around quite overwhelming. As a white European, I felt in my bones what I had only mildly contemplated in my head up until then, the accusation that our exporting of the Nicene Creed, the so-called Apostolic Faith, is the latest-to-be-detected instance of that cultural imperialism which we all recognise when it takes the form of knives, forks and trousers. For, to many in the rest of the world, that is an irredeemably European formulation – redeemable, rather, so long as it is capable of recognising its own cultural relativism, but utterly to be resisted as a global norm of faith-affirmation.

As a woman too, I felt sucked into a tide of anger which I find it hard entirely to share (for reasons which largely baffle me, but which may need more attention in case they merely rationalise a lack of solidarity), and yet which clearly challenges the whole legacy of official credal orthodoxy as a construct of exclusively male, patriarchal ways of thinking.

And I must confess to an immense dividedness in my response to them, at both the intellectual and the gut level. Part of me wants to say, with Wittgenstein, that intelligence is bewitched if it insists on hunting for necessary and sufficient conditions for something to be itself. Most realities of any complexity bear a common name in virtue of overlapping layers of what Wittgenstein calls family resemblances, even if no single property is common to all.

And a part of me wants to say that the characteristic ethos of many denominations is so palpable as to be smelt! So that, even if definition is impossible, we all know as soon as we cross the thresholds that we are inhaling different air.

The Christ and Culture issue – and both these challenges are manifestations of that – will not go away. And part of your privilege as a worldwide communion is that you have to tackle it as a communion. For us, Presbyterian traditions with exported variants, the primary identification is national, and it takes something like the World Alliance of Reformed Churches to knock our heads together. But that body has almost nothing of the cutting edge on provincial sensibilities that the Lambeth Conferences or the existence of the Anglican Consultative Council seem to me to have on your national insularities.

At any rate, the point I am making is this: in the face of the massive questions which challenge all the Churches to ask if their supposed original unity is a flawed ideological construct, questions of denominational identity are trivial. If your quest for what authority and identity mean in the Anglican Communion does not include at least a massive preamble on these issues, I am afraid that I can do little to service your reflections. But I do want to suggest that panic is an inappropriate response, and that putting a cordon sanitaire round some specified bounded range of past definitions of faith and Christian life is unworthy of the openness we owe to an eschatologically active God!

My own conviction is that we have to find a way of demythologising the monolith Scripture and Tradition, and of beginning to articulate different concepts of identity and authority. I know that I speak within all sorts of cultural limitations, but I am so far persuaded that within the New Testament, and from then on, Christians have not, in fact, always believed the same things.

I find it, so far, no less problematic than the sacrifice of Isaac, to deny that a Western-originated biblical criticism is right in identifying fairly basic divergences in, for instance, Christology, within the canon of scripture. What we, the world Church, make of this is an underdeveloped conversation. It seems to me clear that the standard procedure has been to smother the fact that within scripture there are significantly different Christologies. That is why, for instance, Ernst Käsemann (New Testament professor in Tübingen) feels himself to have become *persona non grata* with the World Council of Churches after the Faith and Order Conference in Montreal, because he has pointed this out. And why a book like Geoffrey Lampe's *God as Spirit*, or even more subversively, Professor Chung at Canberra, scarcely appear over the horizons of consciousness for most practising Christians.

It was, of course, innocent and natural for the first seventeen Christian centuries to use a hermeneutics of conflation and convergence, but it is not innocent any longer, and there is a deafening silence in the ecumenical scene, as in most denominational ones, about the relationship between dogma and biblical scholarship.

Many simply argue that it would be tactically premature to raise the question. The poor old Orthodox, for instance, couldn't cope with the shock of the suggestion that Luke, say, has an adoptionist Christology, at variance with John's incarnationalist one! And anyway, biblical criticism of that sort is a provincial activity of European-influenced scholars, and has no claim on the rest of the world's time and energy, which is going on worthier causes like prophetic articulation or missionary outreach.

But if, as I suspect, the root of this silence is fear of boat-rocking, or of theological unpleasantness, then we should be ashamed. For the central hermeneutical principle of the Christian reading of anything is, is it not, that perfect love casts out fear? And that means that however crazy, however naive, however menacing anything seems, in the context of faith it can be received, absorbed and transformed. I find it curious that we accept this so much more readily in the realm of morality than in that of epistemology or hermeneutics. And I find it insulting to the rest of the ecumenical community that we do not trust it to wrestle, with all the intelligence and integrity at its disposal, with this issue. For, until we do, our apparently unanimous affirmation that Scripture and Tradition are our norms seems to me to cheat people.

I have gone on about this at possibly inordinate length, because I think the question of identity and belonging, and their relations to questions of authority, can no longer be answered by a self-evident appeal to Scripture and Tradition. It is disingenuous for those who know that these are both more like plural nouns than singular to use them consentingly as singulars. But what identity do we have in plurality? And with what authority do plural voices speak?

Having confronted you over Scripture and Tradition, let me make one further potentially subversive remark about Reason, the third member of your historic triumvirate of norms for appraising truth by, and for identifying Anglicans! For Canberra made it abundantly clear that there is no consensus of confidence whatsoever about what reason is, or what it involves. The resentment of the two-thirds world is now turning its attention to what may be imperialisms of thought form, even at levels as basic as the elements of formal logic, which were, in my undergraduate days, offered as the preconditions of any intelligible speech.

This challenge may, of course, be dismissed as the ranting of barbarians, intellectually unsophisticated tribesmen, soft-headed feminists and others known to be underequipped in cognitive skills! But at our peril! It should already have been clear from any depth of encounter that Christianity has had with other religious cultures, particularly those outwith the Judaeo/Christian/Islamic axis, that even Aristotle is not unchallengeable. One only needs a close encounter with a Hindu who finds self-contradiction a vehicle of truth rather than a frustration of it, or more alarmingly still with a Zen koan, to appreciate that what counts as reasonable thought by one group appears as slightly surreal nonsense to another.

We are used, I'm sure, to the cosmopolitan recognition shared by most who have the privilege to travel, or to read, or to engage with a foreign visitor, that we tell different psychological, historical and cultural stories. That is becoming almost a truism in a world where the impact of cultural pluralism bites deep into every complacency of thought.

But, though the social sciences are, on the whole, impressed enough by cultural relativism to have generated a sub-discipline called the Sociology of Knowledge, few philosophers I've met, and fewer dogmaticians, begin to ask the question whether their most basic structures of thought can be dismantled, and they still be themselves. Descartes' passion, often trivialised as the mere whim to doubt for the hell of it, was in fact a willingness to test his certitude against any challenge he could conceive of. And, though his range of self-questioning seems curiously one-dimensional and restricted to us who live in a post-Marxist, post-Freudian universe, I think it deserves a better press than dismissal as an Enlightenment cul de sac. It is not only corrosive scepticism which forces such radical self-questioning on us, but also the recognition of our capacity for making idols, and the need for their dethronement.

The outcome of all this, I am suggesting, were that not clear to you paragraphs ago, is that we are unlikely to be able, in the age after Mannheim, to identify ourselves substantively in terms of Scripture, Tradition or Reason. Where, then, does that leave us in terms of being able to say anything positive, let alone distinctively Christian, about the definition of our identity? And how does the concept of authority look in the light of such an account?

In his fascinating and suggestive paper, *Differentiated Participation* (2005), Harding Meyer finishes by recommending that we pay attention to the logical category of equivalence as one which allows us to encompass change in our self-definition. It seems to me an improvement on the classical Aristotelian account of identity to make the shift from the intactness of things and beings to any ontology which can cope with dynamism as constitutive of reality.

But I wonder if equivalence is generous enough to do justice to an identity which comes about in the specific dynamism of creation and salvation. For the ontology of the God who calls us into being and healing is a God for whom equivalence is too meagre. It is the ontology of a generous potency of communion and freedom, willing and able to confer being and value and mutuality on what is not already there. More simply, the identity of God is as one who loves others into being and keeps them there as vital to himself.

The existence of all that is testimony to the inclusive imaginativeness of that creativity; and the specific modality of incarnation is, in the most universalist accounts at least, the wrestling of God for the sustaining of that inclusiveness, at the cost of his own passion, and in the teeth of all that threatens it.

But the inclusiveness is not totalitarian. As Irenaeus put it, 'The Spirit never does constrain of necessity.' It seems to me that the core identity of the Church, whether described primarily Christologically as the body of Christ or pneumatologically as the community of the Holy Spirit, is to be that microcosmic body which invites and suggests, and enacts, and by its constancy of love promises the world its own proper future, without coercion and without despair. This is no matter of cheap or sentimental camaraderie, for if we take on board the malevolence and will to exclude and be separate which poisons our co-existence, and do it in the Christological mode, we really do risk our skins.

That means that we are identified as those who say, and mean, and manifest, without limits: 'You are welcome in the love of God.' That is not, of course, the elimination of the category of judgement. It is the precise searching and testing of that invitation which confronts us with the demand that we be transformed: from beings who want our identification to be by the distance and over-againstness we have from others to a willing and costly and constant commitment to be with them and for them. And not a commitment which is an option, leaving us intact if we renege on it, but one which is so self-involving that we put our own being on the line for it. We are undone in the loss of the other.

I find it, so far, impossible to reconcile this vision of our ecclesiological identity with the common understanding of the Church's practice in separating orthodox from heretical, on grounds of doctrine or practice or whatever. I can see certainly that if the depth identity of the Church is grounded in the embracing life of God, it will repel and alienate those who are determined to exclude some people from God's salvific intent. And in practice, such inclusive and exclusive visions of the saved community are existentially incompatible.

It seems to me to follow from what we are called to be, as bearers of the unconditionality of God's love, that we should never be the agents of exclusion, though people may exclude themselves in horror from what we are. And though the presence of God may, in the end, spell the damnation of any of us in the freedom of our separatedness, it is not for us to anticipate that for one another from the complacency of our own belonging. Certainly, insofar as the Church has procedures for arriving at a common mind, it owes it to the world to say what it believes. But the practice of formal or informal excommunication seems to me disastrous, both because it presumes an impossible access into the interiority of another's understanding, motivation and love, and because it signals a rejection diametrically opposed to the 'bearing all things' of the God who gives us our identity.

What in fact seems to me to lie behind most of our natural, political and pragmatic desire for firm identification criteria is the terror that we do not know who we shall be – a promise which strikes most of us not as Gospel, but as threat.

That our distinctiveness should lie in us being un-boundaried people, resisting all the classifications of dogma, ethics and piety, is such an openness as to explode the security of the worlds we make to inhabit, the gardens we name, the properties or things we've got taped. And yet it seems to me to present the most significant evangelical counter-culture to the world which it is possible to articulate.

Now, that is no particular help to you as Anglicans, but if you agree at all that this is the mission of the Church, your own particular contribution may fall more easily into perspective. For it will consist in reaffirming and reinforcing these elements in the life of your communion which enact such inclusiveness, and in resisting those which seem to tighten up for the sake of weeding out the deviant.

It will be patient of the future ahead of all specification, and impatient of any use of the past as a straitjacket for the definition of faith. Its mode of operation will be exploratory, aware that transcendence is not encapsulated in any language, nor perhaps denied by any, at least at any level of ultimate significance. What denies God is lovelessness, and the only convincing denunciation of that is the ironic one of loving the loveless.

If this is the constitutive identity of the Church, the authority issue follows almost as a corollary. For it is never, in fidelity to that understanding of its being in freedom and mutuality, about control, thought control or behaviour control. It is about convincingness. And what is convincing is the hanging together of life and belief which constitute palpable integrity. Given that we exist, as Lutheran ecclesiology would insist, and Orthodox deny, even institutionally as *simul iustus et peccator*, we need not expect to manifest that fluent and constant goodness which presumably flows from beatitude; but at least it is the glimpsing, the tasting of that possibility which exerts leverage on our existence, and forces us to confessing recognition of that as our horizon.

On the whole, however, the Church's history in relation to authority has been terribly at variance with the authority of a Christ who won by losing, who ruled by serving, and who seems to have teased his contemporaries to the point of documented frustration: eating, to the horror of some, with Pharisees; to the horror of others, with publicans and sinners. Allowing a Matthew to portray him as the ultimate fulfilment of the law, and a Paul as its abolition. Telling impossible parables of a father who invited two incompatible brothers to a party. Refusing to be quietist or zealot, and constantly meeting questions with further questions.

There is, I suppose, one sort of Niebuhrian line which the Church often takes. Recognising that in the Kingdom of heaven there will be no constraint, no coercion, no forcible exclusions, it pleads the need for disciplinary sanctions, for instance, as a concession to our weakness as mortals in mortal institutions. It is not the eschatological condition of the Church which requires the exercise of authority, but its pre-eschatological condition. Human beings can't cope with being at sea. They need marker buoys, defined channels, lighthouses saying 'Keep off these rocks!' The need for authority is a correlate of sin, and vulnerability to sin.

This position does not merit facile dismissal, but I find it shading imperceptibly towards the stance of the Grand Inquisitor, who knows better than God what's good for people. And I wonder how often what is quite sincerely meant as benevolent paternalism is in fact an inability on the part of the paternal to risk the adulthood of their 'children'. The subversive Christ of Dostoevsky seems to me to have more in common with the Christ of the Gospels than with the self-vindicating authorities of magisterium, normative exegesis, or General Assembly.

For as identity was, for Christ, a relational term, to do with his relatedness to the Father, to the Spirit, to the cosmos, to the inhabited earth, so authority seems to have been for him a counter-cultural openness to the testing of the common people as to whether what he said rang true. Certainly it was a counter-culture to the mode of the Scribes and Pharisees, even if we allow for a certain amount of later anti-Pharisee propaganda in the New Testament. The riskiness of that is clear. For popular consensus is obviously no guarantee of truth. Yet the character of the truth which 'defined' the Christ was so dynamically open to the willingness and ability of the other to receive it, that it would not defend itself against attack, except by silence and suffering.

That again, I'm afraid, does not help you much in the nitty-gritty of decision-making about your structures of power, consultation, episcopal authority versus or alongside synodical, and all the other specifics for which the Communion presumably hopes for guidance as a result of this process. All it suggests, perhaps, is that you should be happy rather than sad that you lack a pyramidal model of truth-speaking and legislation; that you may be blessed and not cursed in having structures of dispersed authority, since these are more liable to require the kind of receptivity to the other involved in a genuinely evangelical account of what it means to explore and share the truth of the self-disclosing God.

A Church which has the inbuilt structures to keep living with the complexity of how it seems across lay/clerical boundaries, in diverse cultures through time and space, and in ongoing conversation with the rest of the Church catholic should not be in a flap. The pressures of this particular era seem to me to be regressive ones in terms of mounting demands for ecclesiastical self-justification, and of a sinister competitiveness between past and present, top and bottom, academic and practical, male and female. I am sure it is not a vision of which Anglicans have the monopoly, but I hope that as you embark on this decade of evangelism, so open to abuse and recidivist imperialism, you will keep pioneering, for the sake of all of us, structures of painfully collaborative authority which image the delicacy of God. If you can manage that, I am sure that your identity as a communion will look after itself, and the question will evaporate in the hilarity and passion of knowing who you are in the give-and-take of that imaging.

5

We Still Have No Small Distance to Go*

And when the day of Pentecost was fully come, they were all with one accord in one place. (Acts 2:1)

In the 1980s, ACTS was a twinkle in the eye of the Division of Ecumenical Affairs in the old British Council of Churches. It was a long twinkle! Fifteen years of careful gestation – prayer, study, consultation, analysis involving a million grassroots Christians. The Interchurch Process, 'Not Strangers but Pilgrims', was, for us, an Emmaus journey, a time of burning hearts. May the adventurous spirits of Alastair Haggart, Philip Morgan, Martin Reardon and the like hover over us today!

ACTS and its sibling ecumenical bodies were conceived in an act of mutual desire that the Roman Catholic Church could become a full and equal partner in agreed ecumenical structures. Active and creative collaboration had been accelerating since 1935, with the inauguration of the Week of Prayer for Christian Unity, which itself picked up on a proposal from the 1860s for a crusade of prayer for 'Unity in Truth', inaugurated, against the disapproval of John Henry Newman, by a Roman Catholic convert, one Father Ignatius Spencer (collect 2p on the way out if you've heard of him!).

In the Glasgow winters of my childhood, the two nearest primary schools hurled snowballs across the street to shouts of 'Dirty Catholics/Dirty Protestants'. Civilised neighbours could say, innocent of malice, about a newly arrived Italian family: 'They're Roman Catholics but they're very nice'; and the Orange Lodge reacted annually on 12 July along Clyde Street with triumphant hatred on its corporate face.

* Sermon delivered at the Members' Meeting of Action of Churches Together in Coatbridge, Scotland, October 2011.

The 1987 Swanwick Declaration was the culmination of the Interchurch Process. With the rest of the famous *Marigold Book*, it should be compulsory annual reading for our ecumenical bodies. It said:

> We now declare together our readiness to commit ourselves to each other under God. Our earnest desire is to become more fully, in his own time, the one Church of Christ, united in faith, communion, pastoral care and mission.
>
> It is our conviction that, as a matter of policy at all levels and in all places, our churches must move from co-operation to clear commitment to each other.

We still have no small distance to go. Behind the sheltering phrase 'reconciled diversity', we maintain our denominational tribalisms with too little shame. We have, on the whole, learned civility with one another, even trust and warmth in some cases in the context of ACTS. But we still have to grasp the nettles about what divides us: that we cannot share a common eucharist, cannot fully recognise one another's ministries, grapple too little with deep difference of understanding, within as well as between denominations, on issues like sexuality, bioethics, authority and biblical interpretation.

That little child ACTS has now come of age. For a birthday present, I wish her passionate longing and risk-taking courage!

In the 1980s, Father James Quinn, who wrote hymns like an angel and pronounced dogma like a Denzinger, would stand at the door of the room where Mass was to be celebrated during Division of Ecumenical Affairs meetings. 'Catholic discipline as usual,' he would say politely – which meant crudely for the rest of us, 'You may not have it!'

One weekend, in Father Quinn's absence, the presiding Catholic was Bishop Patrick Kalilombe, first director of Selly Oak's Centre for Black and White Christian Partnership. He began by saying: 'If I were in my own diocese in Malawi, you would all be welcome to receive, for it is inconceivable in Africa that some share food in the presence of others who are excluded. But here, I am under the jurisdiction of the Bishop of Birmingham, so I may not invite you.'

He then preached a homily on the Prodigal Son, and the baggage of the elder brother – in a room full of tears.

We all, of course, have baggage!

ACTS has just decided to sell Scottish Churches House, which, for fifty years, was a dedicated place for exchanges of faith and life. If the property market picks us, it should make a tidy sum for the depleted ecumenical coffers. Its disposal is, however, to many lovers of the Swanwick Declaration, an act of ecumenical vandalism.

The poet, Louis MacNeice, wrote 'Prayer Before Birth'. It is spoken in the voice of an unborn child, a voice which might have named ACTS' antenatal fears:

> I am not yet born: O hear me . . .

> I am not yet born: O fill me
> With strength against those who would freeze my
> humanity, would dragoon me into a lethal automaton,
> would make me a cog in a machine, a thing with
> one face, a thing, and against all those
> who would dissipate my entirety, would
> blow me like thistledown hither and
> thither or hither and thither
> like water held in the
> hands would spill me.

> Let them not make me a stone and let them not spill me.
> Otherwise kill me.

6

*The Stillness of the Heart**

The collapse of ideas, of dogmas, of even the hallowed creeds, is a positive move towards the inexhaustible nature of transcendence.

I am no mystic! Temperamentally, I am much more of a turbulent activist than a contemplative. So, I am a strange choice to speak about the stillness of the heart, and I want you to be absolutely clear that I make not the slightest claim to 'inside expertise'. I have read the writings of some of the Christian mystics since I was a teenager, but I love them from a distance, being not very confident about claims to direct, immediate experience of the divine, and having very mixed feelings about the unity and harmony of the cosmos.

Like many Christians, I suspect, I have a somewhat ragged and fluctuating hope that the world is cradled by a God of love and freedom, inviting us towards transfiguration. Like many people, I have occasional moments of feeling at one with everything smelling of summer grass on a hot day: watching the sun reach over the sea to the horizon; feeling the wind in my face; meeting some perfect articulation in music or paint or words; Blake's sense of seeing 'a world in a grain of sand, and heaven in a wild flower'.

Such situations are widely shared by human beings of all faiths, or no specific one, but for most of us they are occasional and gifted moments rather than a sustained consciousness. How to weigh them against the atrocities in Kosovo, or the other grisly substance of our daily news, is a matter not so much of rational choice but of risky commitment.

In my own fifty-odd years of existence, I can recall only one moment which stands out for me as resembling the quality of technical mystical experience – a moment of startling, out-of-the-blue clarity which I

* From a talk given at Christ Church, Morningside, Edinburgh, 9 October 1998.

cannot explain, but which has had for me a meaning out of all proportion to its duration.

I was a student, at university in Glasgow, going home on my normal route on the Glasgow subway, which thirty years ago was a fairly grubby and ramshackle affair. One afternoon, four people were sitting opposite me across the cigarette-strewn carriage. There was a workman with overalls and a dark blue donkey jacket. There was a wee headscarfed housewife with a battered shopping bag, and two vacant youths with jeans and studded leather jackets. Out of one pocket of the workman's jacket peeped the head of a small doll.

For an instant, without warning, these four people were transfigured. Nothing changed. I wasn't thinking about them. But suddenly they were amazingly beautiful, as if all the grime and wear of their lives had gone. And then they were themselves again, ordinary passengers on this shoogling train.

I don't think about it all that often, but against all my subsequent experience of the malice and stupidity of the world, I believe that I had in that moment a glimpse of how creation looks to God: a glimpse of love-knowledge . . .

What I want to do is to identify some of the characteristics of the mystical tradition which have helped me to interpret my own experience, and which continue to enlarge my sense of who I am.

My first encounter with some of the classics of mystical spirituality came in my late teens, when I was recovering from a bad bout of Protestant evangelical fervour which had sent me rampaging around home and church for two years, denouncing my parents, my minister, my congregation for refusing to fit the model of conversion I had learned from my school Scripture Union!

My generous and gentle minister quietly laid on for me some of the riches of Catholic devotion – Francis de Sales, St John of the Cross, Von Hugel – and, after the somewhat bleak Calvinism of my evangelical phase, I devoured them almost to the point of indigestion! Some of it, I suspect retrospectively, was the transference of adolescent virginal longings, for much mystical writing is deeply erotic. But it was certainly an exhilarating expansion of horizons from the cramped biblical dogmatism which had overlain the modest and moderate home–church environment of my childhood.

The God of these mystics was a beckoner: covering, sheltering, sweet as honey. I longed for such experience!

It never came!

What came instead was seven years of hard agnosticism, triggered by a close encounter with British analytical philosophy. God dissolved. Prayer disintegrated. Creeds fell into meaningless syllables. A painful but, for me, necessary scepticism about all religious experience challenged not only the accounts of my mystics, but, much more alarmingly, all that I had hitherto taken as God's presence in my own life.

Almost the only holding factor for me at that point was the mystical category of 'the Dark Night of the Soul'. To my evangelical friends, the only way of describing my invincible doubts was to see them as backsliding. To my philosophical interrogators, the only way of explaining my desire for the possibility of faith was cowardice. But, between the two, the mystics whispered that as often as not the loss of faith was a strange gift from God: something to take us from the relatively shallow levels of verbalised religious affirmation into the depth of God's darkness, the cloud of unknowing.

This tradition, the *apophatic* tradition of theology, from a word that means 'speaking away from', is deeper in Eastern than in Western theology, but the mystics seem to share it in all faith-traditions, even non-Christian ones. 'Every concept formed by the intellect in an attempt to comprehend and circumscribe the divine nature can succeed only in fashioning an idol, not in making God known' (Olivier Clément).

Speechlessness is a stage on the journey to God. The collapse of ideas, of dogmas, of even the hallowed creeds, is a positive move towards the inexhaustible nature of transcendence . . .

What is wonderful, but not really surprising I suppose from a God who connects with creativity, is that the artist or writer need have no explicit religious faith at all. The faith is somehow *in* the seeing, the doing, the making . . .

Mystics often testify to a sense of transcending time, and in some cases to a sense of absorption in the totality of things. That seems to be a skilled faculty for some, developed by disciplines of prayer and vigilance, what St John Climacus called 'keeping awake in the silence of the heart'.

These are not skills I can lay claim to: I suspect that I enjoy time too much! But I am sure that in the play of human encounter we are not meant to lose identity but to find it. The specificity of form, the irreplaceable particularities of creation are not obliterated by being suffused with the love-knowledge of God; they are enhanced. That is perhaps what it means that we affirm the 'resurrection of the body'.

For me, reading the mystics makes me feel a bit as I do when I climb mountains with my leaner and fitter husband: usually I'm glimpsing the back of his kilt from about 200 yards away, and by the time I catch up, he's had a puff on his pipe and is ready for the next bit!

That's not much of an image of stillness to end with!

As I said, I am no mystic. I am, however, haunted by this intuition that we inhabit a world depth-charged with love, where the letting-be of God gives us space, freedom, irreplaceability. How I reconcile that with my often frazzled existence is probably a matter for the confessional!

I am sure, however, that our frenetic, 'doing' world, and our often frenetic, 'doing' Churches, can learn hugely from these men and women who worked at the stillness of the heart and found it growing into a love-song to all creation. Evagrius of Pontus called it 'ontological tenderness'!

That's quite a mouthful for someone who was registering the merits of speechlessness, but I think I actually have a glimpse of what it means. May we go together into the deep darkness of God, at least in the direction of the stillness of the heart.

PART 5

LIVING, LOVING
AND DYING

Introduction

Lesley Orr

Liz's theology was all about living, loving and dying: she wrestled with the tragedy and the joyous possibilities of embodied human existence throughout her own life. Elsewhere in this collection, she observes that the price of life is death, and argues that our attitude to death is the starting point of theology. For her, death is the enemy because it is the final rolling of the stone against the deep, restless energy of connection, intimacy and love in relationship. And such love can only be experienced and expressed because we are carnal – we don't *have* bodies, we *are* bodies.

The five talks and lectures in this section reveal Liz the complicated flesh-and-blood person for whom being a theologian was always contextual, always addressing the hard questions about the particularity of real lives which resist and transcend efforts (religious or otherwise) to impose categorisation and control. And so, as Liz acknowledges, 'pain, passion and conflict are always involved'.

That seems particularly true when human beings – and especially their religious institutions – confront sexuality and gender. In recent decades, the Church of Scotland has been rudely jostled out of the pulpit from where it had long presumed the God-given right to issue injunctions forbidding sex between anyone except a man and woman bound in wedlock. In May 1994, as convener of the Panel on Doctrine Working Party on the Theology of Marriage, Liz presented its report to the General Assembly. As she stepped forward to the lectern, she may have felt the atmosphere was more akin to the lions' den. The report marked a genuinely significant shift of theology, perspective and tone, for it not only recognised but also affirmed different patterns of intimate relationship (both heterosexual and same-sex) beyond traditional marriage and suggested that moral certainties based on form rather than quality of sexual relationship were neither helpful for actual people in their lives, nor truly faithful to a loving creator God. The report concluded: 'the struggle over these questions of marriage and sexuality is itself a gift to the Church and not simply a problem'. A dissenting minority of Panel members issued their own report, claiming that the Working Party had been 'dismally defeatist', led by the nose, cravenly capitulating to changing social norms, and that their report was a 'Trojan horse to breach our moral defences' against incest and paedophilia. Meanwhile, the Board of Social Responsibility also presented a report on human sexuality in 1994, upholding the traditional Church line of 'loving the sinner but hating the sin' of homosexuality. It was into this febrile setting that Liz spoke, seeking to frame the issue theologically as concerning the nature of God and the responsible freedom of committed Christians. And she challenged the Church to face these contentious issues with candour and integrity.

The following year, Liz was invited to address the 1995 World Alliance of Reformed Churches, European Area Council. This gathering met in Edinburgh during the last week of the Festival. I know, because I was there – in fact, I was on the planning group for the event! We knew that the majority of delegates would be white European men – mostly ministers and theologians. Given the stern patriarchal reputation of Calvinism and its ecclesiastical legacy, we reckoned that gender relations and justice should be a key theme – particularly during the World Council of Churches Decade of Churches in Solidarity with Women (1988–98), which had laid bare the global reality that so many women in church and wider society continued to experience exclusion, and silencing, violation and oppression. In this context, it was important to create a safe and supportive space for the female delegates to share their stories and concerns. But we also wanted the social construction of gender (and its theological implications) to be a matter of self-critical reflection and scrutiny for the men who attended: Reformed traditions, practices and norms were shaped around potent and still largely unexamined assumptions that masculine authority and status are normative. Women, on the other hand, were historically regarded as the Other whose divinely appointed role was service and subordination. When their claims for recognition and equality began to take organised shape, the establishment (with some honourable exceptions) was less inclined to take a close look at itself than to treat 'the place of women' as a conundrum upon which the fathers and brethren would pronounce the appropriate response. With this background, the plan was to set aside one day during the Council when women and men would meet separately, with different programmes. (It turned out that a lot of the brothers in faith were bemused at the notion that it might be worth thinking about their own gendered power, privilege and attitudes, or the patriarchal structures and history of their Churches, so they went shopping instead.)

Before the two groups went their separate ways on the appointed day, Liz was invited to give the opening plenary address. She chose 'Nature, Nurture and Grace' as her subject. It generated much disquiet, debate and indeed anger among some of the participants – especially feminist theologians and activists. Many thought her lecture lacked accuracy and depth in its characterisation of 'feminist orthodoxy', and that she was tilting at windmills which did not represent the realities or complexity of Christian feminism. The tone seemed inappropriate and unfair – was it really the case that 'one of the greatest difficulties in this area is to avoid pomposity'? That seemed harshly dismissive of women's real struggles and the tenacious denial of rights rooted in structural gender inequality, while the strategic value of women-only spaces in the wider context of women and men in community received short shrift. And there was a sharp intake of breath at the off-colour 'jokes'. Reading the presentation again reminded me that many Christian feminists loved Liz, appreciating her friendship, seeing her precarious employment situation (and some-times her lack of due recognition and reward for all that she contributed to the Church) as something shared by countless women; but also find-ing it difficult that she didn't seem to 'get' feminism, or the engaged soli-darity which was so necessary for taking on hegemonic masculinity in Church and society. She recognised this herself, and puzzled over it, as in her 1991 sermon, reflecting on her experience at the WCC Canberra Assembly: 'as a woman I felt sucked into a tide of anger which I find it hard entirely to share (for reasons which largely baffle me, but which may yet need more attention in case they merely rationalise a lack of solidar-ity)'. Reading her address in the context of this collection, I still disagree with much of it, while recognising that it is more nuanced, positive and thoughtful than I recall – and appreciating the distinctive theological worldview which is reflected in the best of it.

It may be that the Hastie Lectures, delivered at the University of Glasgow in 2004, represent Liz's most sustained attempt to articulate the core themes of her work into a coherent theological argument. She explicitly claims that intention in 'God the Phoenix', which was the fourth and final lecture in the series. At the time, I was working in the Department of Theology and Religious Studies, which hosted the lectures, and I recall attending them. (There was a particularly lively question-and-answer session following her lecture on sexuality – but in a good way!) They were densely argued, but also full of arresting images and ideas. This *summa theologica* resounds with recurring themes – a critique of the Western dualist tradition, the primacy and risk of relationship, the material body as the vital heartbeat of personal identity, inseparable from any disembodied 'soul', and the existential need to resist all that would constrain the fullness of individual personhood. And it is all flung into a cosmic, ek-static eschatology of God's freedom beyond the negation of death.

What does all that mean for ordinary people dealing with the messy realities of living, loving and dying? As a freelance theologian, Liz found her calling in the opportunities of encounter and engagement with folk in all kinds of situations. This book is full of her efforts to shake theology (and sometimes the Church) free from its stultifying reputation and to animate its connection with the business of being human. She told stories and didn't pretend to have answers; she provoked and challenged; she came at things from unusual angles. Standing on the threshold allowed her to be both insider and outsider. You can see why BBC Radio invited her to give the Thought for the Day on 11 November 1992. Later that day, the Church of England Synod would vote on the ordination of women to priesthood. As a Scottish Presbyterian laywoman, Liz would not be particularly identified with either side of the debate, and her wee talk avoided any direct endorsement of a position. Instead, she shifted the debate itself off centre, and found a way of locating it in much bigger questions about love.

Likewise, in the final address of this section, Liz speaks to hospital chaplains about sexuality, spirituality and bereavement in language which is personal and honest and grounded. I warm to her reclaiming of spirituality from the clutches of a heritage which 'has made it a thin, spooky, bloodless thing', and the refusal (so clearly an outcome of her incarnational eschatology) to seek comfort in the notion of any disembodied state of being 'beyond death'. It is poignant to read these words from 1997, some time before her son Alan disappeared and the eventual confirmation of his death in 2012: 'Heresy though it is, I want to affirm that dying of a broken heart is an appropriate response to the death of someone loved.'

Did she find, in her own journey around the strangeness of God, that her risky hermeneutics of trust and desire were strong companions through uncharted territory? Was she sustained by relational cosmic love which frees human beings from the bounds of necessity? I hope so.

I

*Sexuality and Marriage**

These questions emerge from actual, faithful lives, and we owe it to our belonging together as one body to share them.

Moderator, on Monday I had a bad moment. Not being a seasoned commissioner, I arrived too late for a seat in the main hall, and was sent to the students' gallery. I feared that meant I could only watch communion, along with other latecomers and foolish virgins! And when the bread and the wine were brought there too, I was hugely comforted, having expected exclusion.

This report speaks for many who love God, desire to be openly among us, and feel not welcome. It is not about modern culture versus the Gospel, as its enemies and some of its friends present it. It is about the nature and will of God, about the responsibility we share as people made in his image, and about the faithful witness of the Church to the inclusiveness of the Gospel. We want to invite the whole Church to calm, searching conversation about these things.

Like many other denominations, we are clearly and painfully divided about them (though it is significant that the Working Party, far from uniform in the theology or experience of its members, produced, through study and sharing, a unanimous report).

Being divided hurts. But there are, it seems to me, two kinds of hurt in scripture. There is the hurt of Jacob at Peniel, wrestling with God for his name. Or the hurt of Peter, invited by God to eat food which he knew God had forbidden him to eat. For it was there in scripture, as plain as plain could be. And then, on the other hand, there is the hurt of the righteous elder brother, saying to his father: 'You are making

---

* Address to the General Assembly of the Church of Scotland, May 1994, presenting the statement of the Working Party on the Panel of Doctrine on Sexuality and Marriage.

this vagabond brother the moral equivalent of me. I will not eat with you.' There is the hurt of the disciples who wanted the wheat and the tares separated as soon as possible, and were told to wait for God's last day.

This report is no Gadarene slope to laissez-faire permissiveness. We all weep for the sad and ugly abuses of sex which so preoccupy the glossy pamphlet you have all had – promiscuity, paedophilia, incest. We share a deep concern that young people should not feel pressurised into premature sexual experience, that sex should not be made a commodity, that chastity and fidelity should be honoured.

We love and commend the things which make marriage precious: steady tenderness, mutual communication and responsibility, secure and trusting commitment, bodily joy, the renewal of forgiveness, the flow of shared strength into the wider world. These are not abstract, slippery criteria. They are things we know and recognise and long for in the fabric of our ordinary lives. And they are of God.

But we also know – many quite sane, everyday, normal, decent parents and grannies and uncles and children and elders and pastors know – that these things are found also in some partnerships which are not marriage, where men and women, and men and men, and women and women live together lovingly. That is perplexing, as Peter's Acts vision was perplexing. But it is faithless and untruthful to deal with perplexity by denying facts. We want the Church at every level of its life to explore, in faith and freedom, how to come to terms with such relationships, which are already among us as well as beyond our doors. We offer this report as a tool to help that exploring.

We are not saying 'Because something goes on it must be right.' We are saying 'There are responsible and loving people, claiming, as God-given, relationships which a traditional reading of scripture seems to disallow. Is it possible that God is in this, teaching us something that we were not ready to hear before? As he was in Peter's vision, revising the faithful tradition of centuries?'

Moderator, there have been, in the run-up to this Assembly, rumbles of schism, ugly and menacing for the Church. There is some sense that this is the Rubicon issue, holding the pass for Christian truth or selling it. But what would sell the pass would be the evasion or suppression of all that is involved in this report: the failure to trust our people with these key questions for any maturing Christian about how the living Word of the living God emerges as we grapple with scripture, tradition, experience and culture.

People are not having these questions foisted on them by alien academics or by vice-rings in the back of parked cars! They emerge from actual, faithful lives, and we owe it to our belonging together as one body to share them. From Paul's first battle with the Jerusalem Church until now, pain and passion and conflict have always been involved in identifying the will of God. We should not fear that. But we should fear our fear of it – for that might betray the 'God of surprises', who leads us, sometimes, to bear new things.

I trust, Moderator, that the Church which nurtured me can face these hard questions with candour and intelligence and integrity and lovingkindness. And I hope it will.

2

Nature, Nurture and Grace[*]

I am convinced that the deepest Christian suggestion is that you cannot know, you cannot perceive truth, you cannot get at the reality of things, if love is absent.

I am well aware, as I embark on this subject, that it is not what is often called an abstract exercise. The very existence of this day, with its split agenda for men and women, has been a cause of heart-searching, controversy and some pain. So, you have already, no doubt, some theological perspective, explicit or implicit, on the range of topics often called 'Women's Issues'.

I am not, myself, convinced that there are any interesting topics which are women's issues but not men's issues. Or vice versa. So, what I hope to do is to look at some shared theological themes with which we all have to wrestle. These themes seem to me to underline a lot of the recurrent debates about power, participation and representation which are so much a part of current ecclesiastical life, especially where gender issues are concerned.

In spite of the Decade of Churches in Solidarity with Women (1988–98), or maybe even because of it, I find that a great deal of the explicit discussion of 'Women's Issues' happens with a measure of male cynicism and distrust. I have overheard several 'over-the-bar' conversations where nice, polite, diplomatic men talk with relief about having got through sessions to do with women's agendas, with a feeling tone which is dismissive and even contemptuous.

I have also been present at women's groups, days, tents, etc. where the feeling tone among the women has been triumphalist. 'Here we are doing

* A lecture delivered to the European Area Council of the World Alliance of Reformed Churches meeting in Edinburgh in September 1995.

splendidly on our own, without these power-crazed autocratic men who don't know how to do it. I suppose we have to keep them on board, but by golly, they've everything to learn from us, and nothing to teach us.'

Both of these stances seem to me shameful and sub-Christian. For they manifest what might be called 'a hermeneutic of distrust' (an official term in Mary Daly orthodoxy which has some support in theory and in practice in international feminist discourse).

There is, admittedly, much point in 'distrusting'. When we look at the question of culture, and the manufacture of sexual stereotypes, it will be evident that deep and searching questions need to be asked about who 'constructs' the world of sexual identity – and it will, I hope, be clear that 'deconstruction' is both possible and desirable. But, at the same time, I am convinced that the deepest Christian suggestion is that you cannot know, you cannot perceive truth, you cannot get at the reality of things, if love is absent. And 'love' is not sentimental attachment. It is being so bound up with another that their life and yours are not detachable. You are who you are only in relation to this other.

This will, I suggest, indicate a way of thinking about gender issues for Christians which is not compatible with self-sufficiency models of existence for women or for men. Many of you will already be familiar with the World Alliance of Reformed Churches' publication on Women's Ordination, *Walk, My Sister* (1993). I shall spend no time in this paper talking about women's ordination, but I would like to acknowledge that text as one of my sources for the international Christian feminist voice. I would also like to acknowledge a recently produced Scottish study which will be launched next month, commissioned by the Network of Ecumenical Women in Scotland. It is called *To Have A Voice*, and is an analysis of the feelings of a cross-section of women from all the Scottish Churches about their needs and aspirations in Christian community here. That, I hope, will give a bit of local colour to our reflections, and will allow you to judge how similar or different it is on your patch.

It seems to me that one of the greatest difficulties in this area is to avoid pomposity. Of course, the questions about how men and women relate in creation, in culture and in Christian fellowship are serious. But one of the difficulties about much conversation in this area is that earnestness can become, easily, 'as sure as death'. (That is one reason, perhaps, why the presence of the clown figure at these proceedings will be a blessing.) I am quite sure that there will be no healing of the animosities, no hearing one another 'from inside' until we can laugh together.

So, in indicating where I begin in this lecture, I share with you two jokes.

One was a car sticker, which I saw once but have celebrated many times. It said: 'Women who seek equality lack all ambition'. I will return to that later, for I do not believe that 'equality' is a particularly helpful category in Christian discourse, and will try to say why. The other was told to me by my eleven-year-old son. What is interesting is not the joke but the fact that he warned me in advance that it was a bad joke. Expecting some piece of playground pornography, I said I thought I could stand it when he asked if he could tell me it.

'Well,' he said, with the shamefaced look of one who knew he was breaking the rules, 'What do you do when your dishwasher breaks down?' 'I don't know; what do you do?' 'You kick her and say, "Hurry up, get on with it."'

I take that as my cue, then, for the question of male and female identity. Why are we men and women? What are men and women for? Would an imaginative creator not have done better to make us all androgynous? Does the differentiation of the sexes in nature not cause most of, or at least many of, the problems of co-existence which blight our political and social life? Is there not some plausible case for rejecting 'vive la différence!' and suggesting that 'la différence' is in fact one of the blights of human happiness? But what, precisely, is 'la différence'?

Clearly, the biological differentiation in body structure and chromosome identity is a given (though a given complicated by the much-neglected and shunned minority who feel sexually at odds with their body structure). From this, most cultures have evolved social structures in which pairing across gender is normative. This can be explained in Darwinian terms, or, as most theologies have done, in terms of some divine purpose of complementarity. Myths about 'halves' needing each other to be whole abound both in religious terms and in more secular ones such as Jungian psychotherapy. Yet, when one moves beyond the sheer biological differentiation – and, with what we now know about hormones, biology itself looks less and less like an absolute parameter – the question of how men and women differ generically is extremely elusive.

It is, of course, hard to separate out in this area what is fact and what is ideology. On the one hand, women are aware of, and increasingly hostile to, what they see as male stereotypes – stereotypes which have too often landed them with mopping up the tea dishes and mending the socks. On the other hand, it is almost feminist orthodoxy that there are womanly virtues which men tend not to have, though whether this is innate or not is not much discussed.

Some of Margaret Hart's respondents in the Scottish study I mentioned, *To Have A Voice*, say this, for example:

> The feminine is one way of describing all of humanity's more intuitive, spontaneous, feeling, caring, compassionate, non-competitive, sharing, nurturing, creatively quiescent qualities. The masculine tends to be more intellectual, logical, assertive, individualistic, competitive, active and hierarchical.

This, I must confess, strikes me as highly questionable. If it means that most women share the former characteristics and most men the latter, then it seems to me, on empirical grounds, simply false. There may well be cultures, among them the one we inhabit as Europeans at this stage in the twentieth century, in which there is some truth in that account, but would it be true of Polynesian men and women? Or even of British or German boys brought up, say, in a Rudolf Steiner school?

Certainly, there is now work going on in the area of brain research which claims to identify objective differences between male and female brains: differences of size (men's are bigger), and differences in the areas of the cortex used for different functions. Women, for instance, according to recent research at Yale University, use both hemispheres of the brain in performing certain speech functions, whereas men use only one for the same function. But what one makes of this – whether, for instance, it suggests that women are more holistic, or men more intellectually economical – is not a matter of fact but a matter of interpretation. And what one values as desirable is, again, highly subjective.

Over a hundred years ago, one early anthropologist, Gustav le Bon, writing about the human brain in 1879, made suggestions which would now be greeted with outrage by even faint-hearted feminist sympathisers.

> In most intelligent races, as among the Parisians, there are a large number of women whose brains are closer in size to those of gorillas than to the most developed male brains. This inferiority is so obvious that no-one can contest it for a moment . . . Women excel in fickleness, inconsistency, absence of thought and logic and incapacity to reason. Without doubt there exist some distinguished women, very superior to the average man, but they are as exceptional as the birth of a

monstrosity – as for example, of a gorilla with two heads: conse-
quently we may neglect them entirely.

For me, the theological question is not about the data, which presumably
will go on emerging as brain sciences refine themselves. It is about what
we make of the data. Most philosophies of science, of course, recognise
that there is some interaction between what you are looking for, how you
set up a question and what you find. So, in one sense, no data is absolutely objective. But even if genetics, or brain chemistry, or some branch
of medical research establishes beyond doubt that men and women are
genetically different in precise respects, there is still the theological and
human question: 'So what?'

Behind that question lies one that divides theologians. Does God set
nature as a fixed and normative structure for human behaviour, or is
nature given to us as something to transcend, as a provisional starting
point, but one which we have freedom to modify, to alter, even to resist?
Natural-law-type theories, whether in the Catholic or the Calvinist
traditions, tend to the former view. Those of Eastern Orthodox traditions, and some forms of anarchic Protestantism, have more sympathy
with the latter.

My own theological position is that God is an anti-determinist
whether the determinism be biological, social, economic or whatever.
Being made in the image of God, then – if we take seriously the idea that
our sexuality is part of that – cannot be about our definition in terms of
closed natures, male and female. It must, rather, be about our interaction
as men and women, our openness to new possibilities which we give one
another, the possibility of encounter, of overcoming aloneness, of finding identity in difference, of sharing the unpredictability of beings who
are free, and open to one another's freedom.

It is, it seems to me, in terms of freedom and not of nature that we
need to construct our theological critique of cultural structures of oppression. For nature is liable to be, in terms of the Christian myth of fallenness (I use 'myth' with no pejorative undertone), as much a place of
un-freedom as culture is. Sin is not merely moral. It is cosmic. It pervades
the structures of space and time and causality as well as the domains of
ethics and politics. We cannot find the Kingdom of God simply by following nature, even if we can isolate what we think nature is.

I think, then, that one of the distinctive Christian contributions to a
counter-culture would actually involve us in challenging some forms of
feminism while supporting others. I think we should be perennially

suspicious of generalisations about women's nature and men's nature, those which are favourable to women as well as those which put them down.

Indeed, the Margaret Hart extract quoted above about feminine and masculine natures seems to me a rather shocking piece of reverse stereotyping. What would the father cradling his hurt child, the gardener who watches the slow processes of the soil, the artist, the lover who responds to every nuance of his partner's mood, make of 'intellectual, logical, assertive, individualistic, competitive, active and hierarchical'? And what indeed would women make of it, who love the dance of the mind, or the lucidity of good arguments for things, or the sense of their own power?

It is clear that the feminist culture of the twentieth century has, both on global and local scales, done much to deconstruct the axioms of Europe's Enlightenment culture. A kind of excessive rationalism has been challenged, as has the linking of power to that kind of rationalism. A sense of our existing as separate atoms, going back at least to Descartes in the modern period, has been questioned, and new models of participating democracy explored.

But I doubt, myself, whether it is because they are women that they have discovered these models; and I deplore the kind of feminism which is Messianic, as if men had a monopoly of sin, and women were prelapsarian. I know, of course, that the 'orthodoxy' is that we tend to sin in different ways. Men are proud and fail to consult, to share, to include. Women fail to assert themselves, and collude in the structures of their own oppression.

This again seems to me unconvincing as an empirical claim, if it is meant to be universal and not culture-specific. It doesn't need much international ecumenical experience, or even much experience of the Church of Scotland, to discover women who like power as much as men, who fail to consult, who are offended if rank is not recognised.

The gift we have to give the world is not, I believe, in reproducing the common and partially true recriminations of the women's movement about hierarchy, patriarchy and the lack of proper equality between the sexes. What we have to do is to create models and structures of co-existence in which we let people glimpse what it is to have moved beyond self-consciousness. The grace of Christian living, if we take it in terms of the ministry of Jesus to the world, is to be so unselfconsciously with and for the other as to lose self-preoccupation.

This, naturally, sounds sinister, as if it could be the back door to another form of asking women to be doormats, forgetting their own claims to empowerment and to all the justice they properly seek. I do not know, in theory, quite how to distinguish between the wrong kind of self-forgetfulness and the right kind. But I am sure that graceful co-existence must transcend the kind of self-consciousness which bedevils so much of the relationships between women and men, especially when we meet to discuss gender issues.

I must admit that I am deeply ambivalent myself about the model which has become normative, of separate women's meetings, mirrored increasingly by corresponding men's ones. That seems to me to reinforce the sense of collectivity which actually helps us internalise the myth that women are one sub-species, systematically different from the other sub-species, men. I know all the arguments, and in other spheres I even find them plausible: about the need for confidence-building, the process of conscientisation, the fact that many women can't risk being themselves in contexts where they expect male domination, in large, formal assemblies and so on.

Nevertheless, I suspect that the longer we go on structuring our ecclesiastical encounters in this way, the harder it will be to break through to images of graceful co-existence which really image the 'belonging together' of Christian community. On the psychological level, for good reasons or bad, many men feel nervous and embarrassed by the sense of their exclusion from women's events. Of course, they have often effectively, if not formally, excluded women, and they need to acknowledge that. But the only creative motive for good positive action has to do with desire. It cannot come simply from remorse, far less from reluctant and grudging concessions to a strategy of power.

But, quite apart from the tactical, practical question of what the outcome is likely to be if we continue to encourage separate men's and women's agendas, it is, I believe, inappropriate as a theological symbol. There is still a huge way to go in overcoming the sense of alienation which is articulated so forcefully by the Christian feminist voice. The Margaret Hart book makes it clear that in every denomination in this land, large numbers of women still feel that their needs are unmet, their gifts are unused or underused, they are not trusted and respected, and there are tragically low expectations of their contribution to the life and ministry of the Church.

It seems to me that we have to move on to a level of mutual risk-taking and vulnerability where we are together going through the pain barriers before we can expect anything analogous to resurrection as a wholesome community. We have to risk the exposure of caricature, of women by men and men by women. We have to test out these generalisations about men's nature and women's nature. We have to recognise that we are all, in different ways, caught as victims, and we are all, in different ways, capable of oppressions. And we have to go through the baptismal drowning which offers our joint failure to God's judgement and healing.

There is, of course, facile talk about 'mutuality and acceptance', which fails to deal with the awfulness of actual, concrete abuses. And it is anger and frustration about some of these abuses which have often led women to protect themselves from hurt by creating their own safer circles of empowerment. I do not want in any way to denigrate those, though I think we women need a little bit more self-criticism perhaps about our rhetoric of renouncing power.

All I wish to suggest is that we clearly cannot confuse 'woman-church' with the Kingdom of God, any more than we can confuse with it most of our tattered and sullied institutions. Nor can we mistake a community in which we wrest power out of dominating male hands for a communion in which each really lives for the sake of the other with unforced delight.

I am sure that the politics of feminism have made a major contribution to men's awareness of some of the tragedies of history, in which sexism has been a large component. For those who haven't done so already, there is a need to realise how little our social and ecclesiastical gender roles are natural, and how much they are cultural, 'constructed and reconstructable'.

But, if I may use a Lutheran metaphor, all this seems to me to remain at the level of law. If we are to be, as an ecclesial community, an image of grace which actually offers hope to the world, I think we have to enact the freedom of the sons and daughters of God. That means that we all enter a critique of power structures which is mandated by the ministry of Jesus and the ministry of God which lies behind it. It means that we renounce all ideologies of self-sufficiency, individual, sexual or whatever. For we are invited to live in the image of a God who cannot be except in communion. And this, not as a matter of political correctness, but in the spontaneous imagination of love.

And it means that we enter an understanding of 'representation' in which each of us represents all of us, male or female. Just as any of us, poor, blind, beggar, child, represents us all to ourselves.

This is not very helpful in terms of offering detailed blueprints of Church life. But I hope that it is enough to start some reflection about how we can move forward creatively in the somewhat stale debates which whizz around the area of Church and gender politics.

We are not defined by our natures. We are free to reconstruct our nurture, the 'Adamic' responsibility to name creation which we surely share across gender differences. And our vision of how to do that comes from that other sense of grace, of the giftedness of being made in the image of God to inherit a future whose form we do not know, but in which the preciousness and irreplaceability of every member will be acknowledged by every other.

3

*God the Phoenix**

The particularity of body is vital to the identity of the self.

Brian Patten's poem 'Angel Wings' is suggestive of the way in which relationship can be destroyed by being 'investigated' in inappropriate ways. The poem gathers many of the themes I have been trying to explore in these lectures, about language and knowledge, about the erotic, about nature, and about what it means to find oneself and the cosmos created by God for God.

Let me try then to recapitulate the previous lectures, and to suggest how together the various themes articulate a sense of theological coherence and direction. First, I have made an appeal for almost the phenomenological recognition of the difference between, in Buber's terms, the I–It mode of encounter and the I–Thou mode. The I–It mode is one in which the other becomes an object of scrutiny, investigation, analysis, classification and so on. It owes its European origin largely to Aristotle, and follows his assumptions about the nature of the identity of anything as its membership of a species, and its capacity to be isolated from other members of the species. The Cartesian subject/object distinction, and its progeny in Newtonian science and the technological developments that it enabled, are part of the same story. That story also involved, ultimately, the desacralising of nature, and was connected with the development of an ideology of human superiority and entitlement to use the earth.

---

* These extracts are from the fourth Hastie Lecture, held in Glasgow in 2004, following others on the hermeneutic of distrust, on cosmology and ecology, and on sexuality. The lecture begins with the Brian Patten poem 'Angel Wings', which describes the discovery of a pair of angel's wings in a cupboard. 'They are mine,' a smiling voice says; but the narrator responds by investigating the wings, pulling their feathers apart, and is left with a dull, lifeless creature.

The I–Thou mode is one in which the other cannot be reduced to the sum of its parts, and in which the other is not object to my subject. In such a relationship, the particularity of the other is not replaceable, not substitutable. The two primary instances of that are the relationships between persons (of which intimate erotic relationship is, at its best, an image) and the relationship between the human creator and the world manifested in the transformative artistic encounter which demands an interaction between the two which is, at least in part, a signal of irreplaceable mutuality. The world is not encountered by Rembrandt as it is encountered by Picasso; nor can it be represented to a third party by one in the same way as by the other, just as no person is the same person to two other persons (which is why perhaps the issue of sexual intimacy with more than one person is not necessarily a matter of competition, betrayal or displacement).

Secondly, I have affirmed, with the consensus of both much contemporary eco-feminism and of the mainstream Christian tradition, that the particularity of form/body is vital to the identity of the self, while recognising that very often, both in theory and in practice, the Church has behaved gnostically.

Thirdly, belonging *to* the cosmos as opposed to belonging *in and with it* cannot produce the permanence of ek-static being which love demands, not for its own sake, but in outrage at the disappearance of the loved other.

Fourthly, if then there is to be a condition of 'rescue' for the particular 'personhood' of creation, human and non-human, it needs to be eschatological, i.e. resourced from beyond the conditioning negation of birth/life/death which are naturally inextricably interconnected. If such a possibility does not exist, then life is ultimately tragic from the perspective of the erotic, i.e. of the passionate one who wants the other's being to be. That means it has to be free from the limitation of the spatio-temporal context which defines the beginnings and endings of things and beings which die.

No ethical proposal or system can perform that eschatological function. It is a lie that even the best ecological practices of sharing and caring can sustain life in the face of death. Nothing arrests the fact that, in a finite cosmos, the price of life is death. That is why it is so ironic that the Vatican currently insists on the bringing to term and adulthood of every conceivable – I use the word advisedly – embryo: for the maximisation of live births means the maximisation of deaths.

The unwritten chapter in these lectures would explore the question of how we do something creative in such a context, in and out of the biosphere but not able to realise and sustain personhood in that context. The probing of that possibility lies, in Eastern theology and devotion, in the anticipation of unrestricted being in communion which the Church is called to be, but of course in almost every concrete manifestation dismally fails to be. The various terminologies, 'stewarding', 'caring for', 'priesting' are, in that 'mind–body' map, related to our offering of ourselves, embedded as we are – and glad to be in the cosmos, instead of resenting it – to the resourcing of a God in whom personhood is not tragically thwarted by individuation and spatio-temporal delimitation, but whose freedom makes possible the non-coerced response of creation from within creation, which was the original 'intention' of giving crea-tion space-time in the first place. That involves themes of Christology/ Incarnation interpreted in a de-individualised way, and of 'ecclesia' interpreted as an eschatological and not a sociological reality – the two, more often than not, being at war.

I am convinced, so far at least, that the disciplined, ascetic mysticism of the great faith-traditions share an exploration of what Rowan Williams calls 'the wound of knowledge'. While I am agnostic about whether they all converge, I am, however, committed to a theology of desire, which I hope, risk, but cannot prove is not the same as wish-fulfilment.

I recognise the outer flicker of ascetic willingness in the recognition that by nature I share all the inclinations to individualism and classifica-tion of the other which block genuine access to the possibility of person-hood and need to be renounced, even if they cannot be moralised out of existence.

Maximus the Confessor, commenting on the Dives and Lazarus story, writes:

> For he [the rich man] neither possessed the present life, which flows away uncontrollably by nature, and which he longed to enjoy by itself, nor was he able to have a share in that which is to come, to which he was feebly moved with little desire. For that can only be attained by those who wholeheartedly love it, and on account of their desire for it eagerly and with delight endure every suffering.

That is an erotic, ascetic theology, and one which I think allows total truthfulness about the fragmentation of perception, the clash of cultures and the awfulness of separation from whom or what one loves, or their reduction to stuff instead of personal presence. But it also affirms the hints of presence in absence, of speech in speechlessness, of selfhood in vulnerability to the dismantling of the other, faithfully held as unfilled longing.

Finally, on one basic methodological point, I differ from the characteristic postmodern hermeneutic of distrust. It seems to me that an eschatology based on the hope of communion can only consistently meet the other, the stranger, the alien even, with a hermeneutic of hope – possibly distrusting oneself, but giving them the benefit of the doubt, until proved wrong – which isn't at all the same as *naïveté* or credulity!

4

*Thought for the Day**

There are people I love, all around England, for whom today could make or break their dreams: if women's ordination to the priesthood is not approved at this afternoon's General Synod, they won't know how to handle the heartbreak and frustration. Some have waited thirty years for the law to change, and feel it's been eternity.

There's a theologian I love in Greece, who fears that if the change *is* made, deepening trust between the Orthodox Churches and the Anglican Communion may be set back terribly. To him, thirty years seems a very short time for the Church to decide such a monumental issue, especially by a single-digit majority (though I seem to recall one early Church council where a vital vote was narrowly carried only because some key bishops missed a ferryboat).

There's a friend I love in New Zealand who couldn't credit that *anyone* thinks it's a monumental issue. To her, it's plain common justice that women should be ordainable – obvious to anyone not cut off from normal human evolution on Galapagos islands of weird theology!

There's a fierce layman I love in Edinburgh who thinks clergy are, almost universally, a problem, male or female, and would be, on balance, better abolished, so that the people of God might regain dignity and sister–brotherhood.

There's a bishop I love in Durham, who tells with relish the story of the little boy at his father's ordination, rather anxiously watching the heap of apostolic hands laid on his father's head: 'Mum, what are they doing to him?' he asked. To which the whispered reply came: 'They're removing his backbone!'

There's a child I haven't actually met, but love at one remove, because he's precious to my best friend. He is called Joel, and is two years old,

* BBC Radio 4, 11 November 1992.

and doesn't care whether the people who play and cuddle and sing with him are Jewish or Christian or German or Israeli or ordained or not.

There is a God I love: made flesh, some hope, in an unordained Jew, whose relationship to this afternoon's debate is problematic. Is he on one side? Are divine promptings being telegraphed to undecided hearts or closed minds? Or is that election-rigging? Will angels be biting their wing-tips in suspense as BBC2 goes out this afternoon? Or is it a comedy matinee for them? Or a cosmic yawn? Or does God weep for a Church consumed by passion about this, while Joels around his earth starve and stiffen for lack of food or love?

And me? I just wish I had an inkling of how to hold all these people I love into a common future, where the pain and the hope and the anger and the boredom aren't wasted or dismissed, but reaped, somehow, into an edible harvest we can all profit from.

5

*Bereavement, Sexuality and Spirituality**

Involvement with one another and the other's pain is properly called 'erotic', a tribute to the specific desire for and absence of the other.

Let me risk beginning with a moment which was, for me, quite recent and quite intimate. So, hear me with tenderness. Twelve days ago, I had to take the funeral of a friend – not a thing I have done often. She was not a bosom crony. Sometimes we weren't in contact at all for months or even years. But, over the twenty-odd years I had known her, the friendship had become one where we could trust each other with a lot of pain, and, whenever we met, could take up where we left.

Several months ago, Anne learned she had terminal bowel cancer. In April, I went for a walk with her on a warm bright day, her first time out after a recent further kidney operation. She reminded me of Dennis Potter in his last interview with Melvyn Bragg, revelling in the glory of the blossom. On that walk, she told me that the doctors thought the operation might have given her anything between three and nine months' more time. A fortnight later, she was dead.

Two nights before she died, her children and the home-care visitor asked me to come to the oncology ward to say goodbye. Anne was quite conscious, but very tired, in an oxygen mask. I was there for a couple of hours, until I sensed the family wanted to be left alone with her. As she lay, her nightdress was open at the top, and I was struck by the beauty of her collarbone. It reminded me of the *Tempest*'s lines:

* The Stobhill Conference on 20 May 1997 was primarily for chaplains and clergy but was also open to the wider public. Stobhill Hospital in Balornock Road was a major hospital in Glasgow.

> Full fathom five thy father lies;
> Of his bones are corals made . . .

I wanted to touch it, but was afraid that would be too intimate a gesture for what the friendship had been, so I made do with holding her hand, which gripped fiercely, for a long time. But, when I was saying the words at the crematorium, committing her body to be burned, it was her collarbone I saw.

I speak with some diffidence, because this vast interlinked agenda for the day is one in which I feel no sort of expertise! Certainly, I have moved for many years in networks which explore both spirituality and sexuality – and that has only convinced me that neither is definable in terms of any single agreed definition. Both terms are controversial, even polemical sometimes.

I should confess a certain lingering unease about the word 'spirituality', a whiff of emotional negativity. This may simply be a hangover from my Protestant background (only Catholics of unsound doctrine go in for spirituality!) – but I doubt it. For, in my teens, my wonderful parish minister was putting me through the great classics of the Anglo-Catholic tradition, St John of the Cross, the Cloud of Unknowing, Evelyn Underhill, St Teresa: in fact, I think retrospectively, they were probably a kind of erotic substitute for a sexually unadventurous but religiously precocious teenager!

I think the negativity comes from later, as my sense of shame and anger grew that much of my historical Christian heritage has made the spirituality a thin, spooky, bloodless thing: to do with souls not bodies, with the inner private world of a religious minority, not with the whole life and death of the earth. I think there are better Christian traditions than that, particularly in Eastern Orthodoxy, where God's desire is the spring of creation, and the spiritual quest is about learning to enter the 'eros' of God: but that's another story. Most of us in the West have been at least subliminally influenced by the dualist, anti-body view of spirituality.

In their wonderful anthology *Sexuality and the Sacred*, James Nelson and Sandra Longfellow come up with a fairly abstract but very inclusive definition of spirituality: 'The ways and patterns by which persons relate to that which is ultimately real and worthful to them.'

That's to say, it's about having one's bearings, about not drifting, about the focus and directedness of the self in relation to what it encounters. For some people, that will emerge within a specific religious tradition; but I'm assuming, rightly or wrongly, that within a secular hospital, as in a secular school, it's a dwindling number of people, whether patients, staff or relatives, who have any explicit positive religious convictions or would feel at home with the word 'spirituality'. I say that, even if the impact of New Age bookshops with their 'body and soul' artefacts has created or reflects a more religion-sympathetic culture than existed thirty or forty years ago.

'Sexuality' is also a term which has been much more thoroughly explored in recent decades than it was before. Far wider and subtler in its range than 'sex', it has come into cultural prominence largely through the impact of the feminist and gay and lesbian critique of how our society deals with issues of sex and gender. My starting point is an acceptance of that critique: that we have a vast amount to learn as a culture about more adequate ways of sharing the preciousness of embodied existence.

So, my working presupposition in relation to sexuality is that we are talking about the deep energy of being embodied, of concrete relationships, of the human, spiritual need for touch, for intimacy, for contact. As with 'spirituality', I aim to use it as inclusively as possible, to cover small children, the accidentally single, the intentionally celibate, the partners, the polygons, the disabled, the old.

Whatever the genetics, the moral choices, the impact of circumstance, the geography of genitals, people are – unless terribly damaged – bodily relating beings. Both these uses of 'spirituality' and 'sexuality' leave open a horde of questions about evaluation. One can, I think, have sinister, infantile, destructive or manipulative spiritualities as well as life-enhancing, mature or authentic ones. And the same is true of sexuality. But the basic, inescapable fact is that all of us are, from cradle to grave, involved in both. This is not, however, a simple truth. And any brief canter round the myths, social practices, religious taboos and commercial investments of the centuries in relation to sexuality and spirituality would make that clear.

Where we are, in contemporary Britain, is a strange, unsettled place. We are in the death throes of the forms of Christianity which have belonged to Christendom – socio-politically dying for about two hundred years, but emotionally lingering in a society deeply uneasy about sexuality, deeply inarticulate about spirituality, and almost without a common myth. The replacement myths for post-Enlightenment Western Christendom have been largely centred round the idea of the 'individual' and the idea of 'the market' – and to many people these also are both collapsing – not just in Tory-free Scotland – as inadequate to bear the weight of human reality.

Modern European culture seems bankrupt to many of its inhabitants. Leaving aside the economics for the moment, the worst thing about the individualist myth is the burden of loneliness it leaves us with. Ultimately, it says, we are atoms. The deepest truth about us is not that we belong, but that we are separate: that we cannot really know and be known; that it is dangerous to look in someone else's eyes; that we are safest condemned to privacy.

Bereavement, for many, I suspect, is experienced as the sealing of that privacy, the rolling of the stone against entry to the separated self. For the dying person, it is the bereavement of losing company, of losing access to sense and sensibility, of losing identity, of making a journey where there is no trail. For the mourners of the death, it is the palpable absence of this one, who is irreplaceable, who may be remembered, of course, but who can no longer be spoken to, smelt, touched, with any mutuality.

There are, of course, beliefs and belief systems which deny that analysis. God is there waiting with the angels and saints as replacement company: the soul survives the death of the body and continues to commune with us. Or, in less theistic terms, from the Buddhist tradition, as Christine Longaker puts it in *Facing Death and Finding Hope*, when the vase shatters – when the ordinary mind dies – our true nature is released and freed, becoming indistinguishable from the space outside.

It may be a matter of temperament or education how one relates to such accounts. Personally, I find them not remotely meeting the existential sharpness of death which is the gut of the bereft lover, parent, child, friend. But that may be my limitation or immaturity. I am not, I think, particularly afraid of dying, in spite of having no speculative certainty about there being a 'beyond death'. And I have certainly known situations where I wish for the death of people I love simply as the ultimate analgesic. But I cannot, so far, rid myself of the conviction that death is our enemy, and the enemy of God; because its function is to undo that specific forming, embodiment, relationality by which I believe is our meaning as human beings. Our spiritual responsibility is to hate it, if we love our embodiment.

On the level of farewell-saying, returning to life, picking up the threads, not being morbidly obsessed with the past, I live with average sanity and equanimity in relation to my personal losses over the years (though not exposed yet to any which have made me not know who I am). But I calmly and steadily refuse to believe in 'letting go', because I think it is in our affirmation that nothing less than body will do that we are true to our particularity. I am not interested in being 'indistinguishable from the space outside'. It is the dynamic, irreplaceable form of eyes, skin, voice, collarbone which are the bearers of spirit. That is the love-knowledge which makes the stomach tighten as the coffin slides away, or makes it so important for people to have a place of burial, an earth space to connect to, to be visited at.

Let me then try to make some summary of my links between sexuality, spirituality and bereavement which may rumble around in the conversation for the rest of the day, whether you find them right or wrong, convincing or unconvincing, strange or obvious. I put them in the form of some theses:

- People do not *have* bodies; they *are* bodies. We are bodies born with the need and capacity for intimacy, for free relationship, for ecstasy, with spiritual hunger.
- The fact that we are bodies means, tragically, that there is a continuous process – subject to the laws of biological development, etc. – of progression towards death. That is experienced, sooner or later, physically, e.g. as people lose faculties, cells, hair, teeth, mobility, etc. even long before the stages of their terminal illnesses or sudden death.
- It is experienced emotionally in the bereavements of irreversible closing life-options: e.g. the sense that you can no longer (or never) have a child; that a certain career is now closed to you; that you are too old to play rugby; that your kids have stopped coming into bed for stories or cuddles.
- With luck, this bereavement is matched by gains: maturity, wisdom, friendship, deepening love; but it is not eliminated by them, and it is the invariable pointer to the final transition from life to death, where, if there is any sense of further communion, it is ethereal, not corporal.
- The recognition of our embodiedness, our need and desire for company as embodied beings, our interdependence, is, with difficulty, resistible. People can barricade themselves in. But fruitful human living accepts the interdependence.
- It is therefore deeply vulnerable to loss, and has to accept and affirm that vulnerability. Bereavement is the key recognition of that vulnerability, and the pain is an obverse of our involvement with one another. It is not something to 'get over' like a bout of 'flu.

- That involvement and pain are properly called 'erotic'. They are a tribute to the specific desire for and absence of the other's 'form' or 'body', the particular mode of their existence, and our longing to share bodily life with them and to receive life from them.
- Now the judgemental bit! Any spirituality which denies or avoids those elements of reality is bound to be lacking in something.
- Bereavement, sexuality and spirituality all, at best, involve the recognition that we do not possess either God or another or ourselves. But that dispossession is not either about self-sufficiency or about recognition.
- The renouncing of possession is, in all three spheres, compatible with the recognition of intimate, inextinguishable desire for the other's presence, for the possibility of specific mutual contact. (Maybe that is why, within my Christian context, at the eucharist, the giving and receiving of bread and wine, especially if giver and receiver risk eye-contact, is an erotic act.)
- Proper comfort need not/must not, in some sense, involve reconciliation to the death of the other/one's own death, but may simply involve the recognition of the intimacy of love, longing, body, pain and absence as proper and truthful. Heresy though it is, I want to affirm that dying of a broken heart is an appropriate response to the death of someone loved.
- Confidence about afterlife, a sense of palpable presence, etc. may be bonuses – but not if they allow people to cut the nerves which connect them body and spirit to the dead.

I am clear that this may seem a long way off from the specific of your professional responsibilities – and I know it does not sit easily with much orthodoxy in the community of, say, hospice care. It does, however, I hope, open up a conversation.

PART 6

ON BEING THE CHURCH

Introduction and Epilogue

Rowan Williams

Two of the most challenging questions that could be put to any theologian: 'Who wants to know?' and 'Who isn't in the room?'

As theologians, we are regularly trying to answer questions no one seems to be asking. This doesn't mean that questions have to be current or fashionable or widespread to be worth working at (otherwise, I imagine, we wouldn't have made much progress with string theory or black holes); only that theology is supposed to connect somewhere with a knowledge that is joyful, nourishing and supremely desirable (Bonhoeffer saying that preaching should be like holding out a juicy apple to a hungry child), and somewhere along the line it ought to be possible to say why it matters, and to say it in terms that connect with actual hungers as experienced by actual humans. At the very least, the theologian might worry about having an answer to the question, 'Why do I want to know?'

This connects with the second question. It's been pointed out rather often in the last few decades that theology – like a lot of supposedly humanistic disciplines, to be honest – has historically been conducted as if most of the human race were absent, not only women and 'subaltern' communities but children too. Rather like the commentator who asked, in relation to Virginia Woolf's famous lecture, 'Who cleans a room of one's own?', the question of exactly whose liberation or flourishing is under discussion needs to be asked, even in what are meant to be emancipatory styles of thinking. It is sobering to think that the overwhelming majority of the major thinkers of the West have been childless. What sort of difference does this make? Who exactly is the 'we' that we write about or in the presence of or for?

What struck me from the first about Elizabeth's writing was that these two questions were never muted in her work. Her first book, *The Nature of Belief* (1976), impressed me for all kinds of reasons, but not least because of the wit and fluency of the dialogues scattered throughout it

– and because of the fact that at one point she casually mentions a point made by a teenager responding to a lecture of hers. Again and again (as the wonderful pieces in this present collection show), she turns from the conventional audience to open a door to those who aren't usually there for the theologian, and to imagine what could possibly be said to draw them into conversation. Her accounts of various exercises in persuading groups to come clean about the question they would actually like taken seriously, and to persuade theologians to imagine such a level of engagement, ought to be required reading for all students for ordained ministry and for anyone trying to think through the rationale of theology as a human exercise.

A *human* exercise: you come away from reading something by Elizabeth (as you would always come away from listening to something of hers) aware that a deep and significant level of human excitement and enlargement has been opened up. I read that first book when I was beginning to teach theology in the 1970s; and, while I wanted to argue furiously at a lot of points, what mattered most was that it seemed to be the work of someone who inhabited a world of living relation and who was not ashamed of letting us know something of why these discussions might matter for a person of manifest human insight, warmth and imagination.

In other words, I was pushed towards examining why it mattered to me to teach and study theology, and to acknowledge that without keeping this somewhere in focus I would be failing at the most important level. 'I find it suspicious that you can't say things in sober prose,' says one of her dialogue *personae* crossly at one point – and her great gift was to acknowledge that crossness and suspicion as a proper part of the theologian's equipment without either letting it win (tight-lipped rationalism) or shutting it up (tight-lipped fideism). To do the job anything like properly, you need never to lose your ear for the way your intellectual or spiritual rhapsodies might sound to the people who aren't there, the people who are hungry for something to hope for.

This has at least two kinds of consequence. First, there is in all that Elizabeth wrote an unusual honesty, in the sense that she recognises that what she writes will not be the end of discussion, that it comes from a very specific place which is bound to be compromised and partial, that it is always at risk of being subtly slanted. She is a passionately non-ideological writer – not because she has no commitments (as if), but because she wants to leave us with the sort of discomfort that we need in order to do theology in an appropriately relational way – to do it as if (to deploy one of the great themes of classical and biblical thinking) it were an activity proper to the Body of Christ in which no one is without a gift to give and no one is without a need to receive. When she muses on the various ways in which we cope with profound conflict in the Church or with the compromises around power and purity, she does so with a humane awareness that there are all sorts of ways in which we make our peace with where we find ourselves in the diversity and unevenness of the Christian community.

She is never collusive or ready to offer easy absolution ('it's all very complicated'), because she wants us to go on asking ourselves whether we are selling out, even though we have no template for what our integrity might look like. All she wants us to keep in view is that we are capable of betrayal *and* that one form of betrayal is to forget the integrity (and the human hunger) of the person we are at odds with and would rather see removed from the scene. Apart from James Alison, there is hardly any other modern theologian who has so acute a sensibility in this area, unsparingly interrogative but always as wary of radical triumphalism as of any other variety. And all the more disturbing to any and every kind of complacency because of it.

So, second, what she has to say about the Church is worth hearing because she is serious in her belief that the Christian community exists not to promote another sort of ideology but to be the environment where something completely basic to reality itself is made visible. Hence her deep debt to John Zizioulas's theology, superficially so far from what some might have thought her native intellectual and confessional territory. She is never simply a 'liberal' in theology (at least as some would define a term that has sadly rather come down in the world), to the extent that she is not particularly worried about shifting around the awkward bits of doctrinal furniture, or even about proclaiming the value of inclusiveness and non-closure. She takes for granted, I think, that plenty of the doctrinal furniture is every bit as awkward as some say, and that inclusivity is indeed a good to be pursued. But pervading everything is a deep belief that our identity as Christians is rooted in a response to truth. It is a truth that defies possession and manipulation, but we ignore its toughness and givenness at our peril.

If the Church is anything like right about what it is responding to, then we need to remember constantly that we die when we deny our relatedness, when we forget the need to receive life at each other's hands. And this entails the possibly paradoxical recognition that we need to be able to receive from those right outside the frame of reference we comfortably inhabit – religious, orthodox, yes, but also liberal, middle-class, prophetic, disruptive, intellectual, anti-intellectual, inclusive, exclusive, whatever, to the extent that these have become markers of an identity other than that given by trust in the good news of the Kingdom. Witness is borne by all sorts of people: no theology, whether it thinks of itself as iconoclastic or traditional, is licensed to forget the need to watch out for this witness. As she says wryly in one piece, she knows that ultimately, before the Throne of God, she and Ian Paisley are going to have to do something to sort out their relation to each other. For Ian Paisley, read whoever you would least want to spend eternity with. If the Church is an anticipation of the heavenly Commonwealth of God, it is so – from one point of view – in giving you ample opportunity to contemplate and experience this challenge. That's why it matters that this community is not an ideological one.

As usual with Elizabeth, and as hardly needs saying, this is not an abdication of the responsibility to argue and indeed struggle. But it is a massive question mark against our urge to reduce such struggle to the terms of success and failure, victory and defeat, as we usually think of them. I suspect that the reason she was so often invited to address gatherings both of ecumenical activists and Church leaders was that she could be relied on to give a perspective that was at right angles to such seductively simple maps of the ecclesial territory, but without any attempt to avoid the discomfort and challenge of the Church as it was and is. I can only say that, for myself, the style and content of what she offered in such contexts was consistently life-giving – and never just reassuring. She writes at one point about 'a catholic God significantly absent from our quarrelling Churches' as one of her discoveries in encountering Zizioulas's thought. And in the often bitter disagreements which my own communion experienced during my time in office (and is still experiencing), and in the bitter sense of failure and of disappointing everyone that came with this, it mattered to hear a theologian who believed that whatever needed to change and to be confronted in the dismal historical corruption or tone-deafness of the Church, there was some level of our ecclesial life where the catholic God might not after all be absent. So, that grace was, after all, working.

All this brings us back starkly to the opening questions I noted. Who wants to know? Who's not here? Elizabeth always made it clear that the first question would begin to open up once I had started to be honest about why I, as the person I am in this place and this moment, in this particular humanity that is mine and my culture's, might want or need to know. Not that theology then becomes therapy or autobiography; just that I will have begun to locate it humanly – the prime condition for communicating it intelligibly. And, as for who's not here – as this last bit of reflection has suggested, the deepest problem may be that *God* isn't here, not just that this or that bit of the human race isn't – or rather that the absence of some part of humanity, and of some part of *my* humanity, *is* God's absence. It's a bizarre thing to say from one point of view, because God is, for Elizabeth, supremely present in every human and cosmic setting, 'bidden or unbidden'. But we are all too capable, we who speak and write about God, of so configuring God's nature or character as to create a God who *could* be absent; and once we've done that, of course, 'he' is. What if Jesus Christ simply shows us the God who cannot be absent? What sort of Church life does that mandate/enable? Reading Elizabeth, that is so often the challenge that we're left with. I think it is the sort of question that every serious Christian theologian has to return to.

Marilynne Robinson, in the third of her astonishing *Gilead* trilogy (*Lila*), imagines her central character wondering how, if she can't bear to be separated from those she loves, God could possibly endure such separation. Reading the Gospels through that sort of lens is a salutary exercise, not one that has shaped, let's say, quite *all* the great theological enterprises of the last two millennia, or even the last ten decades. But what made Elizabeth so remarkable and – in the fullest possible sense – evangelical a theologian was that this was the lens of her reading.

Always intellectually rigorous, always with that edge of wit and irony; always with that openness to the voices usually silenced or ignored; always at once compassionate and imaginative; always informed by her own rich and sometimes devastating human experience, love, appalling bereavement, sickness, passion. She was never the sort of writer or person to produce a 'systematics'; it is still possible to regret that there isn't more of a literary legacy, but I think she (and probably Douglas) would have said that 'literary legacies' are monumentally not the point. She left us not only the animating and troubling questions but also, just as important, the inescapable sense of a 'lightness of being', translated into a theological voice not quite like any other, and profoundly, profoundly necessary for Churches uneasily aware that they might just possibly have been talking about an absent – and so an unreal – God because they have been talking too much to themselves.

I

You Cannot Know What You Do Not Love[*]

I want to explore one version of the Christian story of knowledge.

It is doubtful if there is such a thing as impartial knowledge.

> Once upon a time there was a story
> It was not a long story . . .
> It was a short story . . .
> A good story . . .
>
> It had neither a beginning, a middle
> Or an end . . .
>
> First of all the story was told to a child
> The child smiled and said 'Tell me another'
>
> And the story was told to a man of influence –
> The man of influence ignored it
>
> The story was told to a critic –
> The critic stuffed his shirt with it
>
> The story was told to a theologian –
> The theologian doubted
>
> The story was told to a soldier –
> The soldier tore off its wings
> And wore them on his helmet

[*] Sermon on Graduates Association Sunday, Glasgow University Chapel, 15 May 1977.

The story was told to a historian –
'These are not facts' said the historian

The story was told to a government
Who debated it, amended it –
And, finally, refused to pass it

The story was told to a judge –
'What is a story?' asked the judge

The story was told to the hangman
Who wove it in his rope like hair

The story was told to a man in chains
Who made good his escape in it

The story was told to a juggler
Who threw it in the air and caught it
And threw it in the air and caught it
And threw it in the air

The story was told to a painter
Who signed it in the corner
And hung it on the wall

And the story was told to a young girl
Whose mirror it became

The story was told to a bird
The bird built a nest in its branches

The story was told to a poet
And the poet passed on the story

And this was the story . . .

Once upon a time there was a story
It was not a long story . . .
It was a short story . . .
A good story . . .

It had neither a beginning, a middle
Or an end . . .

This morning, rather than preaching from a text, I want to explore one version of the Christian story of knowledge.

It is the story of God who loved a world into being, and imagined into it men and women who might be free and know joy. To ensure their freedom, to stop them being attracted to him coercively like seabirds to a lighthouse glass, he gave them sufficient time and space and evolutionary history to keep their distance in, and confronted them only as a possibility of the impossible, a suggestion of the transformation of things as they are.

One possibility was that man might know things *only* lovingly, as the God, who *was* love, did. But, to do that, he needed to go out of his tight skin, and to drown a little. For the God had no will to exclude anyone from his love, so, to be one with him, or to know as he knew, meant a quite new launching. It meant being willing to say 'There is no person and no thing in the world which I can be myself without.' And that meant inviting invasion, for of course, as a matter of psychology, man wasn't up to that: he could, given the structures of his existence, only cope with letting one or two people really make or unmake him. The rest were virtually irrelevant, except that they punched his bus ticket, or delivered his milk. He knew them in a more normal way, as part of the furniture of the world. They didn't provoke in him any question of who they were, or who he was, or whether he could be himself at all without them.

However, when he stood on mental tiptoe, and heard the hints of transformation which were in the air, he could imagine everyone being irreplaceable to him, as they were to the God, and he shuddered. 'That would be too much of a good thing.' For he knew the shape of his tidy privacy of thoughts and feelings and nightmares, and did not want the explosion of identity involved in saying to Tom or Dick, 'I will not know myself unless I know you and you know me.' So, he chose to go on knowing as he knew, that being more manageable: to know in detachment, and with precision; to know impersonally and selectively; to know in ways that could be measured and publicly attested, and which would allow him to develop his intelligence apart from his love.

He learned therefore to judge the criminal from the good man, the sane from the insane, the stabilities of nature where mountains didn't skip and wolves ate lambs; and he enjoyed knowing where he was. There was only one problem: knowing like that, he couldn't quite look God in the eye, for he felt overexposed when dealing with one who was involved in love with everything. So, he sewed himself diploma certificates, and shaded his eyes with them, and offered the fruit of his knowledge instead to a non-existent God who was willing to have it, and whose name was objectivity. And he had, as his reward, the guarantee of perfect separability from everything, which is death.

That is one way of glossing the strange, haunting story of the Fall of Man, which refuses to be flattened into doctrine. It offers one suggestion for what might be called a Christian critique of knowledge: you cannot know what you do not love (and 'love' means being so bound up with whatever 'other' you have to do with that your identity stands or falls with his or its). It was the former Professor of Divinity in this University, Ronald Gregor Smith, who translated Martin Buber's *I and Thou*, describing how, if I have both will and grace, even a tree may, in a given moment, become irreplaceable to me. For artists, I suppose, the world is like that more often than for others. But, quite commonly, people know it in their bones in love, or at another's death: without the other, you do not know who you are. 'Love's function is to fabricate unknownness' (e e cummings).

The man called Jesus, to return to our story, refused to be intact or to know anything in isolation. He seems to have been unable to define himself or them without reference to the God, and to the people he bumped into, and to the past, and to the future, and to the death-assaulted world.

He was cavalier about standards of knowledge. He didn't apparently know the difference between decency and indecency, given the people he affirmed. He didn't much classify, except between those who were willing to be involved out of their depth in the future of God, and those who would maintain their moral or religious intactness. He didn't know that you have to come to terms with the world as it is, and constantly proposed images of an alternative world where people not only didn't kill but also didn't hate; not only didn't abuse sexuality but also didn't lust; not only didn't ditch their neighbour but also didn't die.

What became of him is another story, with many variants, but some think that he made concrete the reversal of the Fall, showed how the limited flesh, with its tiredness and perishability, if it gives itself into the sufficient love which is God, may become a new thing, able to clap its hands and sing even through the sharpness of death. For others, it seems enough that he refused to know people as the sum of their past, and insisted on knowing them as the sum of their future, which was to belong to the Kingdom of God (or, if you want it one way demythologised, to be transformable by being loved enough). Paul himself, and the writer of the letters he maybe didn't write, had to do battle with an intellectual/religious option in the early Christian world which seems to have been fairly seductive. Its exponents, the Gnostics, 'those in the know' (almost a religious Graduates Association), thought of themselves as a spiritual elite, able to dispense with the conventions and norms of the religious rank and file. It may be that in Corinth, as certainly at Colossae, some Christians were beginning to claim superior knowledge in relation to more scrupulous Fellows in fairly Gnostic terms. Certainly, Paul keeps hammering the association between *gnosis*, knowledge and 'being puffed up'.

But the real issue is not just a preacher's warning against pride, or even a demand for courteous recognition of others' scruples (kindly don't display the whisky bottle when teetotallers come to tea). Paul, in other contexts, had no qualms about tramping on tender moral or theological toes (for instance, on the circumcision question). And, like Jesus himself, he seems to have been sometimes deliberately provocative about his freedom *not* to be bound by others' scruples. Rather, it is the thrust of the letter to insist that knowledge, Christianly speaking, can only be in the context of love. Apart from that, for Paul, it is 'knowledge' only in inverted commas, hollow, ironically self-defeating. Of course they know, unlike the average man in the pew, that nothing material can do them semi-magical spiritual harm. Of course they are theologically superior. 'Other gods' *is* a figure of speech. They are not wrong about the facts.

If, however, they can dissociate themselves from their brother and his condition, then ipso facto they are not in the knowledge of God. The body of Christ is not one where an eye is independent of a foot. It is not a matter of a new ethic of niceness. It is a new seeing, a new knowing of self-and-other as involved in the identity of either. I am not myself, and then your brother. I am myself because I am your brother. And without you, I am not myself.

Iain Crichton Smith begins a poem written after the death of his mother:

> The chair in which you've sat's not just a chair,
> Nor the table at which you've eaten just a table,
> Nor the window that you've looked from just a window.
>
> All these have now a patina of your body and mind,
> A kind of ghostly glow which haloes them a little,
> Though invisible.

That is love-knowledge of the chair. So Paul: the taboo of which you are afraid is not just a dismissible taboo, for *you* are afraid of it. The food you cannot touch is not food I can lightly enjoy, for I am involved in your inability. The knowledge which has been offered to the God of objectivity (who has no real existence), if it can destroy our neighbour (by letting him, for instance, evade the question of what and whether he loves), is fruit not to be eaten (though most of us eat it daily).

God give us appetite for new eating, where we know one another only in the ending of isolation, if our story turns out to be true.

The Unity We Seek[*]

The Anglican Church has been conspicuously unclassifiable, a kind of ecclesiastical duck-billed platypus, robustly mammal and vigorously egg-laying.

'Let there be a tree,' said God, once upon a time, 'which grows from the birds down.'

And the Church came into being. And its branches spread and its trunk grew downwards, until it rooted itself in the dusty ground. And theologians and clergy of many nations nested among its roots.

After a time, a dispute arose among them. 'This tree does not flourish as it should,' they said to one another. 'We should pull up our roots, and move to richer soil, for one can see the quality of the earth here is abysmally poor. Other trees are improved by such transplanting. Let us have courage, and follow their example.' (For they saw from other trees that it was so.)

'No! No!' said others. 'We have seen trees wither and die when you tamper with their roots. There are bad years and good ones, and we must take the rough with the smooth. It would be colossal folly to pull up our roots, which give us all our sustenance. Let us wait, and things will improve.' (For they saw from other trees that it was so.)

Meanwhile, the noise of the debate reached some of the birds in the topmost branches, and they were puzzled. 'Do they not know,' said one small sparrow, 'that we give this tree its life? Shall we not fly down, and stop them grubbing around in their roots?' 'No,' replied a wise old

---

* This response to Archbishop Runcie's paper at the 1988 Lambeth Conference was widely acclaimed. Richard Randerson, a leading Anglican from New Zealand, commented: 'By far the wittiest and most compelling speaker at the conference was Elizabeth Templeton, a theologian from the Church of Scotland.'

pigeon. 'We can only sing when we are touched by the sunlight. But we must sing louder, so that they remember the possibilities of birdsong.' And he began to coo with all his might.

It is a great honour to be here, but I do not quite know who I speak for as to the unity we seek. For I am, I suppose, in the context of this conference a kind of cut-price bargain specimen of those who are mostly not here – female, lay, Presbyterian and (by the skin of my mother's teeth) post-war. So, I will try to respond to the Archbishop's searching paper by speaking for the 'we' who relate to you as 'outsiders'.

There are, of course, many, even more outside, not only unable to find themselves in any Church, but actively sceptical about this alleged God of love we claim to represent. I speak for them by analogy. Then there are those outsiders, whom many of you rub episcopal shoulders with at home, who, like me, begin their search for unity from a denominational base which is resolutely without bishops. From such outside positions, any comment at all on the Archbishop's exploration of inter-Anglican unity may be incompetent and presumptuous; but I will, in the end, take the liberty of saying how, from my perspective, what happens to you 'on the inside' has a bearing on us 'on the outside'.

So, I risk speaking on the nature of the unity we seek in all the Archbishop's three senses, though in the specific Anglican case I use 'we' in that honorary sense which my husband recognises when I say 'Dear, we must put out the rubbish!'

Of course, in a sense, my first conviction is that there are no outsiders, or that all 'outsiderness' is to be regarded as provisional, since God's lively and inviting love is without bounds. The Church exists to represent, cradle and anticipate the future of all our humanness, which is hidden, with the healing of creation, in the love and freedom of God.

Any unity we seek must be to enact and articulate that. It cannot then be the unity of a strong and exclusive club, which makes the outsider more outside, more alien, more at bay. Rather, it must be the kind of unity which allows those outside to recognise their own humanness, to glimpse their own future with delight and hope, to get a whiff of their own transformation, their own wholeness. To put it a little provocatively, the Church is the world ahead of itself. It is not a separate enclave, not separable. As Hooker so gently puts it in his Sermon on Pride: 'God hath created nothing simply for itself: but each thing in all things, and of everything each part in other have such interest, that in the whole world nothing is found whereunto any thing created can say, "I need thee not."'

This lovely and haunting understanding of the Church, making real and concrete the relatedness of all things in love and freedom, is wonderfully deep in Anglican tradition, and will, I trust, be what sets the agenda for our attempts at inter-Church relations, as well as for our 'mission', our 'ethics' and our 'spirituality'.

That alone will stop us making of the Church yet another apartheid in creation. That alone will give us the courage to keep hearing all the outsiders. For we too rarely acknowledge, we who love this unity of the Church, that it exists in terrible combat with the actual churches so many people encounter – stale, nervous, nostalgic, authoritarian, self-preoccupied in word and deed. Non-Christian credulity (and even Christian credulity) is strained sometimes past breaking point by the pretensions of such churches to express the courtesy and refreshingness of God.

Outsiders, too, are properly sceptical about much of our inter-Church activity, recognising in it, better than we may ourselves, the permanent lure of a Superchurch, corresponding to the Superman God of much popular religious longing, and created in his image for our exclusive self-preservation.

Such a Church would speak with one reassuringly unanimous, unambiguous voice on everything: doctrine, sexuality, politics, liturgy. It would have a uniform pattern of ministry. Its authority structures would define and quash heresy and insubordination. This Superchurch tempts many in all our churches, offering instant relief from panic, from the pain of facing the complexity of life, and the diversity of human responses to it. It even tempts some in the world, battered as they are by the threat of nuclear winter, sexual catastrophe, economic disaster and ideological impasse.

Precisely because we learn from our 'outsiders' how unlovely we can be, it is important that we do not brush aside too quickly their questions about our desire for theological or structural convergence, for clear and unambiguous authority. For, at our best, we believe the unity we seek is not an ecclesiastical protection racket. But we must beware of ourselves at our worst.

One central theological question, which I find deeply embedded in all our internal and ecumenical debates about authority, is what level of provisionality we can properly live with together, under a God who is for us, ahead of us, but not within our grasp. I felt this as almost the deepest theological issue when I was privileged to share in a conversation, five years ago, between Cardinal Ratzinger and a group of joint Roman

Catholic and British Council of Churches representatives. Finally, in the course of explaining why magisterial encyclicals could not be described as 'approximations to the truth', the Cardinal argued that if God had not disclosed himself and his truth in absolute, determinate propositions, then salvation was at risk.

Many a good Calvinist would agree with him, but I do not. And the conversation focused for me the hardest underlying polarity in all our interdenominational and intra-denominational battles. There are among us those who believe that the invincibility of God's love discloses itself in some kind of absolute, safeguarded articulation, whether of scripture, Church, tradition, clerical line management, agreed reason, charismatic gifts, orthopraxis, or any combination of such elements. And there are those among us who believe that the invincibility of God's love discloses itself in the relativity and risk of all doctrine, exegesis, ethics, piety and ecclesiastical structure, which are the Church's serious exploratory play, and which exist at an unspecifiable distance from the face-to-face truth of God.

What unity is possible in concrete existence between those on either side of this transdenominational divide seems to me our toughest ecumenical question. If we can find a way through that one, I suspect that all our specific problems of doctrine, ministry and authority will come away as easily as afterbirth. But, if we seek in any of our bilateral or multilateral shifts to mask, suppress or smother that divide, our so-called unity will be a disastrous untruth.

While that is my pre-eminent concern about the unity we seek at the inter-Church level, I have another shade of worry – the only point where I suspect I reflect my own denomination's self-consciousness. (Since I am well aware of Scottish Anglicanophobia, I hope I speak without Presbyterian huffiness.)

Clearly, in the galloping ecumenical progress among Anglicans, Roman Catholics, Orthodox and Lutherans, episcopacy is cherished as a sign (some would say *the* sign) of the apostolicity and continuity of the whole Church. Now, I belong to a denomination which, with some others, like the Archbishop's atheist, not only happens not to have bishops, but is also, so far, determined not to have them (though, of course, God may surprise even Free Church persons by his future).

Certainly, as a Presbyterian, I sometimes entertain the question: 'Was I told the truth at my baptism, that I was now received into the one, living, holy, catholic and apostolic Church?' But it is not because we lack bishops that I entertain it, but because we lack, over and over again, love, grace and truthfulness. And surely, of all our Churches, episcopal or not, that is true. Indeed, it was partly because at some key points in Church history prelates were so unconvincing as custodians of the Gospel that the so-called Protestants thought it better to risk God without bishops than bishops without God! Or, to put it more lightly, as Sydney Smith, that devout Anglican, suggests: 'I must believe in the Apostolic Succession, there being no other way of accounting for the descent of the Bishop of Exeter from Judas Iscariot.'

Now, much of this is mere historically fossilised resentment, and must be undone. But perhaps it must be gently said, even to a gathering of bishops, that for some Christian bodies within the ecumenical movement, episcopacy itself is a theological problem. All our denominations have so much to learn, to understand, to forgive, to confess in mutuality, that I rather hope the episcopal Churches will not take off with the collective consciousness of a clump of front runners, leaving what you perceive as a handicapped assortment of Methodists, Baptists, Presbyterians, Quakers and others hobbling around the back straight! I too celebrate the immense advances made in these rich bilateral encounters between Anglicans and older episcopal Churches. But I hope that it might be your particular gift, after four centuries of 'Reformed Catholicity', to bear into the heart of these encounters the significant absence of the non-episcopal Churches, and to interpret it.

In a way, I am merely reflecting on my experience of BCC or WSCF encounters, where the lived working assumption is that all member denominations are equal in their status as 'receiving contributors' to the truth. That, of course, may become bland, evasive, superficial, complacent. It needs constant theological scrutiny. But it is extraordinarily healing as a presupposition. It is, of course, also a procedural necessity. For such Federations have no executive authority structures over their members. But precisely that fact actually enacts the hope that the truth is among us, around us and ahead of us, that the truth is our custodian, not we the custodians of the truth. That relaxes us into the real mutuality of those who can risk being ecclesiastically in love.

Finally, may I venture an outsider's longing about internal Anglican unity, as you face especially this testing and delicate issue of women's ordination to the priesthood and episcopate. In preparing for this Conference and reading something of your history as a communion, I have been constantly struck by the best generosity of your recurrent insistence that across parties, camps, styles and dogmas, you have need of one another. Both internally and in relation to other evolving Christian life-forms, you have been conspicuously unclassifiable, a kind of ecclesiastical duck-billed platypus, robustly mammal and vigorously egg-laying. That, I am sure, is to be celebrated and not deplored.

As a guest, I am sad to feel that you are under some pressure to renounce this remarkable openness of being, to tighten up the structures of dogma, ministry and pastoral discipline, to align definitively either with the lions or with the hens. For I find your costly openness a gift to the other Churches and a gift to the world.

How you sustain this now, whether you sustain it, seems central to this Lambeth Conference (though, of course, the survival of formal unity can never properly be used as a blackmailing pistol at the head of perceived truth).

My hope is, at least, that the women's ordination issue does not become a scapegoat for all the questions that potentially divide you in your communion, though it may be a focus of them. It is, at best, that you can see the issue as gift, calling us all to earthed exploration of what Christ and culture mean for each other, how a human Church bears God to people, how sacrament and sexuality relate. For these are questions which reach into the wider world, where on the whole people couldn't care less about the ordination of anyone to anything, because they are too busy living and dying. And if it is gift, it is gift not just most because it opens up deep and wide theological questions, but because it also touches the levels of pain and passion which test what it means that we love our enemies.

The world is used to unity of all sorts, to solidarity in campaigns, unity in resistance, communities of party, creed, interest. But it is not used to such possibilities as this: that, for example, those who find the exclusion of women from the priesthood an intolerable apartheid and those who find their inclusion a violation of God's will should enter one another's suffering, wash one another's feet. Somewhere in there, authority lies.

I suspect that only from such depth of exploration, which Churches rarely expose themselves to, will unity or authority emerge, at least in any sense which makes us credible as agents of God's healing to the nations.

3

*The Ritual Dimension of Faith**

The central image of Christian ritual is of an encounter where all divisions of race, gender, age, wealth and so on are transcended, for they plough, inevitably, into death.

I have no specialist expertise to bring to this subject. I am a lay theologian, brought up in the Scottish Presbyterian or Reformed tradition. Neither 'liturgy' nor 'ritual' were words I heard in my childhood. What we had were 'services'; we were vaguely aware that Catholics had Mass, and there was a kind of subliminal sense of that as a strange and superstitious practice. But it was only as I moved into ecumenical circles in my student days, and had real contact with Anglicans, Catholics or Orthodox, that I began to have any consciousness of liturgy or ritual as a significant or challenging issue. My central question, which I hope we will be exploring during the week, is whether we can still have any confidence that the specific ritual that is Christian liturgy can actually connect with issues of life and death for the whole world. If not, the interest is basically sectarian.

But what makes Christian ritual connect with the life and death of the world? The classic vision of the Eastern Orthodox tradition runs something like this: corporate worship, the manifestation of the Church as the body of Christ, is an enactment of salvation. It presents a community in which all the natural differences which normally divide human beings – race, gender, age, wealth and so on – are transcended; in which people acknowledge that they cannot be themselves without the other. The central image of Christian ritual is of an encounter where such divisions are transcended, for they plough, inevitably, into death. It is this sense of liturgy, the act of the whole people,

* Address to the Theological Summer School at Agape, Italy, August 2000.

which makes it impossible, in orthodoxy, for priests to celebrate the eucharist without the presence of a lay person, or to contemplate 'dedicated' eucharists for students only, women only, children only. The ritual has to embody catholicity, not just in will or intention, but in concrete reality.

This is a significant aspect of ritual. It embodies things. Christian ritual is characteristically about *embodying* the *future*, the so-called 'Kingdom of God'. If we cannot make the connection between liturgy and the *presence* of that *future*, we are back in a state of regarding Christian rituals of worship as matters of taste rather than matters of life and death.

The future which is claimed by the Gospel is characterised by two things, communion and freedom. The communion is not simply human. It involves the whole of creation being transformed from a state of internal dividedness and hostility into a restored harmony. This means that the ritual of worship is seeking to express and articulate not just moral or emotional transformation, but also the transformation of matter, of space, of time. The 'offering', the 'work of the people', which is at the heart of liturgy is the dedication of everything, the senses and what we know through them, to the divine creativity which can free them from their natural condition of impermanence and fragility.

I am sure that it is worth bringing this analysis into the ecumenical dialogue, but I am no longer sure that it can stand as the whole truth. Again, I need specialist help both from biblical exegetes and from early Church historians, especially those involved in liturgical reconstruction. My impression is that Jewish studies in recent decades have softened the polarisation between cult and prophecy. Certainly, if one looks at the continuing history of Judaism, the annual cycle of festivals and the daily rituals of household observance culminating in Sabbath co-exist in harmony with commitments to social and political justice. To many Jews, the Christian elevation of the prophets over Torah is a piece of religious imperialism, distorting the Mosaic revelation as much as the language of 'Old Testament' and 'New Testament'.

New Testament scholarship too suggests a more ambivalent stance towards Temple and synagogue than that of hostility. It is clear that Jesus wanted the reform of cultic practice where it had become a mere formality – and that he deplored the abuse of the Temple for exploitative and self-serving purposes. But there is no sense that he wanted to turn his back on Jewish observance: his instructions after healings that people should present themselves in the Temple; his participation in synagogue worship, even (if some commentators on John's Gospel are right) that the structure of that Gospel reflects Jewish festivals still present in the consciousness of the late first-century Church – all that belies the dissociation of the early Church from the Jewish structures of relationship to time, to ceremony and to community identity.

Orthodox and Catholic scholarship in this area claim a liturgical tradition which predates the conversion of Constantine, with the Didache and the writings of Irenaeus in the second century as crucial. They argue, with some plausibility, that it was for liturgical reasons that scripture came to be written down, rather than left to oral traditions.

I believe that Protestantism needs to rediscover, and to some extent is discovering through its ecumenical pilgrimage, something of what it means to be a eucharistic community, not just looking back in a commemorative act, but also looking forward to the fulfilment of the Kingdom, in which earth and heaven are not fused but are in constant dynamic relationship. I believe also that there is a lot of well-intentioned moral urgency which, if it is not to collapse in burn-out, needs to recover the sense that we offer ourselves and the inanimate creation to a transformation beyond ethical management, a transformation of the structures of our being. The narratives of the presence of Christ in the New Testament seem to me to be saying that, somehow or other, presence needs public form.

If, on the other hand, ritual and liturgy are important, it is because they actually *embody* who we distinctively *are* as a Church – *both* how we are world, for example, *and* how we are not world.

I take it for granted that whichever view we take, there has to be a connection between ritual and praxis in the wider life of the community, the liturgy after the liturgy. I cannot offer myself in a ritual of inclusive love and then return to the tribalism of my prejudices as if nothing had happened.

An anthropology teacher at the beginning of one term went into his class and silently handed out a stone, indicating non-verbally that it should be passed on. Every day for the next ten weeks, the class began by the passing of the stone from student to student, and back to the teacher, who laid it on his desk until the next day. One day, the second last day of term, he came in, but didn't pass the stone round and began to lecture. There was visible distress, and as the class ended the students expressed their consternation.

'But sir, you didn't hand the stone round. Why didn't you hand the stone round? What's wrong? What does it mean?'

'Oh,' he said coolly, 'it means that now you understand what a ritual is.'

4

The Weakness We Are Learning[*]

*The Church is called to image a future where God's freedom disman-
tles everything that separates us, while reaffirming the distinctiveness
and personhood of each.*

> Fiona has no words for it, no thought even.
> She has narrowed down in being
> to a pair of childish hands.
> and yet the weakness she is learning now
> will stay with her
> > Alasdair Maclean, 'Waking the Dead'

The weakness we are learning might be summarised as the vulnerability
of being trusted to hold the world in our hands as it palpitates in need of
release like the wee mouse in Fiona's hands. And what I want to try to do
here is focus on some aspects of that holding.

Last month, Dorothee Sölle died. I had only met her twice, and both
times found her luminous. It was by chance a few months ago that I came
across what may well be her last book, *The Silent Cry: Mysticism and
Resistance*, where there is a rather remarkable, if occasionally slightly
strained, fusion of two themes not so often connected in Christian
consciousness: the intuitive, immediate recognition of the presence/
absence of God which is at the heart of mystical spirituality, and the robust
commitment to hard-nosed naming and shaming the powers and to living
against the world for the sake of the world – the Johannine paradox.

Since the Church is too often itself a power in the pejorative sense, as
well as a bearer of vision and a cradler of the world's weakness, we must

* For the second time, a most unusual distinction, Elizabeth was invited to address the
Lambeth Conference of Bishops, convened in 2003 by Archbishop Rowan Williams.

have a somewhat ambivalent sense of our own identity – which none of the standard moves contrasting true Church with empirical, or institutional Church with a coming Church, can really eliminate. I know that, for Orthodoxy, confessing the sin of the Church is conceptually impossible; but I suspect that for most of us there is a fair level of malaise about the tensions between vision and practice in this actual body we make up.

One way of living against the world for the sake of the world is to be quite clear that the things which are unmanageable are as important for us to concentrate on and seek to address as the things which are manageable. At one level that seems like masochism, but at another I suspect it is a real question to a deeply Pelagian culture – which runs from performance criteria for nursery children to the almost total social marginalisation of the infirm elderly.

The unmanageabilities I am going to name are, on the whole, obvious, and need little rehearsing. Some of you may disagree that they need or should be so unmanageable, were we only more faithful to God, to Jesus, to Scripture, to Tradition and so on. But I believe it isn't just feeble capitulation to the *Zeitgeist* which makes it necessary to say: 'It can be seen in this way and that way.' Whatever is going on in this ambiguous phenomenon of globalisation, its turbulence has to be the context in which the early twenty-first-century Church lives its earthed life.

Of all the vital things which John Zizioulas taught me, one of the most suggestive – and he would locate this in Maximus the Confessor – is the sense that tradition is the shadow of the future caught by the past and committed to us now. One implication of that is that what has been believed in the past is not the fullness of truth, but a faithful anticipation of the fullness of truth, so that there has to be a constant ongoing conversation between the deposit of faith and the pneumatological pressure of the *eschaton*, which in simpler Johannine terms is 'truth we cannot yet bear'. There is a startlingly gynaecological metaphor in *Being and Communion* about the Spirit dilating time and history: those of you who have watched childbirth will know what that entails in terms of weakness and exhaustion!

The transformation of the heart which is, I think, involved in our learning faith is that which makes it second nature for us to renounce both domination over and dissociation from those with whom we profoundly differ (first nature being, for most of us, to seek either or both!). If, on the personal level, such transformation of intention is rare, costly and dependent on a huge discipline of attention to the weakness of God, for institutions it is even more of a miracle. Reinhold Niebuhr's *Moral Man and Immoral Society* has some relevance here. Somehow, en masse, structures, including ecclesiastical ones, have a tendency to accumulate what Simone Weil would have called gravity, the capacity to be pulled into the orbit of power and ownership and control. The Grand Inquisitor is alive and well.

Especially Churches which have a formally symbiotic relationship with state and nation may feel the burden here of discerning appropriate compromise from inappropriate, though I suspect any manifestation of church which engages with the world has to grapple with such dilemmas, since the world, on the whole, confuses God with Superman, as do elements within the Church. The lures of territory, strength and acclaim are immense; which is why I love these tiny white churches which dot the Greek landscape, at the top of stony mountains, on inaccessible promontories, in the middle of virtually pathless fields of scrub and thistle, ridiculous as gathering places for even the locals, but hallowing the impossible land!

If it is the Church's vocation to appropriate and rehearse the Passion, not in timeless or spiritualised terms, but in the specificity of the here-and-now world, then that means face-setting towards our concrete twenty-first-century Jerusalems, the scenarios which properly have us gasping with Gethsemane outrage and horror, and yet, in a more Johannine mode, draw us with a steady sense of calling.

It's important to start from where you actually encounter being Church as creative and energising and empowering, and to try to extrapolate from that to diocesan, provincial or international strategies. That is the thrust of Ian Fraser's *Re-inventing Theology as the People's Work* (2000), with its deliberately provocative title, and of Jeanne Hinton and Peter Price's *Changing Communities* (2003). Sharing best practice is certainly one of the ways we all learn. All I know is that when I hear my own denomination talking about success and growth and even the Great Commission, I often have a sinking feeling that I am very near landmines!

I would like to pick out three issues to dwell on a little bit further: one, because I think it is vitally important and not yet treated seriously by the Church; the others, because they are treated seriously but, I suspect, in no-through-road manner.

The first is the not-enough-happening dialogue between Christianity and paganism. For me, the concrete context of encounter was an application by the Pagan Federation in Scotland to join Edinburgh Interfaith

Association. The initial response was an immediate 'Yes' from the Hindu, Buddhist and Sikh communities, and an immediate 'No' from the Jews and Muslims. The Christians were divided!

So, we embarked on two years of 'Meet the Pagans'. I will never forget the joy, at one forum, of hearing a wee, prim-looking, shilpit (Scots, untranslatable: pinched, underfed-looking) woman of about sixty, with a tight bun, NHS spectacles, a pink crimplene suit and cheap white shoes, introducing herself as: 'I'm an Aberdeen witch.'

As she spoke, with immense modesty and diffidence, about her sense that she had a gift of healing, for pagan witchcraft cannot be intentionally used to do harm, I had a curious sense that there was hardly a broomstick's breadth between her and many Christians' intentions and hopes in what they call intercessory prayer. Indeed, the experiment currently in progress in the USA with Templeton Foundation funding, where control groups of hospital patients – prayed for/unprayed for/ prayed for knowing they are prayed for/prayed for not knowing they are prayed for – are being monitored for cure rates, seems to me to be based on a worse-than-witchcraft view of prayer.

Pagans – still, of course, an eccentric minority in our culture – are people of huge tenderness and ecological concern. They have a vision of life harmonised with the rhythms of nature, accepting birth and death as part of the divine cycle, celebrating the bipolarity of male and female and the triumph of regeneration.

But far more significant than the 10,000 or so formally signed-up pagans in the UK are the thousands and thousands for whom there is effectively no God but nature. The groundswell of the veneration or love/ worship of nature is not, I believe, malevolent. It is a genuine, often idealistic, perhaps utopian attempt to recover the perceived wisdom, harmony and rhythm of many indigenous cultures, whose depth of community, integrating human and non-human, is viewed with wistfulness by a fragmented and mechanised society.

Leaving aside the ethical issues about where and how to draw lines about our proper rights and responsibilities in modifying nature (cooking, medicine, technology), the Christian exchange with paganism must, I think, be about the fragility and pathos of the cosmos: the way space and time frustrate the relatedness of things and people as well as mediating it; the impersonality of the causal processes which turn us into earth mould. Pagans are not only resigned to that: they appear to celebrate the process, accepting the psychic force of bereavement as a mere blip, a mere emotional phase almost, in the context of a deeper long-term acceptance of the cosmic synthesis. But to be a person is to insist on the irreplaceable particularity of selves who cannot be mashed into cosmic soup, no matter how nutritious. And, at the same time, it is to resist the standard Western modern equivalence of person with individual.

A person – and this is the core anthropology of John Zizioulas's *Being as Communion*, with its deep Trinitarian roots – is a self who can only be a self-with: and indeed a self whose identity is constituted by relationship with other selves. Unless you are a self-in-relation, you are not a person at all. You are a thing. Or you are in hell. Human beings are pulled simultaneously in two directions – the split being what, in Christian code, we call fallenness. On the one hand, we are gasping for love-knowledge, for the mutuality of recognition which makes those we love irreplaceable, and us too irreplaceable as loved.

On the other hand, something in us is terrified of such anarchy, of the abolition of the boundaries which make us feel we know who we are, even negatively. That's why Iain Crichton Smith's guilt is so seductive, 'that's small and black and creeps in when the door swings on its oiled hinges!' It's also, I suspect, why the outward projection of guilt into judgement of others is so prominent a feature of Church pronouncements and practice.

The dialogue with paganism, if we risked it, would, I believe, recall us to aspects of the cosmic issues at stake in being Christian. It was not the worst of paganism which threatened Christianity, but the best of it; the celebration of natural rhythm as disclosing ultimate reality, stoic dignity which accepted death, and which makes paganism, like Gnosticism, a serious perennial contender for the hearts and minds of good, devoted and caring people. It is the outrageous, extravagant claim of Christianity that the cosmos needs transformation and is, in the light of Christ's incarnation, death and resurrection, capable of it, which scandalises commonsense paganism, Stoicism and the Karmic patience of classic Eastern cosmology. I suspect that it is a primary evangelical and apologetic task for the Church at this point in the twenty-first century to rekindle the desire not to accept the universe.

The sad, funny predicaments of the human race: a priest advising a parishioner to resort to prostitutes rather than abandon a sterile marriage: a planeload of environmentalists jetting off to an international conference on air pollution: a Church, called and claiming to represent the catholicity of creation, riven by anathemas and exclusions – these are ironies too deep to be dismissed as hypocrisy. They represent entrapments which seem beyond moral ingenuity to solve. And that is the human condition – what the trade calls original sin, and what David Jenkins, in a more lively contemporary idiom, calls 'the buggeration factor'. That too is what I mean by 'weakness'. We do not help the world, ever, I suspect, by nagging at it. But we might help by sharing with it, in dismay, in humour, in candour, the absurdity of utopian solutions. That is not, I hope, what Tillich dismissed as 'secularised Methodism', but a more precise analysis of the encounter with the unmanageable. And my hunch is that the dialogue with latent or explicit paganism might be, at this juncture, an important creative way into that.

The second, unfinished business, which is still, if unfashionably, vital for the Churches of Europe and its ex-colonies, and possibly for the rest of the world, is to catch up with how it is going to handle the Enlightenment agenda: whether it is going to ignore it, renounce it or, in some way, advance it.

Two vignettes here:

One is that of Frances Young leading Bible Studies on Galatians at the Faith and Order Conference in Santiago de Compostela (1993). After day two, most of the Orthodox delegates left, never to return, because she had been suggesting a serious rift between Paul and the Jerusalem Church. 'But it is impossible', was the major criticism, 'because we cele-brate the Feast of St Peter and St Paul on the same day.' Is this *lex orandi, lex credendi* at its best or its worst?

My second vignette is a memory of my first participation in a Society for the Study of Theology meeting in Durham, around 1970, when I had just been appointed to teach in Edinburgh's Divinity Faculty. Christopher Evans had given a paper on the non-dominical institution of the sacra-ments, which certainly at the time I found historically convincing.

What impressed me even more was Ian Ramsey, all five foot four of him, jumping up after the paper and saying: 'Well, if Canon Evans is right, we'd better stop baptising, then.' Did he mean it? Was he being ironical? Would *lex orandi, lex credendi* mean that, a priori, Christopher Evans's question was illegitimate?

Clearly, this is a neuralgic point in relation to current sexuality issues, questions of ministry and decisions about relations to non-Christians, as well as being the unfocused malaise among many ordinary churchgoers about whether they are being asked to inhabit at least two incompatible worlds. Since I live with a New Testament scholar who is not convinced, on biblical critical grounds, that Jesus ever dreamt of founding a Church, or thought of himself as, in any unique sense, the Son of God, this is for me more than an academic question.

The third area, once you have mopped up modernity, which seems to me still to need engaged attention, is postmodernity. So far, I detect two broad responses from within the Christian community. One is dismissive, even hostile. Postmodernity is a dangerous climate, in which private ideologies, spiritualities and worldviews are given carte blanche by a laissez-faire consumerist world to market themselves as they will for potential customers. It marks the collapse of any confidence in truth, and depends instead on a cynical recognition of the spin factor in behaviour and utterance.

For others, postmodernity is something to take advantage of. If the basic cultural axiom is 'You tell your story and I'll tell mine', then the Christian narrative need seek no justification in terms of coherence or consistency with other accounts of reality.

Neither of these approaches seems to me adequate. The latter is impossible if we are really affirming the relationality of all things, all knowledge and all loving. Yet I welcome, on the whole, the postmodern challenge to scrutinise stories for spin, conscious or unconscious. For certainly we have been complacent about our dubious, un-self-critical allegiances and how we rationalise them.

So, at the level of ethics, postmodernity may be nudging us towards humility, a kind of correction to the hubris of thinking we've got it taped. More deeply, perhaps, this postmodern chaos can be read as a distinctively twentieth/twenty-first-century variant of the drive back to silence: a rejection of the hubbub of claims and counter-claims which work for washing powder and insurance deals. This is *God* we're on about. But the culture has hardly a glimmer of what *apophatic* silence means. It expects, and too often finds, Christianity to be busily marketing itself.

Just, in closing, a word about tactics; or, if that sounds too managerial for someone advocating attention to the unmanageable, a word about courage. I actually believe that public Christian discourse is virtually poisoned in the ears of most people in this culture. It is poisoned partly by the vices of the Church – dogmatism, moralising, judgementalism and dullness. It is poisoned also by the vices of the culture – false expectations, intellectual laziness, luxury, insularity and individualism. Most people are victims of that.

To release them into fresh hearing, there has to be real decoding (which can probably only begin when we live so surprisingly that people want to ask us questions). But, in preparation for that decoding, I think there has to be an absolutely massive programme of what I might call adult theological literacy.

For most of the last twenty years, I've been doing theology with people who, one way or another, have been seriously infantilised in their Christian environments. What I have been learning, ever since then, is that people really can cope with all of it: with the complexity, with the unanswered questions, even with serious conflict. What they cannot, and shouldn't have to, cope with is furtiveness and fudging.

I leave you with some lines from a poem by the Orcadian, Edwin Muir:

> The heart could never speak
> But that the Word was spoken.
> We hear the heart break
> Here with hearts unbroken.
> Time, teach us the art
> That breaks and heals the heart.

5

*The Word of God**

In all the traces of how the Word has been heard and misheard, there has been passion, a sense of crisis, of being forced to levels of self-scrutiny full of pain as well as promise.

All around Scotland, in the last hour, people have been urged to 'hear the Word of God' in the reading of the scriptures and in the exposition of many hundreds of sermons. The framework of ritual expectancy, that God will address us simultaneously around 11:30 on Sunday mornings, is not a naturalistic one. Simply compare the normal lack of 'frisson' when you listen in, in the context of public worship, to 'Hear the Word of God', and your likely reaction to a stranger in a bus queue saying 'God spoke to me last night' – if you're like me, in the latter case, probably reaching mentally for the nearest psychiatrist's phone number.

This theme of the given Word is particularly dear to the Reformed traditions of the Church – quite different from mere human reflection or collective wisdom – the bare, sharp, promising word which God himself speaks. But, every so often perhaps, we need to look at what we actually expect, to relocate ourselves personally and communally around this idea of 'the Word'.

The opening verse of our Samuel narrative is one to chill complacency. 'And the Word of the Lord was rare in those days: there was no frequent vision.' One translator, Ronald Knox, makes it even more sinister: 'In those days, a message from the Lord was a rare treasure: he would not openly reveal himself.' There already, even at the most obvious level, the Hebrew-less hearer depends for the Word he hears on a community of interpreters!

* Sermon in the High Kirk of St Giles, Edinburgh, 5 November 1995 (1 Samuel 3:1–14; John 8:43–59).

But the rest of the story has the sweet simplicity of a good folk-tale: the voice in the night three times; the absence of a human source: it has to be God; the message is clear and unambiguous and irresistible. We have all inherited Samuel as an archetype of listening faith, but behind this story lie centuries of controversy in the religious life of Israel. Under the surface, this is a significantly political narrative. It celebrates the destruction of the sanctuary, the priesthood of Eli, and his line in favour of Samuel, seen retrospectively as the first of the prophets. The subsequent story is full of irony, of course, because Samuel, who brings word of the doom of Eli, is involved in inaugurating the kingship which leads to the building of the Temple – but it looks as if this is one of the traces of a conflict which surfaced over and over again in Israel.

There were those who believed that God's Word was at home in the accredited places, in the Ark of the Covenant, in the sanctuary, in the care of the legitimate priests, through the proper performance of hallowed ritual. And there were also, especially in the north of the country, traditions clustering round prophetic figures – presented usually as ungroomed hearers of the Word, compelled to speak, and more often than not speaking against the cult, saying 'Your worship gives God no pleasure'; challenging the 'prosperity theology' of priests who said 'We'll be all right. God is with us'; reading history with a more pessimistic, critical eye.

Were there two Words of God? Both certainly survive in what we inherit as scriptures. Perhaps, awareness of the tension is a gift to us if we are tempted to complacency about the predictable presence of the Word, about who are its custodians, about where we may expect to hear it, or if we're tempted by nostalgia for far-off days when everyone agreed about the Word of God! As we sit, poised near the cusp of the Christian calendar which is Advent, it is a vital question. Richard Holloway in his recent book, *Stranger in the Wings*, suggests that for our day, annunciation is borne by the homeless on Edinburgh streets, or the community of those who are HIV. Not a Word many want to live with, that one!

For most of us, I suspect, isolated voices in the night are not what we expect, even if our modes of listening for God take many forms – checking out the vividest convictions of heart and conscience against those we trust in the faith, the occasional startling sentence that jumps off a page at us, unexpected gifts of sustaining friendship, or less dramatic senses of 'being in the right or wrong direction' as our experience knits together in certain ways.

Whatever its immediacy, we always have to wrestle with the question: 'But is this really God?' And we have to do that because, in the history of the Church's claims and counter-claims about what the Word is, we recognise that what has been live Word for some ceases to speak for others – or causes battles.

So, for example, it has to be a question for us, though it isn't for the writer of 1 Samuel, whether God who promises the destruction of Eli and the Shiloh sanctuary because of the misdeeds of his sons is in character – in character with the God who doesn't break bruised reeds, for example. Does our Word of God invite us to see events of death and destruction as divine vengeance, or to refuse such a reading as too crude, too vindictive?

Turning to John 8 does not provide much for our immediate comfort. Here too, we are embroiled in a conflict about the Word: who knows it, who speaks it, who keeps it. For the Johannine community, the Risen Christ is the Word, transcending space and time, but visible in the concrete life of Jesus, whose presence generated crisis after crisis for the unresponsive world – a world which John's Gospel represents almost entirely as 'the Jews' or 'the Pharisees'.

Because it is scripture, and Jesus speaking, we easily somehow miss what our normal reaction would be to someone using language like this: 'Why do you not understand what I say? It is because you cannot bear to hear my Word. You are of your father the devil, and your will is to do your father's desires.' With the awful hindsight of history, we know that words like these have been used by Christians to justify the most awful persecutions of the Jews, right down to the Holocaust. And there they are, as part of our inheritance as the Word of God. What do we do with them?

There are, of course, various devices to deflect the blast of this blazing, if stylised, row. We know something of the rhetoric of anger, the conventions of Semitic hyperbole.

We have clues too, that the feeling of the Christian community which produced John's Gospel late on in the first century was actually much more polarised against the Pharisees than Jesus himself half a century earlier. Relations had worsened. There are traces of conviviality and some mutual respect in the historic ministry of Jesus, but relationships between the synagogue and these Johannine Christians were at a life-and-death stage.

They may have been expelled from the Jewish community that had been their roots, and were needing desperately to believe that, in that vulnerable position, the eternal God really was with them and against their persecutors. But, whatever the elements of caricature and polemic, it is clear that the Church has, for most of its history, endorsed the ringing denunciations of John's Gospel as the very Word of God. And that properly worries us. Is it just liberal squeamishness which recoils from this, and tries to atone, as much contemporary scholarship does, by reconstructing the Pharisees – not as a bunch of die-hard conservative obscurantists, but as people who wanted the Torah, the gift-word of God, to be accessible within the structures of everyday life – even as radicals of a sort, wanting themselves to reduce priestly power? Was their complaint against Jesus that he out-radicalled their radicalism? Was that what explained an intensity of shared concern, yet different vision, which became mutually venomous? The questions are hard to answer, but important to ask, as we watch the Gospel traditions harden in their anti-Pharisaic hostility.

But in any case, whether we believe that these angry words are consonant with the mind of the historical Jesus, or the anger of the living God, they are part of the burden we carry in inheriting this 'Word'. For we know, over the centuries, how often they have been echoes in the accents of fanaticism. And we dread, most of us, to claim the confidence to say categorically to another person: 'You are of the devil: I cannot share life with you.'

Yet that kind of crunch seems, in a way, to be part of the burden that goes with taking seriously that God really speaks. For, in all the traces of how the Word has been heard and misheard, wrestled with and interpreted, there has been passion. There has been a sense of 'crisis'; of someone in world or Church being forced to levels of self-scrutiny which are full of pain as well as promise – making the two ears of everyone who hears it tingle – precisely the things which are most precious, which make us most ourselves, which define us as a community, are not bland platitudes of laissez-faire co-existence. They are sharp commitments to handle life in ways which others find stupid or menacing. That is why John's Gospel plays so prominently with the theme of cross.

I am not sure that the Churches in Scotland at present really live such passion in any manifest way. Perhaps that is why the haunting emptiness of the Samuel opening verse may be our best description.

Yet, if we approach Advent with a sense of our poverty, our inability to get matters of life and death into perspective, our flight from conflicts which involve facing real enmity, we might be just a shade more open to the God who waits to speak.

Contributors

Tim Duffy retired in 2016 after thirty years as Research Officer for the Scottish Roman Catholic Justice and Peace Commission. He was party to the ecumenical initiatives of those years with Elizabeth Templeton and others and through Scottish Churches House.

Now a writer and broadcaster, Richard Holloway was Bishop of Edinburgh and Primus of the Scottish Episcopal Church until he stood down in 2000.

After a spell as Scottish Secretary of the Student Christian Movement at the end of the 1960s, Alastair Hulbert worked off and on for twenty years in missionary and ecumenical organisations in Europe. His last job was as Warden of Scottish Churches House.

Peter Matheson is a Reformation historian, born a Scot, married to a German, living in New Zealand.

Charlotte Methuen studied mathematics at Cambridge and theology at Edinburgh, where she also completed her PhD on science and theology in the sixteenth century. She is Professor of Church History at the University of Glasgow and an Anglican priest, with a strong interest in ecumenical theology.

Lesley Orr is a historian and activist, currently Research Fellow at the University of Edinburgh Centre for Theology and Public Issues. She has been engaged for many years in Scottish, ecumenical and international movements for gender justice and active citizenship, and is a member of the Iona Community.

Rowan Williams was Archbishop of Canterbury from 2002 to 2012. Since then, he has been Master of Magdalen College, Cambridge.

Acknowledgements

The Publisher and Editors acknowledge copyright permission to use the following: Polygon (Birlinn Ltd) for 'Grandchild' and 'A Man I Agreed With', from *The Poems of Norman MacCaig* (2005); Carcanet Press for 'None is the same as another' and 'The chair in which you've sat's not just a chair', from *Collected Poems* (1992) by Iain Crichton Smith; Faber & Faber for the first verse of 'The heart could never speak', from *Collected Poems* (1960) by Edwin Muir, and for lines from Burnt Norton V, *Four Quartets* (1936) by T.S. Eliot; David Higham Associates for lines from *Waking the Dead* (Gollancz, 1976) by Alasdair Maclean; Oxford University Press for 'Anything rather than an angel', 'The Paradise of the Theologians' and 'Mythology', from *Selected Poems*, translated by Carpenter and Carpenter (1977), by Zbigniew Herbert; Curtis Brown Ltd for lines from W.H. Auden, *The Dog Beneath the Skin* (1935); Orion Publishing Group for 'The Word' and lines from 'Emerging' by R.S.Thomas, from *Collected Poems 1945–1990* (1993); David Higham Associates for lines from 'Prayer before Birth' (1943) by Louis MacNeice, from *Collected Poems* (Faber & Faber, 1979); Weidenfeld and Nicolson for lines from 'Do not go gentle into that good night' (1951) from *The Collected Poems of Dylan Thomas: The Centenary Edition*. USA permission for lines from 'Do not go gentle into that good night' by Dylan Thomas, from *The Poems of Dylan Thomas*, copyright 1952. Reprinted with permission of New Directions Publishing Corp.

Index